Blue Collars and Hard-Hats

Books by Patricia Sexton

Education and Income: Inequality of Opportunity
in the Public Schools

Spanish Harlem: An Anatomy of Poverty

The American School

The School in Society

The Feminized Male: Classrooms, White Collars
and the Decline of Manliness

with Brendan Sexton

Blue Collars and Hard-Hats: The Working Class
and the Future of American Politics

The Working Class
and the Future of American Politics

New York

Blue Collars and Hard-Hats

by *Patricia Cayo Sexton*
and Brendan Sexton

Random House

For Walter and May
Victor and Sophie

and for Charlie Kerrigan,
who is surely in paradise
if there is such a place.

So I returned
and considered all the oppressions that are done
        under the sun;
and behold the tears of such as were oppressed,
        and they had no comforter;
and on the side of their oppressors there was power;
        but they had no comforter.

                              —*Ecclesiastes*

I am the people—the mob—the crowd—the mass.
Do you know that all the great work of the world is done
        through me?

                              —Carl Sandburg

ACKNOWLEDGMENTS

The idea for this book came from my husband, Brendan, who wrote and talked about the subject long before its current popularity. As usual, his vision saw beyond his time, into the neglected and inarticulate grief of that great mass of people who live on the modest streets of middle America.

Applying his compelling persuasive powers—and some arm-twisting—he convinced me (as with so many things) to develop the idea. I take responsibility for the growth of the idea, the research, and the actual writing of this book. Yet even here his suggestions and comments have been invaluable, and several key chapters are largely derived or taken verbatim from materials he wrote.

The work was facilitated by a Guggenheim Fellowship and a year's leave of absence from my work as professor of sociology and education at New York University. I thank Irving Howe, S. M. Miller and Amitoi Etzioni for their help and examples in winning that year's freedom. I am indebted to Angus Campbell and the Survey Research Center at Ann Arbor for their generous assistance in analyzing survey data, and to the American Jewish Committee for the material they have supplied. I am grateful to Dick Wilson for reading the manuscript carefully and critically. Above all, I must thank Jason Epstein for his usual responsiveness and encouragement and for his rare perceptive powers as an editor.

The year at Black Lake was a serene and happy one for me, thanks to the kindness of my friends, old and new, at the UAW Family Education Center. Its tranquillity, however, was ruthlessly shattered by one awful event: the deaths of Walter and May Reuther, Oscar Stonorov and Bill Wolf. We loved them, miss them deeply, every day, and we shall always grieve for them and for us.

Patricia Cayo Sexton

Black Lake, Michigan

CONTENTS

I : A Case

1

An ex-Smug Society

In almost every generation, political soothsayers—
right and left—have predicted doom for American society.
For a time in the thirties, before the New Deal came along,
the flammable tinder that could have lit fires of revolt lay
all around. But Roosevelt uncovered regenerative powers,
and World War II put the economy in motion and created
a national esprit.

Now once again the nation seems headed for a major
conflagration. Not since the Civil War has internal strife
been so pervasive. The division between black and white—
even though economic and social gaps between the races
have been narrowed—is still wide. Antagonism between

young and old is general. Such polarization is a luxury that our society can no longer afford. The war goes on. Political mechanisms have grown obsolete; instead of the regional governments needed to solve complex urban problems, we shuffle along with archaic state and municipal instruments that only block remedies for the agonies of housing, transport, education, pollution.

Seniority insures almost absolute control of Congress by Representatives (and somewhat less so by Senators) most of whom know little and apparently care less about the excruciating needs of a people who are now two-thirds urban. Rich as the nation is, state and local governments teeter at the edge of bankruptcy, while billions of dollars are poured out for wild dreams of military conquest. At the same time, urban and technological growth almost daily compounds our problems.

The society's complexity makes it vulnerable to the depredations of fanatic and antisocial minorities. The high-powered rifle, equipped with telescopic sight, puts the assassin within arm's length of his victim. The automobile, maneuvering through traffic-clogged streets, takes him from the scene of the crime, and the jet flies him thousands of miles in hours. Though he may not actually escape, the routes to freedom seem open at the time the crime is hatched. Even in the event of capture, he is insured his moment in the sun; TV shows with the highest audience ratings, and mass-circulation newspapers put his picture in every American home. Our technology encourages the grandstand lunatic.

On the lunatic fringe of the left, the maddened middle-class bomber has the means, wit, and learning not only to manufacture explosives but also to figure out the points at which the society is most vulnerable to attack. In general, tiny fanatical groups with homicidal intent can threaten the general welfare as never before. If they attract to their side significant minorities, they can create havoc in the society.

The menace is greatest from the right. The danger at Kent State came not from the handful of student extremists who sought to manipulate the outrage of sensible young people unwilling to die in an unjust war. The danger was from the savage reaction of a brutal Governor whose order to shoot drove thousands into the arms of the "militants," many of whom must have been as gratified by the deaths of the innocents as the Governor himself.

The Black Panthers are unlikely ever to win many black people to their cause on their own. Though they have attracted numbers of apparently able and surely eloquent young blacks, they have made little headway in black communities. The danger is that police and prosecutors, responding to wild and abusive Panther rhetoric, will continue to overreact—to persecute, even murder (as apparently they did in Chicago) members of the Black Panther party. The black community's natural response to such persecution is to close ranks behind the Panthers.

On the right, the danger lies not so much in the handful who plot revolution at the local rifle range, as in the millions of disaffected middle Americans who turn to George Wallace or Spiro Agnew because they alone seem responsive to their problems and needs.

It is out of the anxiety and the relative economic and social deprivation of this group of middle Americans that the sentiments expressed in the hard-hat demonstrations grew. The link between declining jobs in the construction industry—as a result of Nixon's high interest-rate policies that make construction money scarce—and the hard-hat demonstrations should be obvious, though it escapes most critics of these events. Such prosperity as the construction industry has known (and it has been minuscule compared with most heavy industry) has been maintained by a conspiracy of scarcity—one that includes land speculators, bankers, construction companies. (The unions are usually involved only in large-scale projects for which a supply of many kinds of highly skilled workers is indispensable.) In many trades, unemployment was running as high as 15 per cent at the time of the hard-hat occurrences. Despite high hourly wage rates, only a minority of construction workers earn enough each year to live at what the government calls an "adequate" budget standard. They are an insecure lot, in whom hostility has been nurtured by continuing social, economic and cultural deprivation and discrimination. Although hard-hats and Wallace voters comprise only a minority of middle America at present, continuing denial and frustration can push greater numbers of middle Americans into the arms of the fanatics on the right; together they could bring down our democracy.

The middle American is specially distressed. Many of his complaints—those on the top of his mind, in any case— are against the discontented, with those who in flailing out at the society often miss their mark and strike him. But the real cause of his distress—usually unconscious and unverbalized—has to do with the conditions of his own life rather than the disorder of other lives.

This book will consider the middle American's grievances. These grievances have to do with his frustration with the Vietnam war, the inequality of sacrifice in military and civilian life, his own acute impecuniousness in the face of the popular myth of affluence, job insecurity and unemployment, his dissatisfaction with the quality of his life and the nature of his work, the high cost and low quality of housing, transport and medical care, and his inability to influence the institutions of his society. These are only a few of his problems, but they are high on the list of complaints.

The average man, no mistake about it, is not in a revolutionary mood. The flaming rhetoric of rebellion, so popular in many quarters, definitely turns him off, not on. He wants some of the same social reforms as the revolutionary but the call to guerrilla war, assassination, revolution sends chills up his spine. He does not want to assault City Hall, the Post Office, the legislatures, Wall Street—and, literally, throw the rascals out. Indeed if anyone else tried, he would come to defend the citadels. He is in no mood for more violence, bloodshed, physical combat. He sees no more attractive position for himself in alternate models for a better society, were this one to be miraculously overthrown. This is it, he feels, let's make the best of it. Short of deep economic depression or crippling recession, he will want only to convert and reform—not destroy —the social arrangements that trouble him.

2

The grievances of the middle American are many and yet, for the most part, are foreign to most of us. How does it happen, we might wonder, that there is this great well of discontent in our society and yet, until recently, its existence has been unknown to us? Why are we so unprepared, so unable to deal with it, so surprised at what appears to be its sudden manifestation?

Much of our condition can be explained if we look at those people who supply us with ideas and information—writers, intellectuals, artists, scholars, informants from the mass media. Most have simply been remiss in their duty to enlighten the public. The postwar "good times" apparently made many of them complacent and conservative. Among those who are ex-radicals, the failure of "capitalism" to fold up and collapse as predicted, and the failure of the Soviet system to work out an appealing alternative model, sent many straight into the open arms of conservatism.

With a few exceptions, the people who have been interpreting our society for us have had no interest at all in the average man, except to assume that he is a well-oiled cog in an enormously productive social machinery. Moreover, they have generally overlooked the causes for distress among those who have been outside the great machine— the blacks, the poor, the students. Having moved over very far toward what we can only call (with some loathing of the cliché) the "conservative establishment," they have failed to give us much intellectual leadership, ideological direction, or insight into our condition.

Much of the creative dissent and informed criticism that could have helped us through the present period was wiped out by McCarthyism. Almost *all* ideological thinking on the left was leveled by this fanatic Republican Inquisition. Thus when the civil-rights, poverty and student movements came along—with amorphous masses looking for ideological direction—they ran into a vacuum of intellectual sentiment, a wasteland left barren by the McCarthy purges.

The inquisitors, says historian Richard Hofstadter, were trying to gain satisfaction against liberals, New Dealers, reformers, internationalists, intellectuals, and finally even against a Republican Administration that failed to reverse liberal policies. "What was involved, above all, was a set of political hostilities in which the New Deal was linked to the welfare state, the welfare state to socialism, and socialism to communism. In this crusade Communism was not the target but the weapon . . ." [1]

McCarthy's own expression "twenty years of treason"

[1] Richard Hofstadter, *Anti-Intellectualism in American Life,* New York: Alfred A. Knopf, 1963, p. 41.

suggests the range of grievances being attacked by the inquisitors. Right-wing spokesman Frank Chodorov summed it up when he said that the betrayal of the United States had really begun in 1913, with the passage of the income-tax amendment.

What dissenting thought McCarthyism did not manage to demolish, the open embraces of the American establishment, and the awful blunders of the world's largest communist state, finally picked off. We were left with an empty mind (or an "open" one as some scholars put it) and the belief that, except for this and that small issue, we had come upon the best of all possible social systems. Many politicians, unionists, even intellectuals felt they had saved our country by driving the communists out. In fact, the strains in our society remained unchanged.

To those who say that the business of university scholarship in our time is revolution, we reply that the contrary is true, and that because of it many universities are a shambles. Students who seek, as young people might be expected to, a better, juster, saner society have virtually no mentors at the universities. Reformist and critical sentiment has been ousted almost completely by "scientism," neutrality, and a remarkable capacity to understand why the system should function as it does. Many students want to examine the real world and make it better. When they turn to action, they have almost nobody on campus to talk to, almost no intellectual leadership that makes sense. In their confusion and agitation they turn in wild directions—to drugs, freak-outs, Yippies, and the refurbished Stalinist elitism of Herbert Marcuse.

Delivering a Phi Beta Kappa address at Harvard in 1881, Wendell Phillips said that most great social truths are "not the result of scholarly meditation, but have been first heard in the solemn protests of martyred patriots and the loud cries of crushed and starving labor." American scholars, he

contended, had missed five great chances to align themselves with the forces of progress and humanity: the slavery
controversy, penal reform, the temperance crusade, the
women's movement, the labor struggle. "Timid scholarship
either shrinks from sharing in these agitations, or de-
nounces them as vulgar and dangerous interferences by
incompetent hands with matters above them." [2] Distrust
for the educated, Phillips said, was natural in view of the
scholar's aloofness from the great battles of humanity.

Scholars are not warriors. Few of us would ask them to
be. What we might expect, and what many students sought,
was an interest in examining reality firsthand, and analyzing the problems of our society with a view to their solution. What we got instead were apologies, neutrality, unin-
formed speculation.

It was, generally speaking, Merle Curti notes, "not
scholars but farmers who demanded government control
over railroads, rural credit facilities, and an income tax.
Wage earners, rather than scholars, first demanded protection of child labor, the prevention of industrial accidents, workmen's compensation, and the outlawing of
strike-breaking Pinkerton detectives." [3]

While relations between business and intellectuals were
traditionally strained, in recent decades they have become
more comfortable. The Babbitts and robber barons have
disappeared from our literature. Many writers, thinkers,
scholars have gone to work for business—for the radio and
television industries, newspapers, book publishers, magazines and other parts of the corporate world. Thousands
are subsidized by foundations that are funded by business.

[2] W. Phillips, *Speeches, Addresses and Lectures* (Second Series),
Boston: Lea and Shepard, 1894, pp. 331–364.
[3] Merle Curti, *American Paradox,* New Brunswick, N.J.: Rutgers
University Press, 1956.

Representatives of business teach in engineering or business schools of large universities.

"If wealth accepted the intellectuals," said Irving Howe, "it was only because the intellectuals had become tame, and no longer presumed to challenge wealth, engaging instead in some undignified prostrations before it. The intellectuals are more powerless than ever, and most particularly the new realists who attach themselves to the seats of power, where they surrender their freedom of expression without gaining any significance as political figures." Whenever intellectuals are absorbed into the accredited institutions of society, Howe says, "they not only lose their traditional rebelliousness but to one extent or another they cease to function as intellectuals." [4]

The dissenters were absorbed at the very time in our history when we most needed an interested, rational, critical view of our society.

From their secure vantage point, many intellectuals came to view popular progressive movements as irrational and harmful in their effects. In a brilliant analysis of the roots of McCarthyism, Michael Rogin referred to a group of prominent thinkers who attributed the rise of Joseph McCarthy to the populist movement and agrarian radicalism —to the common men and the dispossessed of the Midwest who had produced Senators LaFollette, Norris and Borah. For many writers—including Richard Hofstadter, Seymour Martin Lipset, Talcott Parsons, Edward Shils, David Riesman, Nathan Glazer, Oscar Handlin, Peter Viereck, Will Herberg, Daniel Bell, William Kornhauser—"these movements embody a nativist mystique which, glorifying the ordinary folk, threatens the civilized restraints of a complex society." In the view of these writers, "McCarthyism appealed to the same social groups as did 'left-wing' Popu-

[4] Irving Howe in Hofstadter, *op. cit.*, p. 397.

lism"; agrarian radicalism rejects the "traditional cultural and educational leadership of the enlightened upper and upper-middle classes"; McCarthyism is the "same old isolationist, Anglophobe, Germanophile revolt of radical Populist lunatic fringers against the eastern, educated Anglicized elite." [5]

Rogin, however, carefully examines the Wisconsin vote and shows decisively that McCarthy's support came from the reactionary Republican right rather than from the populist left.

Along with labor unions, the populist and progressive movement, which had broad support in the Midwest, West and South, has been the most significant political creation of middle (farmer-labor) America. That so many writers sought to connect the movement with McCarthyism illustrates the low regard they had for the condition and sentiments of middle America. A few of them (such as Daniel Bell, Seymour Martin Lipset, Irving Kristol) have occasionally taken enough interest in the subject to write about workers and unions. Most of what they wrote was negative. Workers have authoritarian personalities. Unions are corrupt, bureaucratic, hollow.

The authors mentioned above were not alone. Most writers or scholars in this country were tuned out to any grievances from middle America—or any other source. Though they nodded almost reflexively when the word "change" was mentioned, when it came down to specifics, they had no desire to look at real problems, and admit the need for basic change in the society. They agreed to change in principle, but not in fact. Most were concerned with abstractions but not with specific issues. They were more interested in the *idea* of equality than in the actual deprivations of any group of dissenters.

[5] Michael P. Rogin, *The Intellectuals and McCarthy: The Radical Specter*, Boston: The MIT Press, 1967, pp. 6–7.

What they failed to realize is that the alternative to continuing change is social upheaval. Revolution and violence may not succeed in a state so heavily armed as ours, but that will not keep some from making hair-raising moves in that direction. That we are coping so poorly with our rebellions can be laid as much at the doorstep of these writers as anywhere else. At Berkeley, many of them viewed student leader Mario Savio as a demonic agitator, a violator of law, reason, order. Because they were unwilling or unable to deal with such relatively rational student agitators, we are now faced with Weathermen and similar extremists.

The SDS (Students for a Democratic Society) had its origins as a youth section of the liberal-leftist League for Industrial Democracy (an organization of which the authors of this book are board members). The decision of that parent group to expel the SDS because of its New Left tendencies and its interest in agitation, severed all lines of communication between old democratic radicals and the SDS. None of us can be congratulated for what has happened to SDS since then. The founding conference of SDS, incidentally, was underwritten by a five-thousand-dollar subsidy from the United Auto Workers and was held at the AFL-CIO summer camp at Port Huron, Michigan. SDS was a student group, however, not a union group; it was located on campuses, not in factories. Yet at the universities SDS members found almost no faculty who were interested in change and industrial democracy. In the end, radical students lost all touch with their professors.

While sociologist Daniel Bell sat atop Morningside Park at Columbia University weaving the fascinating concepts and ideas that make up *The End of Ideology,* Michael Harrington was on the other side of the park, down in the valley, looking at poverty in Harlem. So much had Bell and others averted their concern from the realities of American society that Dwight MacDonald, a man in touch with the most advanced social comment, could speak of "the invisible poor" in reviewing Harrington's book.

During the period when unions were struggling to win pensions, income maintenance, and protection against the depredations of inflation, Seymour Martin Lipset could find only one thing concerning unions that was of interest to him—whether they had a two-party system. Finding only one union so endowed (the typographers), he turned away from the problems of unions to an examination of the worker's authoritarian personality.

While Nathan Glazer was wondering "are cities governable?" Jane Jacobs was walking around New York, looking at the city's problems and suggesting solutions that, when compiled, added up to the most inspired—and probably the most influential—book of our time on urban affairs, *The Death and Life of Great American Cities.*

These writers who ignore urban realities are all eminently civilized men whose general social views are admirable. But in turning away from the real problems and toward intangible ideas, they concealed the obvious from themselves and others: that under the very thin veneer of stability and equilibrium, the society was rent by injustice, deprivation, inequality, and class, race and sex discrimination.

Most great American universities are located within walking distance of ghettos. Yet until the physical expansion of these universities was blocked by them, these institutions hardly noticed the ghettos' presence. If twenty-five years ago the universities had begun to send into these ghettos the kind of legal, medical, educational and organizing assistance that is now being brought there by radical students and faculty, many of the violent ghetto disturbances might have been averted.

While ghetto and working-class children were struggling with the inequalities built into their schools—inequalities that ultimately denied them entry into the privileged sanctuaries of higher education—the academics were concerning themselves with the problems of the "gifted," a euphemism for children of professionals and the upper-middle class. While the poor and near-poor were leaving school as functional illiterates, the academics were concerning themselves with the school's failure to produce the "well-rounded student," in touch with the classics, the world of literature and science.

When the passionate dissatisfaction of the poor with the schools finally erupted in small-scale revolutions, the academic community had nothing to offer. It was not even aware of the problem. Teachers were then made easy scapegoats, though the school system itself was a monument to social and community neglect.

The insularity of many intellectuals had led them to the arrogant assumption that their abstractions were in fact truth. The effect of their influence was to turn attention away from real problems to heady, exciting concern with pure ideas. The fact that they, their families, their friends had done well in the society must also have deluded them. Many were born to poor parents, grew up in poor neighborhoods, had gone for years without money, taken their recreation in public parks and settlement houses, seen their parents sweat to earn a dollar. Even those who had not been born in poverty had lived through the great Depression, when "everyone was poor." Now they and everyone they knew, while not quite capitalists, were doing very well. What more could a society offer?

Many discovered that in the more civilized industries, such as publishing, on the boards of foundations, and among the university trustees with whom they were in direct contact, there were in fact many enlightened men with a benign if somewhat conservative concern about social problems. The capitalists they met did not conform to the gross stereotype they had heard about in their radical youth.

Since the system had done well by them, and its representatives were men of good will, it was easy for them to slip into complacency, to believe that, inevitably, the system under the guidance of its more enlightened leaders would solve all problems.

As they deserted the field, they took with them their readers, listeners, followers—leaving the young with no continuing radical tradition. They complained later that the "kids are ahistorical and nonideological," as of course they are. But where would "the kids" have found an ideology when those who might have been their mentors had turned so completely to preservation of the status quo?

3

Among the essentially conservative concepts that have come into vogue are those of pluralism, countervailing powers and the self-regulating society. The concept of countervailing powers, popularized by Professor John Kenneth Galbraith and others, held that the system is kept in balance and good working order by conflicting groups: labor and capital, blacks and whites, liberals and radicals, big business and little business, etc. Under the influence of such contending groups, the system becomes self-regulating. With so many power groups contending in the society—balancing each other off—we need no longer worry about the monolithic influences of great wealth and power or the predatory nature of capitalism. Fine. Capitalism is tamed, let's get on with it.

A related idea, the transformation of American capitalism, has also become popular. James Burnham's managerial revolution put the owners (the bad capitalists) out and the managers (presumably a more civilized lot) into power in the corporate world. Earlier, Adolf Berle, Jr., had also insisted that we now have a system of power without property—managers in, capital out.

The phrase "the end of ideology," coined by Raymond Aron and further developed by Daniel Bell, also gained currency. Its message was that class conflict and quarreling about ideological issues is over, so that now we can get down to business. Lipset also proclaimed the end of political man and a comforting tendency toward the waning of conflict between the classes.

Above all, the myth of affluence—alongside the myth of the happy worker—was spread, giving most of us a sense of general material well-being. From this myth came discussions about "leisure" and what to do with all this new affluence and idleness.

At least in academic circles, much has been said about functionalism in the social sciences and about Talcott Parsons in sociology. C. Wright Mills and others established the case very solidly for the essential conservatism of the functionalist view, with its emphasis on equilibrium, stability and social *order* in the society. As a speculative system, it generated almost no interest in change, conflict, or in real people and their problems.

Even over on the left, closer to confrontation sociology, there has also been a singular lack of interest in ordinary people (nondeviant types) and real problems. In Alvin Gouldner's book, *The Coming Crisis of Western Sociology,* for example, the working class, or any synonym for it, is hardly mentioned at all. The "proletariat" has three references in the book. Unions, workers, labor, the working class—none! The "middle class" (in Marxian terms, the bourgeoisie of owners and their kindred) is mentioned fifty-two times, Marxism about one hundred times, and the New Left forty-four times.

Gouldner's book attempts to grasp all of the major contemporary concerns and views of the left and New Left. Without doubt, the "radical left" (aside from the Maoist faction known as Progressive Labor) has been more barren of interest in workers and middle America than even the ex-radicals.

On a different tangent, the conservative ideas of consensus and communication as means of resolving conflict, came into their own. The practical applications of these ideas were sensitivity training and group dynamics, activities which have some validity as therapy but which were often used to pacify workers and dissenters with mere words.

The Oxford Movement, which flourished in the 1930's and reappeared in the 1960's as Moral Rearmament, was based on the idea that the great failure in our society was one of communication. Its exponents wanted the lions and lambs to sit down together and talk out their conflict, the assumption being that people who were fighting for a bigger stake in the society could be placated by such therapeutic "understanding." The movement's ideas were applied with some impact to the political scene and to the conduct of labor-management relations.

The group dynamics movement had a similar appeal to management and others who wanted to get people to forget their grievances. It emphasized talk, which is cheap, and minimized the role of unions in resolving conflict. The movement's message to management was that workers wanted not better wages and working conditions (which cost money) but such intangible and inexpensive items as status, participation, etc. The interest in the Hawthorne experiments (conducted at Western Electric by sociologist Elton Mayo), which demonstrated that attention itself would make workers more productive, ran parallel to the assumptions about participation.

When the poverty program came along, sensitivity training was applied to blacks, in an effort to reduce their anger
and protest.

Communications was considered a related cure for conflict. Industry hired communications experts to treat employee problems. Management lionized Marshall McLuhan,
as did many of the young ex-radicals. They believed that
in communications, specifically television, he had uncovered a new and powerful secret weapon, a means of controlling minds and society.

The idea of consensus had many useful applications, but
it was reduced to absurdity. Consensus was counterposed
to majority rule. Decisions were never taken to a vote in
which dissenting "no" votes were cast. Everyone was supposed to agree; no minorities, no dissent, no conflict. A
fine goal, but it resulted in a watering down of all decisions
and action—to the point of total consent. The goal was
harmony, not justice or truth, concepts that inevitably
divide people. Consensus invaded American politics and
education. It had a natural appeal to educators, a group of
people who have usually abhorred controversy. How much,
we wonder, of the present rage in the schools derives from
the fastidious suppression of conflict over the years?

Though these movements were not Freudian (many
were anti-Freudian), they accepted the basic concepts of
psychoanalytic thought. The rebel was always explained
in psychological terms. The dissenter was disturbed, sick,
crazy. Many far-out rebels are indeed sick, but many others
have legitimate grievances, and often even the sick ones
are driven to their illness by circumstances that need
attention.

The old ideologies interpreted human behavior in political and economic terms. People behaved as they did
because of objective conditions—an imperfect society. The
new ideology—psychology—interpreted behavior in indi-

vidualistic terms. The disturbance was in the psyche rather than the society.

Crime and delinquency were seen as reflections of distorted internal needs. The delinquent boy was sick and must be treated. Criticisms of the society were seen as "neurotic conflicts of our times"; rebellion, as an outgrowth of impaired relations with parents. The absurdity of trying to deal with objective social grievances through psychotherapy should seem obvious.

Thomas Jefferson observed in 1787: "God forbid we should ever be twenty years without a rebellion. What country can preserve its liberties if its rulers are not warned from time to time that this people preserve the spirit of resistance? Let them take arms. The remedy is to set them right as to facts, pardon and pacify them. What signify a few lives lost in a century or two? The tree of liberty must be refreshed from time to time with the blood of patriots and tyrants. It is its natural manure."

In the Declaration of Independence, Jefferson spoke not of property rights but of human rights and the self-evident truth that all men are created equal. When governments fail to secure natural rights, it is the "Right of the People to alter or to abolish it, and to institute new Government . . . Prudence, indeed, will dictate that Governments long established should not be changed for light and transient Causes . . . But when a long Train of Abuses and Usurpations, pursuing invariably the same Object, evinces a design to reduce them under absolute Despotism, it is their Right, it is their Duty to throw off such Government, and to provide new Guards for their future Security."

Jefferson would not lightly throw out governments, unless they moved to "absolute despotism." But neither would he accept the violation of human rights without protest—or even an occasional rebellion—to show rulers that all is not well.

Jefferson advocated an experimental society, rather than a traditional one. He was an advocate of the poor, the people, the popular will, individual civil rights. He would not support the Constitution until the Bill of Rights was included, providing freedom of religion and the press, protecting against standing armies, etc. He believed that the best government was that which governed least. Though he was an aristocrat, gentleman farmer and slaveowner, founder of the aristocratic University of Virginia, he probably would have seen, had he lived into the industrial era, that laissez-faire permits the powerful to reign unchecked by public will and that federal government can be the only resource open to people for creative innovation in the society.

4

This book treats the middle American as victim rather than villain in our current social drama. There is yet time to redress the wrongs from which he suffers and to reenlist him in the progressive coalitions that support social and political equity and a more open and generous society. We Americans are now able to see some of the invisible poor—those at the very bottom of society. The working class and other residents of middle America are still invisible and unattended; perhaps their time is coming.

Above all others in politics, the Kennedys have been able to reach this group—and not just because of the family name or personal style, as some suppose. The Kennedys, perhaps because their Irish Catholicism made them outsiders in many places, were able to experience and express the sentiments of the middle American, as well as the ghetto resident.

Few doubt that Bobby Kennedy would have won a majority of the white working-class vote, as his brother did before him. Though called racists by many, these workers responded to Bobby because he talked to them and expressed their views and needs, even while addressing himself directly to the grievances of blacks, chicanos and poor whites.

It is true that the Kennedys possessed a special magic, but it is one they neither invented nor patented. They simply have had the intelligence to look at and comprehend the whole of the society, and the courage to speak out against discrimination in all its manifestations.

The way is open to others. Indeed, political programs that do not speak to the needs of middle America are losers. If liberal and left-of-liberal politicians continue to ignore the middle American, his march to the right will become a stampede—a right-wing victory of unprecedented magnitude will be won and a truly repressive, perhaps even dictatorial, regime installed in power.

In this book, we shall explore several themes, all of them relating to the middle American. Above all, we shall look at the myth that the average man is living in contented affluence. The chapters on income, workers and consumers will establish the basic features of the middle man's marginality, and the one on grievances will explore the sources of his discontent, financial and otherwise. In the two chapters on survival, we shall see the middle man as a victim of violent dissent in the society, and we shall see his own sacrifices and struggle for survival.

In the section on equity and alienation we compare economic and other aspects of his life to those of groups with superior advantages. In our treatment of taxes we see how even this instrument of public equity is turned against the average family. Chapter 8, on equality, describes the continuing inequities inherent in our class structure, and

Chapter 10, on education, summarizes the persisting educational handicaps from which middle America suffers. Chapter 12, on alienation, deals with the sense of estrangement felt by middle America in relation to those above and below them on the social scale.

We postulate, in this section on equity, the existence of at least two distinct classes above the middle American—the affluent (most of whom are members of the educated New Class) and the rich, those of great wealth and power. Being very special people, the rich deserve very special treatment. It is they who own virtually a controlling interest in the nation's total wealth, and who influence most strategic economic and political decisions. The classes below—the affluent, middle America, the poor—share one characteristic in common: they are, compared to the rich, relatively impotent and impecunious. These last two classes absorb their energies in conflict with one another. Living side by side, they batter each other, while the very rich, who live in detached isolation, need not accommodate themselves to their neighbors' interests.

In dealing with ethnics we explore the identity of many middle Americans, their relations with the black community, and finally, in some detail, look at the qualities of one ethnic group—the Irish—that make them distinct and at the same time typical of middle America. The final chapters on alliances deal with the relation of workers, liberals, intellectuals, New Classmen, unions.

We do not wish to glorify the individual working-class man. Yet as a class, workers possess a quiet strength, integrity, good sense and genuine individuality. It is regrettable that so few of our writers, dramatists, artists have ever seen fit to portray the workingman as more than a slob, menial, buffoon, racist. In a sense this core of our society—working-class culture—has almost never found expression in the formal arts or in the material that finds its way into academic classrooms. Occasionally the media will pick up a working-class type—most notably in the recent past the folk singer Johnny Cash—and find he is a crashing success, instantly and unexpectedly. But neither the media nor others who "express" American culture or peddle the arts learn much from such bright examples. Maybe soon we will begin to notice these people, their needs, and the political and economic organizations they have created.

2

The Myth of Affluence

The myth that all Americans are affluent has made us unobservant of middle America. The idea that the average family is fairly saturated with material goods comes mainly from the economic theories of John Kenneth Galbraith.

Economics can be a dreary subject, as dull as its close synonym "money" is exciting. The economist's prose is liberally studded with baffling statistics, references to cyclical movements, fiscal policy, and other abstractions. The opacity of their prose style causes two very different reactions: either people don't read it at all or they are inclined to accept it as gospel. Readers often suspend their critical judgment where mysteries, especially grand ones such as economists contrive, are concerned.

Karl Marx was perhaps the most notable beneficiary—or victim—of the reader's disinclination to work through even a few paragraphs of a weighty volume. It was enough to know that *Das Kapital* offered a world view, an explanation of many grand mysteries, and memorable phrases such as "historical materialism," the "dialectic," "class struggle." Many felt they need search no further. Once you get the key words, as the speed-reader knows, you have the whole thing; you need not bother with the rest. And if you seek a faith, it is almost better that the gospel be written in a formidable vein, such as a turgid academic German style— that way you are excused from calling on your analytic powers.

For the consumer of economic theories there are many options. All are equally "scientific," all use a common pool of data, all are stridently dogmatic in tone, and all are in sharp conflict. The reader may pick from this bag the one that yields the most suitable slogans for his own purposes.

Most theories are marked by familiar phrases, Pavlovian bells that ring up the right response. "Affluent society" is one such phrase, coined by Galbraith more than a decade ago. So popular did the phrase become that readers often devoured the phrase itself rather than the book of which it is the title. Closer attention to the book's text might have slowed the myth's sudden rise to fame.

The phrase caught on because it seemed to ring the right bell for the educated, book-buying class. This group had by the mid fifties achieved an unexpected level of material prosperity. It was pleased but somewhat conflicted about its good fortunes, for as a class it was presumably committed to intellectual rather than material values. Out of its own prosperity and the guilt that accompanied it (and also some self-interest) the educated grasped at the idea that the average man had consumed enough and should turn to public values. Absorbing the idea was eased by Galbraith's reluctance to press the issue of equality or ask this educated and affluent class to share its fortunes with others. So there was little to lose. A moratorium would be called; workers would give up wage demands and at the same time consent to pay a higher tax rate for public services. The myth was also made easier to accept by class myopia. This class is so numerous that its members often see only one another. Seeing everywhere around them only a thick mass of prosperous professionals, they assumed that everyone had made it.

It is difficult to resist observing that Galbraith began his celebrated book with these words: "Since I sailed for Switzerland in the early summer of 1955 to begin work on this book I have accumulated a large and cosmopolitan set of obligations. Thus a Guggenheim fellowship facilitated that movement as did my wife . . ."

It is equally difficult to avoid speculating that Professor Galbraith was delivering in his celebrated book a familiar yet welcome message to a growing army of Switzerland-bound, Guggenheim-winning book buyers. The trip from Cambridge to Switzerland may be an enlightening one, but it does not cross the path of middle America.

Galbraith made these points:

1. The Keynesian preoccupation with productivity, which still dominates liberal and conservative economics, does not suit the affluent society.

2. The new affluence makes obsolete the old stress on jobs, work, full employment, economic growth, productivity, gross national product.

3. The old issues of inequality and insecurity no longer excite much interest and are also unsuited to our times.

4. We need to deemphasize consumer spending and production, and stress instead leisure, public service, investment in human resources (especially education) and en-

largement of the New Class of professionals (those who seek gratifying work rather than money).

5. While we still have some poverty, median income is well into the affluent level. Increased taxes to support the new leisure and public services are so vital that we must put aside the old liberal insistence on tax equity. Liberals should stop opposing the sales tax and other taxes that bear more heavily on low- than high-income groups. We may then get on with the job of taxing to support public programs.

Aside from a reference to poverty at the very end of the book, Galbraith paid no attention to the problems that accompany limited incomes or to the material deprivation common to middle America.

Man does not live by bread, pay checks, and material things alone. But he cannot live at all without them. Galbraith's mistake was the assumption that almost everyone had as much bread as was needed to satisfy reasonable appetites.

Governor Muñoz Marín "first persuaded me to question the wisdom of our preoccupation with more and more consumer goods as a goal," Galbraith says. Still, Governor Muñoz found a place in history and the hearts of the Puerto Rican people because he brought what was relatively speaking an astonishing new material prosperity to his country. He did not wish to disturb the unhurried warmness and hospitality of the Puerto Rican people but at the same time he wanted to achieve dramatic advances in the material standard.

Galbraith made several major errors of observation and prognostication. Since these errors persist in the revised text of his book and in the heart of liberalism, they may still influence our view of middle America. It is difficult to see how we can boost public programs and real personal income by de-emphasizing productivity, as he suggested. On the contrary, greater national productivity—of *useful* goods—is clearly a prerequisite for better income and public services.

Galbraith's failure to note the material needs of most Americans (in fact his positive assertion that the average man was doing well financially) added to the already overblown complacency and conservatism of the New Class. Indeed, he was as responsible as anyone for the popular belief, held by liberals and conservatives alike, that the "old" issues (full employment, decent wages, health care, housing) are "dead."

When Galbraith sailed for Switzerland in 1955 to write his book, he was moving before a gathering storm. Only one year before, the Supreme Court had ruled that de jure school segregation was unconstitutional. The ensuing national conflict concerned an issue that Galbraith felt no longer meant much to most Americans—equality. Yet equality, and the related issue of poverty, still shape our times. Galbraith never in his book mentioned the words "Negro" or "race." Even though he dealt with poverty briefly, he did not see that it raised the issue of equality or that it was potent enough to shake our social institutions.

Galbraith, we suspect, had his eye on the New Class when he spoke of affluence. This New Class of college-bred professionals, executives, owners, politicians, and organization leaders are quite affluent. Their high income gives them enormous consumer power, which they use unsparingly.

Some members of the New Class spend their money on gadgets, flashy cars, big wardrobes, and wall-to-wall carpets. Others consume less conspicuously. They often disdain what they call gadgetry. Even so, few of them are without new dishwashers, garbage disposal units, washing machines and dryers, freezers. They may deplore Cadillac convertibles, but they will probably own at least two cars—perhaps rather dated and ostentatiously economical. They may not invest much in fancy home furnishings, but typically they will live in fine spacious houses with ample grounds and gardens, situated in expensive and exclusive neighborhoods. Usually they have a place in the country. They will travel extensively; during the winter they may fly to Florida or the Caribbean with their families, and during the summer to their seashore or mountain place.

They send their children to private schools so that they can get into the best colleges. The object of such schooling is often not so much a good education as a passport to continued affluence. They may also buy music, dance, tennis lessons for their children—or send them for an academic year or summer abroad. They dine out frequently—and they are more likely to go to The Four Seasons than Chock Full O' Nuts. With such substantial consumer pleasures, who needs gadgets and flashy fronts?

In Galbraith's view, work satisfaction means more to the New Class than maximizing income. Perhaps. To our view, the New Class tries as hard as anyone to maximize both job *and* pay satisfaction. The shaggy-looking sons of the affluent want money as much as anyone does. This zeal is conspicuous, for example, in the consulting, lecturing, and other financially rewarding moonlighting chores that professors and their kindred do when they can—and in the tough negotiations they carry on with their deans each year over salary. The young lawyers and physicians who work in programs specially designed to serve the poor must be history's most highly paid idealists. Few of them work for less than $15,000 a year, and some earn much more than that.

2

The United States is the wealthiest nation in history. There are probably more truly affluent people in this country than in all other nations combined. The same is probably true of the near-affluent: only a relative handful of Americans are millionaires, but tens of thousands own two cars, two televisions, two family homes.

The affluent and near-affluent form a large and conspicuous mass, whose style of life creates the illusion of general opulence. Yet the central fact of our economic life is that a majority of American families earns less than $9,000 a year. In 1969 the median income of all families, based on the income of all wage earners in the family, was $8,632. Half earned less and half earned more than that amount. According to the carefully devised budget of the U.S. Bureau of Labor Statistics, this is well under the $10,077 required in 1969 for a family of four to live in urban areas at only a "moderate living standard." The people not living in family groups—the "unrelated individuals"—were worse off. Their median income in 1969 was only $2,786.

About 29.6 million Americans live in families earning $15,000 a year or more, a level that is generally considered (by Bureau of Labor Statistics standards) to be the lower limit of affluence. Far less visible than these conspicuous consumers are the 118.6 million Americans who live in families earning *less* than $15,000 but *more* than the $5,000 poverty level. About 65 percent of all white American families are in this category. This great mass of middle Americans outnumbers the affluent by about four to one.

It is true that the number of people who are truly affluent has increased over the years. Between 1955 and 1967, the proportion of families earning $15,000 or more almost quadrupled—from about 3 percent of all families to about 12 percent. Still, only one family in eight is in this group.

During those same years, the proportion of poor families (those earning $5,000 or less in constant 1967 dollars) also decreased dramatically—from 41 percent to 25 percent of all families. The size of middle America (families earning $5,000 to $15,000) increased from 54 percent to 63 percent of all families.

Yet since many writers and scholars live among the affluent and are themselves affluent, they have led us to mistake the affluent minority for the struggling majority. Most Americans rarely enter expensive steak houses. When they do, it's for a special event—a golden anniversary, a union convention, or a meeting of a fraternal order. Most never or rarely go to movies, the theater, concerts. Their entertainment comes mainly from TV and an occasional night out to bowl, watch ball games, play cards, or go to church, a union meeting, a relative's house.

Many buy their houses half finished and spend their leisure time painting, building a garage, fixing up. Some put up their own houses, from scratch. Increasingly they buy and live in house trailers (mobile homes). There are hundreds of squatters' villages (trailer "parks") housing thousands of middle Americans—in barren lots, close to the city dump, or backed up against the factory parking lot. The glib commentators on affluence might spend a season in one of these "parks" or in a typical crackerbox neighborhood if they really want to dig into the mid-American way of life.

Most families are kept afloat by multiple incomes. Since about half of all income-earning *individuals* make $5,000 or less, other earners are needed to bring median family income up to its present level of $8,632. Usually it is the wife who brings home the second pay check. The higher the family income is (except in the bracket over $15,000) the more earners are needed in a family to put it together. More than 60 percent of white families needed two or more earners in 1967 to reach an income of $5,000 or more.

There is nothing wrong with multiple incomes or working wives. In a sense it is a mark of progress, in indicating that jobs are available to what have been traditionally considered marginal workers—women, the elderly, the young. What the average family suffers from is the *need* for multiple incomes. In most families, wives and children *must* work because the family head is so poorly paid. Many wives find it awkward or impossible to take jobs, because they have large families to take care of or are unsuited to the labor market. The hardship is greatest for the young family, where male earnings are low and young children abundant.

We criticize the Soviet system where "a man can't earn a decent living so he has to send his wife out to work." To what extent does the observation apply to our own system as well?

3

A city worker, age thirty-eight, with a family of four had to make close to $10,000 a year in the fall of 1968 [1] in order to live at a "modest but adequate standard of living." [2] That means he had to work forty hours a week, fifty-two weeks a year, and make about $4.80 an hour (about $192 a week). Even the most highly paid industrial

[1] The Bureau of Labor Statistics is slow to compile such data. At the time of this publication, data for the year 1968 were the latest available. However, the index does not rise dramatically from year to year.

[2] "Three Standards of Living, for an Urban Family of Four Persons," U.S. Dept. of Labor, BLS, Bulletin No. 1570-5, and City Workers Family Budget for a Moderate Living Standard, Autumn, 1966, Bulletin No. 1570-1, BLS.

The moderate budget does not represent an ideal standard. The quantities (but not the cost) of items in the budget were determined from surveys of what families actually buy.

workers, as in the auto industry, earned only $3.50 an hour, or $7,280 a year, without layoffs.

According to the careful calculations of the U.S. Bureau of Labor Statistics, $10,000 is a "moderate"—not an affluent—budget for a city family of four. It allows for *no savings at all* and nothing that the affluent call luxuries.

For a "higher living standard," says the B.L.S. (Bureau of Labor Statistics), a city worker must make about $4,000 more each year than what is allowed in the moderate standard—or about $14,000 a year. "This higher standard of living budget will reflect a more comfortable level and manner of living sometimes known as the "American standard of living." It is the only budget that allows for major medical insurance. This higher standard still provides for no savings or luxuries.

The low budget devised by the B.L.S.—described as "austere"—requires a family income of $5,154.

About 63 percent of all white families in the country earn less than $10,000 a year—the "moderate budget" level. In other words, about two in three white American families do not even live at a "moderate" standard.

4

Real income (income after taxes and inflation) continues to rise over the years, but not so quickly as most people assume. Between 1952 and 1962, for example, average family income (after taxes and in constant 1962 dollars) rose from $5,220 to $6,400, an increase in real earnings of $1,180—or only $118 a year over the decade.[3] This pros-

[3] Jeannete M. Fitzwilliams, "Size Distribution of Income in 1962," *Survey of Current Business,* April 1963.

perous decade, in which Galbraith conceived the "affluent society," annually yielded to the average family the equivalent of only one additional week's pay. Progress toward affluence was just as plodding for the average family in the years after 1962 as before.[4] For the average worker and his family, real earnings actually *declined* between 1962 and 1969. In 1962 real wages (for private workers, excluding farm workers, with three dependents—after tax and social security deductions) were $79.03 a week; by 1969, real wages were *down* to $78.77.

We come now to the puzzling matter of standards. What is a proper standard of affluence? Who is to say that the middle American has not arrived at that standard? Compared with Fiji Islanders, Peruvian Indians, and the Watusi, he is a king. For that matter, the poorest black sharecropper in the South is well-off materially, compared with millions of people throughout the world—perhaps even compared with those considered affluent in other societies.

Such comparisons, though interesting, are often not germane to a discussion of American economic conditions. We all live, for better or worse, in America, where we are weaned on a national faith in progress, the belief that one must aspire to the top and that, with enough effort, anyone can become a Carnegie or a Rockefeller. Nourished on this rich diet of rising expectations and belief in equality, we naturally want something better than we have. We want it now. It is the same doctrine America has tried to spread to the developing world—this doctrine of rising expectations. If it's good enough for them, it's good enough for all Americans, including middle America.

[4] The growth in average per capita income (after taxes and adjusted for inflation) was only 10.6 percent during the three years between 1964 and 1968. *Survey of Current Business,* Commerce Dept. Office of Business Economics, July 1969.

The middle American feels *relatively* deprived, just as blacks feel deprived in relation to others. The average man's *absolute* living standard is low enough to warrant dissatisfaction, too low to bring him up to the B.L.S. "moderate" budget. But his relative standard—relative to the affluence of others—is intolerable. And he knows it, even without articulating it. He knows he is not making it. In 1969 more than two thirds of middle-income families surveyed felt they were not better off financially than the previous year.[5] Many felt they were worse off. The number of those feeling worse off almost doubled between 1966 and 1969. Moreover, the sense of slipping financially, falling back rather than going forward, is considerably greater in the middle- than in high-income groups, according to the survey.

5

The affluent (who are mainly managers, owners, professionals) have several tricks up their sleeves to provide themselves tax-free income. If this hidden income is added to the exposed income figures, the affluent are seen to be doing even better than it appears at first glance.

Expense accounts are probably the most lavish of the income substitutes given the affluent by large corporations, but there are others—complete health care, insurance, housing, restricted stock options on which only capital-gains taxes need be paid.

Big business is always searching for tax-free benefits for executives. The search maneuvers its way in and out of

[5] Survey Research Center, University of Michigan, *Survey of Consumer Finances, 1967.*

revenue rules, looking for legal loopholes. Business lobbies make many of the loopholes by influencing what laws are passed, and their expensive tax lawyers search out soft spots and punch holes where none exist.

"Money itself is no longer much of a management lever, especially in the upper echelons," says *Dun's Review,* and quotes a vice-president of General Tire as saying, "Dollars are too expensive. You have to make it up to the man with incentive gimmicks, bonuses, stock options or fringe goodies." [6]

So eager is the search for tax-free benefits, that in the early sixties, Project 777, an organization of sixty-nine member companies, was formed to exchange information about new forms of benefits.

Some companies give benefits cafeteria style. The executive can take his choice. He may be offered, say, $10,000 in extra compensation. The computer then shows him the various combinations of things he can buy with this money and the long-run costs of each. "Frankly," one company vice-president said, "compensation has been a game of cat and rat. For years we have been dodging in and out of tax shelters while staying two paces ahead of the law."

Within some limits, expense spending is tax-free so long as its object is to make a profit. This bending of tax law to suit moneymakers benefits professionals as well as executives. The writer and the college professor, for instance—if they make a profit on their writing—can deduct any number of ordinary expenses from their taxable income. Anyone who is self-employed or who owns anything that he makes a profit on is also in line for tax benefits.

For both executives and professionals, there are car allowances, paid dues in country clubs, professional societies; expense-paid business and professional meetings, travel grants, scholarships for their children, etc.

[6] "Executive Salaries," *Dun's Review,* March 1969.

About 80 percent of the checks in the most expensive restaurants, according to Gabriel Kolko, and 30 to 40 percent of Broadway theater tickets are covered by business expense accounts. In 1954, 37 percent of Cadillacs registered in Manhattan and 20 percent in Philadelphia were in the names of businesses; half of the executives in small companies and a third of those in large ones are reimbursed for expenses in social clubs and organizations; about the same number are provided private cars.[7] Approximately one in five large corporations has its own country clubs and executive resorts. Unofficial Treasury Department estimates in 1957 put total corporate expense accounts at from $5 to $10 billion.

Oddly enough, in view of the tons of statistics reported by government and private agencies, no systematic accounting of expense spending is made. It is, therefore, impossible to know what it amounts to nationally. Spending on executive clubs alone is estimated to be $3 billion a year. Compare this with the $7 billion spent by the federal government alone on public education. And the club is only one small item in a gigantic expense budget.

Dun's Review reports that there are from 3,000 to 7,000 private clubs, including country clubs, in the nation.[8] Corporations devote about $3 billion a year to food, liquor and facilities needed to maintain these clubs. The clubs provide everything from fine living, eating, meeting quarters to the latest in recreation facilities.

The expense account buys almost everything that regular income can buy—breakfast, lunch, dinner, cars and gasoline, night-club entertainment, Mediterranean cruises, elaborate resorts in the Caribbean. Almost anything goes. Only recently has the purchase of call girls for customers

[7] Gabriel Kolko, *Wealth and Power in America,* New York: Praeger, 1962.

[8] "The Booming Clubs of Business," *Dun's Review,* July 1969.

been strictly prohibited by Internal Revenue. For many years it had been an allowable entertainment item.

Expense-account dining has become such a common extravagance for executives that *Dun's Review* offers advice on how to eat in elegant restaurants without gaining weight. "Your problem is this: There you are, making deals in fancy restaurants, coping with frosty Maitre D's, spending your company's money; and gaining weight." You can also gain weight at a luncheonette but it's more difficult to "forego the delectable concoctions provided every day at an excellent restaurant." Dieting requires "a sincere, uncompromising desire to lose weight—and—somebody else's money." With the company's money you can replace cottage cheese with such delicacies "as fresh caviar, hearts of palm vinaigrette, chateaubriand, and champagne." The diet requires one sacrifice—that the executive eat lunch on only $24.95 a day. For an amount below $25, the boss does not require that a receipt be shown.

This $25 ceiling is seen as a plot by the funless staff of Internal Revenue. "The men in the IRS are found each day to eat lunch in some bastion of culinary mediocrity such as the cafeteria of the National Archives Building, and they have decided that the rest of us should be held accountable for having a good time. What they say is that it is okay to have a good time provided it does not cost more than $25.00."

The expense account "is an American cultural phenomenon devised to make creative people trapped in our urban jungles feel as if they were making more money than they actually are—and to allow all corporations a viable and legitimate means of coping with the Internal Revenue Service." [9]

[9] "The Expense Account Diet," Jonathan Dolger, *Dun's Review,* Nov. 1969.

Conspicuous consumption at this level is limited to some 12 percent of the population, at most. The executive may complain about having to account for a lunch bill over $25, but the average man has not much more than that to spend each day for all the costs of his living.

6

Many of the refrigerators, washing machines and other household conveniences that casual observers mistake for affluence are financed by installment debt—and represent voluntary but pressing obligations rather than assets. A majority of American families owe such debts, and the proportion grows each year. In early 1969, total installment debt in the nation exceeded $89 billion.

The middle American is more likely to be indebted than those above or below him on the income ladder, and his debt grows at a faster rate. About 65 percent of average-income families had installment debt in 1969, compared with 48 percent of those with incomes in excess of $15,000.[10] Most families have serious trouble paying off these debts, and many default.

About three in ten families have car debts. Indeed, this is the most common form of indebtedness among families over the poverty line. Young couples are the most likely to be in debt. They have more to buy and less income and savings to buy it with.

When New Classmen talk about the glut of gadgets in our society, presumably they have in mind items like washers, dryers, refrigerators, dishwashers, TV, air conditioning. While many Americans treasure these "gadgets"—

[10] Survey Research Center, University of Michigan, *Survey of Consumer Finances,* Report III, June 1969.

particularly housewives and working women whose labor they conserve—it is not true that they are fixtures in every American home. Television sets and refrigerators, found in 81 percent of all homes, come closest to being standard in American households.

We might assume that by now every household has a washing machine; in fact only 70 percent have them. Only 38 percent of households own clothes dryers, 16 percent dishwashers, 20 percent air conditioners.

Those who write so frequently about excess gadgetry in the home might, in looking honestly at their own households, find the very items there that the average family covets but cannot afford, even on the installment plan.

The desire for more basic material goods peaks in the middle-income groups. About two-thirds of this group say there are things they want to buy or replace. People at the highest income levels are more likely to be satisfied with the material goods they have, simply because they have so much. The greatest longing for more goods is found among the young. Three-quarters of those under age thirty-five, compared with one third of those sixty-five or older, want to buy or replace something.[11]

The two most costly and valued possessions of Americans are home and car. A home is the average man's domain and his major asset in life. Only about 60 percent of all non-farm families were home owners in 1968—a decline from 63 percent in 1964. Home owning varies with income. About 85 percent of non-farm families making $15,000 or more owned their own home in 1968, but only 52 percent of those in the $5,000 to $7,500 bracket.

The average man has been priced out of the market by land speculators and money lenders. In 1949 the average price of a new home was $9,780. In 1969 it was $20,534.

[11] Survey Research Center, University of Michigan, *Productive Americans*, James N. Morgan, et al., 1966.

The proportionate costs of land and financing doubled, while the proportionate costs of labor declined steeply. Even prefabrication, it appears, will not rescue the housing market from the owners of land and money. Only public intervention will do that.[12]

Even among those who do have their own homes, home ownership means vastly different things to different people. For the affluent it usually means a spacious and well-equipped home in the suburbs, with an acre or so of land and perhaps a swimming pool. For most mid-Americans it means a cracker-box on a treeless, shrubless street, or an aging place near the city's decaying slums or a smoke-belching factory. Not tenements, but not far away.

The possession of the average American that is envied most around the world is his car. Far less glamour attaches to the possession of an automobile in the average man's real life than is imagined.

A middle American family generally owns one car bought at a used-car lot and operated in so-so shape for at least several years. Those owning two, three or even four cars—one or all of them new and expensive—usually earn far above the middle man's income.

For the average man the auto is a necessity. He has no choice but to own one. He is dependent upon a reliable source of transportation to and from his job, and good public transportation is virtually nonexistent in America.

[12] HOME BUILDING COST, 1949 AND 1969
(*Congressional Record,* Oct. 29, 1969).

		1949		1969	
Structure		70%		56%	
	On-site labor	33%		18%	
	Materials	36		38	
Land		11		21	
Overhead and profit		15		13	
Financing		5		10	
Average Price			$9,780		$20,534

Many of the leisure activities available to him are designed for those with access to an automobile, so that if he wants to participate he must have one.

Perhaps it can be said that the middle American is too attached to his car—not only does it get him where he wants to go, but it gives him a sense of freedom, mobility, power and a pride in ownership. The need and attachment, however, are matched by a resentment.

Only about one in four middle Americans who owns a car is driving a new one. About 40 percent of middle-income earners report that the last car they bought is at least five years old now, while about half of the affluent report that they are driving a new car. About 63 percent of affluent households against 25 percent of middle-income households own two or more cars. About one in ten middle-income families owns no car at all.

The average man can see that this car is a mixed blessing. The car's exhaust pollutes the air, his lungs, house, clothes. The highways that serve it take up about a fourth of all urban land. It creates indescribable congestion. It kills thousands and cripples millions more. It piles cost upon cost—purchase, repair, licenses, insurance, garages, streets, highways, traffic police, parking lots, etc. Perhaps the biggest pain is poor service. The old vehicle that the average man usually is stuck with just barely makes it through the day. In the end, the automobile is more often an aggravation than a convenience. Though most cars are designed for quick obsolescence, the average man must keep his own vehicle far beyond the limits of its natural life. Again, he is the victim rather than beneficiary of affluence.

Leisure is another big consumer item. Since we are presumed to have increasing amounts of leisure, we are also presumed to spend more on it too.

What we know about leisure (how much there is of it, who has it, how it's spent, what it costs) can be summarized briefly: almost nothing. What we do know is that some people have large quantities of time when they are not at their regular jobs. College professors, teachers and many other New Classmen enjoy three months vacation every summer, during which most travel at least part of the time. Many also use extended winter and spring vacations to go South or visit their country homes.

What is ordinary to the New Class is exceptional to the average man. In fact, the majority of middle Americans take no real vacation at all during the year. They may travel overnight to visit friends or relatives, but the majority do not take real trips (five days or more). In 1967, 70 percent of families with incomes over $15,000 took real trips, compared with 34 percent of families earning between $5,000 and $7,500, and fewer than 50 percent of middle Americans earning up to $15,000.[13]

Those who did vacation could not have gone far, judging by what they spent on the trip—a mean amount of $390. Among the vacationers, the highest income group spent more than twice as much as the middle American. In 1967, families earning more than $15,000 spent $700, but families earning $5,000 to $7,500 spent only $260 and those earning up to $10,000 spent only $270.

The worker's leisure is more a construct devised by armchair researchers than a pressing reality. During his work week the average man is too busy and too tired to play much. It is probably fair to assume, therefore, that most of the money spent on leisure in our country is spent by the affluent and rich. In 1969 that spending totaled $83 billion. Spending for leisure has dramatically increased in recent years, as has the size of the leisure class. Between

[13] Survey Research Center, University of Michigan.

1965 and 1969 alone, spending for leisure increased an estimated 42 percent.[14]

The biggest leisure spending item is recreational equipment—airplanes, boats, camping vehicles, color television, motor bikes, etc. Together with admissions to sports events, $38 billion a year is spent on them. It is not known how these items are distributed in the population, but it is fairly certain that the big-cost items, such as boats and planes, are simply the newest playthings of the affluent and rich.

Some 4.2 million Americans go abroad each year and spend $5.2 billion. It is doubtful that such travel cuts very deep into middle America.

It has been noted that most middle Americans do not take "real vacations," trips of more than five days duration. Beyond that, there are no statistics available on how the average American spends what limited leisure he has. A single shred of information comes from a U.S. Department of Commerce report: the higher the income, education and job status of the head of family, the more likely is a family

[14] Spending for recreation, sports equipment, reading matter, sporting events, other "personal consumption" products and activities	*1969 (est.) (billions of $)* 38.2	*Increase from 1965* 43%
Vacations and recreation trips in U.S.	35.0	40%
Travel abroad	5.2	37%
Second homes	1.5	67%
Swimming pools	1.4	27%
Vacation land and lots	1.3	86%
TOTAL	82.6	42%

Sources: American Automobile Assn.; U.S. Dept. of Commerce; Recreational Vehicle Institute; International Snowmobile Industry Assn.; National Swimming Pool Institute; U.S. Dept. of Housing and Urban Development. 1969 estimates—USN&WR Economic Unit.

to take part in outdoor recreation.[15] If the family head had a paid vacation, the family was also more likely to participate. The further from the city the family lived, the more likely were they to participate.

How does the average man take his pleasures? If any researchers had been concerned enough to inquire, they would probably have come to this big five: TV, sex, cards, booze, bowling—and not necessarily in that order. Judging by the fact that more deaths are attributable to cirrhosis of the liver (28,000 in 1967) than to accidents in the home (24,000), it would appear that booze, a specific for fatigue and pain, is very high on the list.

Because so many commentators on American life are estranged from the object of their inquiries, gross distortions often appear in their observations. Some see American life as rosy, promising, affluent. Others see it as gray, menacing, impoverished. Professor Galbraith sees one set of colors. Professor Ferdinand Lundberg, author of *The Rich and the Super-Rich*, sees a different set altogether. Both men, of course, are respected scientists and scholars.

Most Americans, Lundberg writes, "own nothing more than their household goods, a few glittering gadgets such as automobiles and television sets (usually purchased on the installment plan, many at second hand) and the clothes on their backs."

It would be difficult, he says, for Americans to show fewer possessions "if the country had labored under a grasping dictatorship." How has it been possible, he asks, for a society to strip threadbare a population that at least once owned a piece of virgin land?

Lundberg compares the United States to Latin American oligarchies. Newspapers, he says, are "invariably grieved

[15] *Tourism and Recreation,* U.S. Dept. of Commerce, Economic Development Administration, 1967.

to find a small oligarchy of big landowners in control" in Latin America, with the rest of the population being "sycophantic hangers-on and landless, poverty-stricken peasants." [16] The situation in the U.S. with respect to employees and owners, he suggests, is similar.

Galbraith sees rosy colors and Lundberg muddy ones. The real America—middle America—falls somewhere between the two hues. The United States is not a Latin-American dictatorship or oligarchy. Hence the total failure of revolutionaries to persuade any significant number of "dispossessed" to overthrow their government in favor of something else. The middle American is neither affluent nor dispossessed. And he is neither pleased with his lot nor ready to swap it for a revolutionist's dream.

Yet the myth that all Americans, except the "poor," are floating on bubbles of prosperity, is now part of our folklore. It is so popular that it is hard to dislodge by facts alone, especially cold and lifeless statistics. The facts tell us clearly that, while the rising New Class of professionals and managers has fallen on good times, the great bulk of our citizenry does not even reach a "modest" let alone an opulent level of well-being.

The folklore is nourished by invisibility and lack of interest. The middle American is plain Bill, an ordinary person, making a living, minding his own business. He can be overlooked. Since those who tell us what is happening in our country apparently notice only deviance and violence, the bond is sealed and the myth is perpetuated.

[16] Ferdinand Lundberg, *The Rich and the Super-Rich*, New York: Lyle Stuart Inc., 1968, p. 4.

3

Grievances

We Americans are all educated and sensitive people. We know suffering when we see it, and we are quick to recognize social problems and identify with victims of injustice. We believe we can put ourselves in the other man's place and see the world through his eyes.

Let us try out our powers of empathy on someone who is as strange as he is familiar to most of us: the middle American. So common is he, and lacking in exotic appeal, that we hardly notice his presence around us everywhere. He is no hero in the ordinary sense—no Ulysses, Hamlet, Kennedy—whose fall from greatness is presumed to be the essence of tragedy. In fact, he likes to think of himself as an "average man," no better or worse than the others, trying to get along and do his best without upstaging or pushing out the other guy. Unlike those of us whose preferences run to the bizarre, the extraordinary, the mid-American is not turned off by words such as "common," "average," "ordinary" or the reality they represent. On the contrary, he finds his greatest comfort in this familiar middle ground. He is—in the terse language used to dismiss him—square, not very groovy.

But he is important, if not conspicuous, because he represents a large group of people. If we measure by income alone, and leave out the people below the poverty level and above the $15,000-a-year affluence level, we have left to us about 65 percent of our population. This is middle America.

It takes all kinds to put together middle America— blue-collar workers, white-collar workers, service workers, small businessmen and professionals. This diversity is tied together by some common threads. Mainly the middle American is a wage or salary worker. Most often he is a blue-collar worker. About nine times out of ten his race is white.

Perhaps because of the rise and the insularity of the New Class, the mid-American traditionally lacks articulate spokesmen and interested listeners. The Kennedys came close, as FDR had before them, to registering the sentiments of the average man. But two Kennedys are gone and the mid-American is probably still more shaken by their deaths than by other current acts of violence.

Silent as he has been, the average American still has many unspoken gripes. Some of them found an outlet in votes for George Wallace, backlash, and support for suppression of dissent. On balance, his *behavior* has usually been admirably tolerant of the anger and violence that afflicts us all.

Many of the middle American's grievances are un-founded, selfish, wrong-headed. The average man is often poorly informed. Moreover, his opinions are manipulated by people who practice the old strategy of divide and con-quer, people who would like to see the rift deepen between mid-America and those dissenting groups who should be allies. So, the average man's grievances are too often di-rected at people lower down instead of those higher up on the social ladder—those who really control his fate.

We may reject the grievances but we can at least listen to them. Such grievances are common in the blue-collar working class. Though middle America, as defined by income, includes many white-collar workers, service work-ers, salesmen, farmers, self-employed, etc., the blue-collar worker is perhaps the most typical, being the most com-mon. The following list of grievances is a composite taken from talks we have had with a variety of blue-collar workers about their views and their problems:

GRIEVANCE

I'm supposed to be affluent, but I'm having as hard a time as ever just keeping ahead. Interest rates go up, taxes go up, prices go up. What I take home doesn't keep up with the inflation.

Thank God I've got my home mostly paid for. But my oldest son . . . he's married and got two young children. He makes $160 a week. He can't buy a decent home for less than $20,000 with 9 percent interest on the mortgage and $5,000 down. He can't raise the cash and he can't make the payments ($112.50 a month for interest alone) without going into heavy debt and staying there. He's having a tough time, my son. It's hardest on these young people.

Nobody gives a damn about *them,* men who are out to earn a decent living. All anybody cares about are the people on welfare, and those hippies and all those long-hair college kids.

GRIEVANCE

My sons can't make it to college, neither can my daughter. They say everyone *else* is going to college. But my kids can't make it. I can help them a little, but I can't stretch it far. Besides, they're not too keen on school. Nothing there interested them much, though they were very good about going and there's nothing at all dumb about them. Of course, as things are at the state college, if they went they'd probably get flunked out in the first year. They think they've got too many kids there, so they just flunk most of them out right away. I want my kids to have the breaks and have a better life than I had, but I don't see how they're going to make it.

GRIEVANCE

I've got one son, my youngest, in Vietnam. He didn't have a chance. He couldn't get out of it by going to college. He says that all the men there are in the same boat. They come from average families just like ours, and a lot of them are bitter as hell about being picked to go over there and get killed. They just don't get the same breaks as the college kids.

Of course, my son's willing to do his duty to his country if he has to. And I feel the same way. But we can't understand how all those rich kids—the kids with the beads from the fancy suburbs—how they get off when my son has to go over there and maybe get his head shot off. They get off scot-free . . . and when they see they're going to graduate from college, and maybe get drafted, they raise such a stink.

GRIEVANCE

I've lived in this neighborhood all my life, and my father lived here too. I worked all my life to buy this house, and now it's almost mine—not much, but the only thing of much value besides my car that I own. I built a lot of what's in it with my own hands. We liked this neighborhood and decided to settle here in the first place because the neighbors were like us. Now the black people have moved in. They've got a right to, I guess, just like anybody else. They want a better life. But they're poor people and they don't keep things up the way *we* used to. Most of my friends and my brother were afraid when the blacks started moving in—afraid that everything would go to hell and they wouldn't be able to sell their houses—so they moved. Now they're gone. And the schools have gone down. What have I got left? I guess I'll have to move . . . but, damn it, this is my home. It takes a whole lifetime to make good friends, and now they've all moved out. I'll be a stranger wherever I move.

If more of the blacks moved out into those fancy suburbs, where all those whites who say they're so hot for civil rights live, then maybe there wouldn't be ghettos in neighborhoods like this. But the people out in the rich suburbs won't let them come in . . . unless, of course, they're from Harvard or Yale.

GRIEVANCE

This violence and crime is too much. Houses were burned out in the riots just four blocks from here. I thought they'd get to ours. I sat up for three nights with a shotgun. Now my wife won't go out at night, and I don't feel right about walking around at any time of the day or night. The liquor store down the street has been robbed four times in the last year. All the stores are closing down. I was mugged once and the man in the next house has gotten it twice. Last year they broke through the back door and stole my wife's coat, my camera and the television. It's a hell of a way to live.

GRIEVANCE

The blacks have had a hard time. I don't deny that a minute. But they're always complaining and wrecking things and goofing off. Not all, but a lot of them. The way I see it, they've gotten a lot in the last years. They've moved into the cities, like into my neighborhood, and taken them over. They've moved up into all the top jobs. They're in the offices and the plants. They've done a hell of a lot better than I have—or my family—or people like me. Everybody's getting ahead but us.

GRIEVANCE

All this spitting on policemen and law and order. I don't get that. This is a democratic country. We all vote. We make the laws. The police only see that the laws we make are obeyed. That's their job. They protect us. It's a tough job and it's damn dangerous. You never know when some maniac is going to send you to your coffin. I wouldn't take the job if they gave me the U.S. Mint.

The cops are just like us—ordinary people. My brother was in the force twenty years, and his son's in it too, and I have two cousins who went in. They're all fine men. It's a job, just like being a fireman, or anything else in the civil service. Sure, there are some rotten eggs in the force. Working around crime all the time, some of them are bound to be rotten. But most of them are pretty average guys just like you and me. Their job just makes them tougher than most of us. And people—the good citizens—are always trying to buy them off with one thing or another. They get called to a house that's being robbed and the very people who call them wind up charging them with brutality. How do these punk kids get off calling them pigs and taking pot shots at them?

GRIEVANCE

How come these privileged kids get away with messing up the colleges that we're paying to support? I'd give my right arm to get my son into one of those colleges and all these kids seem to do is parade around and denounce the government. What the hell have they got to complain about? If they don't like it there, let them go out and get a job or get drafted like mine—see how much they like that!

GRIEVANCE

How do these privileged kids get off carrying Viet Cong flags around, saying they want the enemy to win? It sounds like treason to me. My son's over there getting shot at so the rest of us can have more security and a better life. And they want to help the enemy kill him. If *my* son was doing that, instead of kids whose papas have a lot of pull, he'd be locked up damn fast.

GRIEVANCE

What makes these privileged kids feel so smart when all they accomplish—with all their demonstrations and noise—is to get Nixon elected President? I suppose they think that's progress.

GRIEVANCE

These privileged kids spit on us, call us pigs and squares. But what do they offer? Drugs and dope, sex orgies, fiendish crimes, filthy clothes, filthy pads (as they say), loafing around from morning till night, looking for kicks, and living off their parents and off of us. They're destroying everything we struggled to build. They say they're for love, but they seem to hate us, and the government, and the country, and damn nearly everything. Maybe even themselves. They live for themselves, for their own kicks. They have nothing to offer that *I* want.

GRIEVANCE

We're carrying everyone on our backs. The rich don't work. They just clip coupons and order us around. All those people on welfare and those unwed mothers. They won't work. You couldn't *make* them work. They just sit around and collect their checks, and *we* pay for it. Let those women have as many children as they want, each one with a different boyfriend. I don't care. Just don't ask me to pay for bringing them up. I can just barely bring up my own kids.

The hippies and the college kids. They don't work. They just collect on all the things we struggle to pay for. And they all think that we're dopes and drones for doing it.

GRIEVANCE

And the communists. I never went for Joe Mc-Carthy, and all that looking for communists under the quilts, but those communists scare me. They're fanatical, and they have a way of taking over when you're not looking, just like they did in our union for a while. Stalin was the worst, but not the last of them.

They keep saying they're for the workingman, but here's one workingman that doesn't want those fellows ruling me. What the hell does a worker in Russia or China have anyway—except maybe a strait jacket. He doesn't even have a union.

And I don't like to see them moving in on the rest of the world, in Asia and Africa, and places like them. When they get that far, we may be next. Still, we have to sit down more and talk things over with them. They'll change, and we'll change. War is rotten for everybody.

But don't expect me to be happy when I see these kids and professors going over to those fellows. Burning the American flag, spitting on the flag, denouncing their country, and idolizing Castro and Ho Chi Minh. They don't know what they're asking for. If they think they can't say their piece *now*, what do they think Castro would give them?

To tell the truth, I've always thought there's a lot of things wrong with this system. Too few people have too much of the money and all the say about what goes on. And we're way behind some other countries in many ways.

I believe in more justice for all people, full employment, and such things as that. I guess we're moving toward something like socialism, something like the Swedes have. But I'll be damned if I want to see this whole system burned down so those fanatics can run everything. I've got a vote—everybody has—and, if we want to, we can change the things that are wrong. But the more I hear those kids raving about Ho Chi Minh, the more I want to defend this system and everything in it. It's like your wife. You could beat her up every day, but let someone else try to touch her, and you'd defend her. I know one thing for sure, I certainly am not going to trade in this system for something those crazy kids dream up. I know they hate people like me, and wouldn't want anything that would be good for us. If they make me choose up sides, I'll defend what we've got with my life.

GRIEVANCE

I'm not asking for any paradise, but I want some equity and some justice and I want it NOW. To be fair, we ought to trim a lot of the fat off of those rich fellows, and the corporations that run everything and own everything. I'd spread some of this so-called "affluence" around. I'd give more of it to the average guy, and I'd give it to the poor—to all the people who are willing to earn their way, even if for some reason they can't.

Then I'd clean up a mess or two.

Like medical care. It stinks in this country. We should have good medical care for everyone in the country. We've got to stop the doctors from running the whole show.

Like housing. Everyone should have enough room and a decent place to live. No cracker-boxes. Build something good, and build good communities where people can really be neighborly. Make it so that neither the blacks nor the whites get pushed out. Integrate all the suburbs. Don't let the rich segregate themselves and leave all the others to fight it out.

Like jobs. A good job, a dignified job, and a decent wage for everyone—man, woman or child—who wants to work. More part-time jobs for older people and others who can't work full time.

Like schools. Who knows better than *we* do that we need to have better schools and do a better job of educating people? But nobody should be handicapped. Everyone should have the same chance. Everyone should go as far in school as they want to go—free—with no pushouts.

Like pollution. Let's pass laws to keep industry from polluting everything—the air, the water, the land, our lungs, and so on.

Like parks and recreation. There aren't enough places for people in the city to go and play and have fun. We need something that will be better than saloons and opium dens and TV rooms to pass the time.

Like poverty and discrimination and crime. Wipe them out.

Like cities. Make them places where there are things to do, people to meet, things to learn and look at.

Like war. We are not warmongers. The average man wants peace more than anyone. Where do these crazy people get the idea that we want our kids killed in a war? Let's talk it over and over again before we pull a gun.

2

As for the workingman's state of affluence, we must point to some dreary facts. "Production workers in *manufacturing*" are the most numerous, and among the most highly paid, production workers in the country. There are almost 15 million of them, skilled and unskilled, and their average weekly pay (gross) in early 1969 was $126.77. This was an hourly rate of a little more than $3, and a yearly rate of about $6,600.

Take-home for such a worker (with three dependents) averaged $109.33. Taking inflation into account, *the real spendable income of such workers has risen only a few cents in more than five years.*

With a take-home of $109.33, a family of four teeters on the edge of poverty. If they spend $10 out of this pay check on various other taxes (non-income taxes), and $5 for medical care or insurance, and $35 for rent (modest enough), they are left with only $59 in spendable money. *This comes to not much more than $2 per person per day*—for food, clothing, entertainment, recreation, transportation, savings. It is about what the really affluent would tip the waiter for a single evening meal.

Only in Michigan do the earnings of "production workers in manufacturing" come close to $10,000—what the B.L.S. regards as a "moderate" urban living standard.

But what about those considered the privileged workers—the unionized workers, the small group of production workers who earn more than those in manufacturing, and the skilled craftsmen?

1. Auto workers, who are unionized and among the highest paid in the country, averaged in 1968 only about $3.50 an hour, or $7,280 for a full year's work—still well below the B.L.S. moderate budget.

2. Though most "production workers" are paid less than those "production workers" who are in "manufacturing," some are paid more. Those in mining took home $133.02 in late 1969, and those in contract construction (the most highly paid) took home $159.02. Better, but not much.

3. Skilled workers, craftsmen, are the princes of labor. Everyone considers them affluent, and indeed many of them are—those who work at highly skilled jobs, those who work a lot of overtime and/or have working wives. However, *the median earnings of craftsmen (employed full time) in 1967 were only $7,227.*

If a craftsman works at *union* scale he will usually go over the B.L.S. moderate budget. In late 1969, for example, the average union scale in all building trades was $5.67 an hour, or $11,794 for a full year's work. Most building tradesmen, however, suffer long layoffs each year, and only a minority of them are unionized or work at union scale.

The best-paid building tradesman—the plumber—averaged $6.38 an hour on union scale, or $13,270 for a full year's work. Thus, the most skilled and best-paid union craftsmen, working a full eight-hour day, fifty-two weeks a year, will earn about what an assistant professor makes. The professor, however, will not suffer layoffs or pay reductions, and he will get about three and a half months vacation during which he can earn other income. The craftsman too can work overtime, but he is just as likely to get short-weeks or layoffs. The industrial plumber, the pipe fitter, is more likely to have continuous work than the man in union construction, but he makes less money.

A good friend of ours, for example, works for General Motors as a pipe fitter. Last year he worked the whole year, eight hours a day, fifty-two weeks, without vacation. He also worked forty-five Saturdays and twenty-six Sundays or about six and a half days a week throughout the year. His gross earnings were $14,800 for the year. Our friend served a four-year apprenticeship, during which time he earned less than the journeyman's rate. He is now at the very top of his earning capacity, and can go no further.

Other skilled workers in his plant earn about the same—die makers, millwrights, etc. The best-paid craftsman in the plant, the electrician, makes ten cents an hour more than the pipe fitter. Our friend is much more highly paid than pipe fitters who work in small plants, other industries, or non-union shops.

Another friend of ours is a die maker in a large auto plant. He has three young children and a wife who does not work. Because he wants to be with his family, he works very little overtime. He made something less than $12,000 last year, for a full year's work. He lives in a house he paid $15,000 for. Since the house has only two bedrooms, for a family of four, he has been looking for a larger house, but can find nothing suitable for much under $40,000, so he is not buying. He has no cottage, no speedboat, and he does not vacation with his family except on weekends. As a "hobby" he has $4,000 in the stock market, where he is just "holding his own." Seven years ago, he bought three lots in Florida at $500 each. They are now worth $1,500 each, he thinks. He has a "few hundred" in the bank. These are the total assets of a highly skilled craftsman at age forty.

Other skilled workers may put in all their chips and buy that $40,000 house—paying for it in overtime, a working wife, and the imminent threat of layoffs and the pressure of bills they can't pay.

The printing trades are among the oldest, best organized and most highly paid of all crafts. In early 1970, the highest paid printing tradesman was the photoengraver. His weekly rate, for night work, was $220.45 (compared with $193.06 for typographers, $187.85 for pressmen, etc.). This highly skilled craftsman, if he were employed a full year, would make only $11,463.40—for night work.

3

We have been examining the individual worker's income. Examining family income, we find a picture that is different, but only slightly.

Statisticians like Herman Miller point out that median family income of white blue-collar workers was $10,700 in 1969. This looks good, except . . .

—It is still only slightly above the B.L.S. moderate budget and not even close to the "comfortable" one. And from this median figure we learn that about half of all white blue-collar families live *below* a moderate standard of living. Nor does this blue-collar category in Miller's statistical analysis include the families of the lowest paid workers—laborers, farm and service workers, etc., who number about 26 million. This statistic also excludes blacks, who are more poorly paid than white families.

—It is based on the working wife and the multiple income. A high national unemployment rate can quickly knock the props out from under family income, as it has in recent years.

The statisticians also point out that the real income of white blue-collar families is up 30 percent from the early 1960's. This too looks good, except . . .

—The rise was based, in large part, on a decline in unemployment and a rise in the proportion of working wives. Between 1960 and 1969, unemployment among all white workers declined from 4.9 percent to 3.1 percent. Unemployment among white women declined from 5.3 percent to 3.8 percent. This is, at best, shaky security and progress;

employment can and does wane as quickly as it waxes, leaving debts and disappointment behind. Nor is it a sign of progress that so many wives feel compelled to work in order to bring the family income up to a moderate level. The family may actually be worse off in many ways because of it. The worker may have to baby-sit and care for the house while his wife works. Children may not get enough of their mother's attention. The family may be together less, enjoy each other less.

—It is not much consolation to know you're better off than you were ten years ago, if you're still unable to live at a decent standard. When Henry Ford announced the five-dollar day, workers rejoiced and flocked to Detroit to get jobs. Those days, and worse, are behind us; we must face the shortages of our own time.

Increases can even be found in the real income of *individual* earners. The "production worker in manufacturing," for example, had about a 60 percent real-income rise in the four decades between 1940 and 1969 (from $50.64 to $87.05 in constant dollars). It's nothing to celebrate. Workers in other production jobs (laborers, farm and service workers) had even less to celebrate.

Recent rises in the income of *white* workers have been less than rises for *nonwhites* so, even here, white workers have no special cause to celebrate good fortune.

The blue-collar worker falls behind economically as his family ages, Presidential Adviser Jerome M. Rosow points out. The earnings of workers reach a plateau at a point when they most need more income. At forty a worker may have two or more children of high-school age, all requiring a lot of food, clothing, spending money, and in a few years, hopefully, college expenses. By the time he is that age, his family will probably be as large as it's going to be. Payments on housing and equipment will be high, and aging parents will need support. According to the B.L.S. family budget figures, a family needs an increase in income of 60 percent to meet the change from minimum to maximum in its income requirements. Yet this is about double the income rise for blue-collar workers during this period.

Census data show that of white, male heads of families who were age twenty-five to thirty-four in 1959, those who are managers and professionals increased their income in the following ten years by 57 percent. Those who are clerical and sales workers increased theirs by only 41 percent. Craftsmen and operatives increased theirs by 33 percent, laborers and service workers, by only 28 percent. Thus only the professionals and managers were able, through promotions and increased profits and pay, to keep up with the needs of a growing family, as defined by the B.L.S.

In contrast, the young unmarried worker, who perhaps lives at home, can do well on a blue-collar income—drive a fancy car and live "rich." So can the young worker who is married and has a working wife but no children. As soon as children come, bang, he's in trouble. Everything happens at once: the wife stops work, a house and furniture must be bought, hospital bills must be paid for both his wife and his new child. And unlike the professional, for example, who may move up in position and thereby hike up his income, the typical blue-collar worker has a maximum fixed income for his job, and once he reaches this maximum, his earnings reach a dead-end. His choices are to use up his savings, go into debt, or possibly send his wife back to work as soon as his child is old enough to attend school.

A young single blue-collar worker, without children, earns pay that exceeds the B.L.S. moderate budget level. A worker (a steelworker, for example) with two children, one a teen-ager, has costs that exceed his earnings. In 1967 he earned $8,039 but needed $10,347 to operate on a moderate budget, according to Rosow's analysis.

The younger worker with children is harder hit than the worker with grown children. One survey found that the young worker, more than the worker in other age groups, wants to earn more and work more hours than he does. Asked if they wanted a large income rise in the next five years, 83 percent of workers under twenty-five and only 39 percent of those fifty-five to sixty-four responded affirmatively.[1] (Blue-collar workers and the undereducated are more likely than other groups to want more work; more than half of all semiskilled workers said they wanted more work. The desire for a higher income peaks in the middle of the income range—in middle America.)

The young worker usually gets the most poorly paid and least pleasant job. He is somewhat less likely to be able to work overtime at premium rates and more likely to be caught in temporary layoffs, though in some union contracts he is now protected against such loss. No less than others of his generation, the young worker expects more. Why not? He belongs to a generation of rapidly rising expectations.

The largest gains made by workers in the past decade are in retirement income—pensions. Yet, even when "too old to work and too young to die," the typical worker faces financial hardship.

A recent study of auto workers who were close to retirement showed that the median income from pensions and social security to which workers (age fifty-eight to sixty-one) and their spouses were entitled at retirement was around $4,000. Almost one in four was entitled to less than $1,000.[2] Only 1 percent were entitled to more than $7,500.

[1] Survey Research Center, University of Michigan, *Productive Americans,* James N. Morgan et al., 1966.
[2] Survey Research Center, University of Michigan, *The Decision to Retire,* 1969.

All this, under one of the most generous of all pension systems.

Since most would have had to live in poverty (especially considering the medical costs of aging), quite naturally the vast majority of these workers chose not to retire, even though qualified to do so. Quite naturally also, the larger the retirement income, the more likely were these workers to choose retirement.

The common assumption that workers are ambivalent about retirement, or even rather negative about it, is not borne out by this survey. Only 15 percent of these older auto workers were either skeptical or negative about retirement. Overwhelmingly, they looked forward to retirement —even when near-poverty awaited them.

Of these older workers, after a lifetime of labor, almost one in ten had savings and investments amounting to less than $100. About 28 percent had savings of less than $2,000, and 50 percent had less than $5,000.

More than one in five had no hobbies to turn to on retirement. As for their leisure, the strongest preference was for mild recreational activities, and then for working around the house, gardening, etc.

Questioned about their attitudes toward work, a majority—56 percent—reported that their work was repetitious, and 38 percent said they were unable to vary the pace of their work at all. One-third said they had worked for the same company for more than thirty years. Almost 40 percent felt that their work place was either unpleasant or neutral. Some 58 percent said they would miss the people they worked with when they retired.

These workers tended to be as immobile in retirement as during their working lives. Of those already retired, less than 10 percent had moved. Less than 1 percent had gone to a warmer climate or to what they regarded as a more desirable community.

An astonishing proportion of fully employed workers are poor. Among family heads who work full time, about 7 percent earn a poverty income. Among "unrelated individuals" who are fully employed, 30 percent are impoverished.

The working poor are found in all occupations. About 30 percent work in agriculture, forestry and fisheries; about 15 percent in manufacturing, 15 percent in retail trade, 10 percent in personal services, 9 percent in construction, and 21 percent in other nonagricultural jobs. In general, the working poor are in industries with a relatively low margin of profit and a relatively high level of competition.

About two-thirds of all working-poor families are white. Surprisingly, more than three-fourths of people who head working-poor families are in the prime of their lives— twenty-five to fifty-four. About 90 percent of all working-poor families are headed by men. About half of working-poor families live in the South.

Almost all the working poor are unorganized. Most of them work in industries not covered by the Fair Labor Standards Act.[3] In any event, the minimum wage of $1.60

[3] In 1964 the Fair Labor Standards Act (covering minimum wage and premium pay for overtime) applied to only 29 million out of 44 million wage earners. The exempted 15 million workers included about 3.3 million retail trade workers, about 4 million in service industries, especially hotels, laundries and hospitals; about 2.5 million in domestic service and about 2 million in agriculture.

In 1963 the average wage of restaurant workers in the South was 80 cents an hour, as compared with $1.58 in the West. Nearly one-fourth of restaurant workers (300,000) were paid less than 75 cents an hour. Only about a third of restaurant workers receive tips, since only about that proportion are waiters and waitresses.

More than half of laundry and cleaning workers (500,000) are paid less than $1.25 an hour.

More than one in four nonpublic hospital workers (700,000) are paid less than $1.25 an hour.

The nearly 2 million farm workers not covered by the law are among the most miserably paid and treated. In May of 1963, average

an hour is a poverty wage for most workers. Their unionization is hampered by so-called "right to work" laws in
most Southern and a few Northern states.

In fact, about a third of all impoverished families (2.4
million in 1967) are headed by a fully employed person.
Another million "unrelated individuals" are in the same
situation—fully employed but poor. Millions more full-
time workers live at the margin of poverty.

These economic realities confront workers with a long
list of harrowing problems. How, for example, do they
provide equal opportunity for their children? How do they
shelter them against the draft for four years when the cost
of sending a son to state university now averages nearly
$2,000 a year? Working-class kids make their trips abroad
as members of the armed forces, while many middle-class
youths, student deferments in hand, spend their junior
year at European universities. While the college boy usually steps onto an escalator that moves rapidly upward, the
worker's son probably will step onto his father's assembly
line and be doomed to stay on the same level.

Relatively few colleges, social agencies, schools or other
public institutions have mounted programs to meet the
special needs of workers. In many places even the services
provided by "Red Feather" agencies (community and
social-service agencies supported by United Fund drives
for voluntary contributions, much of which comes from
check-offs of workers' wages) seem more closely geared to
middle- than working-class needs.

Inevitably, many workers come to feel they are being
dunned and taxed for the benefit of others. Considering

---

hourly pay of farm workers was 89 cents an hour. Almost half earned
less than 75 cents an hour. For about 75,000, pay was less than 30
cents an hour. Two states now have minimum-wage protection for
farm workers, and federal law covers some of them, such as sugar-
field workers and foreign farm laborers.

the notorious imbalance in our tax structures, they have a point.

Reporters often talk about the sweeper who "makes more than a teacher." True, a sweeper in an auto plant in Michigan probably earns more than a teacher in a backwoods school in Mississippi, but that's hardly a pot of gold.

The sweeper seems to fit a set of hidden assumptions according to which society is divided, along a magical line, between rich and poor. In this oversimplified pseudo-Marxian schema, organized workers are seen as part of the rich half, along with bankers, businessmen, professionals. They are assumed to be well-fed, well cared for, up to their eyebrows in "things," and all-around participants in society.

According to these hidden assumptions, all or nearly all the poor are black. They are mostly mothers of large families living on welfare in big-city ghettos. The rest (except for a few Appalachian whites) are young blacks who can't find jobs because they are school dropouts or because they are excluded from unions by union bosses. The fact is that about 80 percent of the poor are white and, as we have seen, about a third work full time.

Contrary to these popular assumptions, in real life the typical worker has been on a treadmill, except where union contracts have protected him from rises in the cost of living. And to the worker, it has seemed that everyone else—including the welfare recipient and the militant blacks—was moving forward, while only he stood still, waiting in a twilight zone somewhere between hunger and plenty. Some comforts came to him through expanded consumer credit, but the credit exacted high costs in insecurity and interest rates. Increasingly, he paid taxes to the government and gave his sons to the military, and got little in return. Certainly the typical production worker is much better off than the Mississippi tractor driver, or the city mother on welfare, but he hardly lives opulently. He is treading water, financially and psychically.

The mythical middle-class worker is kin to the folkloric Negro who "lives in the slums but drives a big new Cadillac." He's there, all right, but his numbers are grossly exaggerated.

As for the unions that represent the worker's economic interests, they too are part of the myth of affluence. Unions have advanced the interests of workers in many significant ways, but their successes have been limited by the power of the companies with whom they deal and by public responses that are indifferent to workers and antagonistic to strikes. We shall return to this subject and deal with it at length later.

4

Ronald Popham

The image of the blue-collar worker, as reflected in the media, is as distorted, and in some respects as debased and vicious, as Hitler's stereotype of the Jews.

In manner and speech, workers are miles apart from the middle class and light years away from their public stereotype. In the authors' experience workers are generally about as intelligent, though not so academically advantaged, as middle-class people. Their native wit is revealed less in IQ tests than in ability to handle the complicated problems of life. In the working class there are many unusually talented people and many who are untainted by middle-class restraints and individual competitiveness.

At Black Lake, Michigan, an auto workers' union leadership training center, we have talked with many able young men and women who work in the shops and are active in the union. One of them is Ronald Popham, a twenty-nine-year-old worker from a Ford assembly plant in Louisville, Kentucky. In many ways he is different from the people he knows and works with. He tends less to make racial prejudgments. He is more talkative and articulate. Though he has a gentle disposition, he is tough mentally and physically. But in one literal sense, he *is* representative of his fellow workers: they chose him—"strange" as his attitudes are—to be their union committeeman and to represent them on the job.

In a small arena—his plant—he managed to win support from workers who were overwhelmingly in favor of George Wallace. He did what Bobby Kennedy did in a larger arena—he gained the confidence of many "racists" by fighting militantly and well for a program that promised them relief from their pressing job and economic grievances, proving that racism quickly takes a back seat when leaders have sense enough to raise and press real issues.

Popham has been an unskilled assembly worker for the last five and a half years. Before that he worked as an unskilled laborer for an oil company, and before that he spent five years in the Marines. His father and brother now work in the plant with him. His father is a mechanic; his father's father was a doctor. Popham is of mixed stock but probably is mainly Irish on both sides. He is Catholic and attended Catholic schools for all but one year of his education. After completing the ninth grade, he dropped out to join the Marines. Popham is good-looking, clean-shaven, wears his hair in a brush cut, and looks as tough and strong as a pro-football player.

RONALD POPHAM, WORKER [1]

In Louisville, you know, we're the sophistry capital of the world. We have to make an excuse. Down South, in the Deep South, their racial attitude is that "we don't like niggers." Up North they'll say, "I don't mind the black people, I just don't want them taking what I've got," or something like that. In Kentucky, most people won't talk about race. They'll cut you off. They have to make excuses. They give you a long story about why their attitude is this way, and most of it is phoney. It's not so very different from the way they've always felt. They've gotten something to back them up now. It used to be enough to say, "I just don't want to be around black people." It's not that way any more because nobody likes to seem stupid.

When I was in the service I saw a whole lot of guys with tattoos. After they get them, they get to feeling it's stupid to have a tattoo. But they'll never admit it. They'd much rather admit that they're drunkards. I never heard one of them say I got it because I wanted it. I got drunk, they'd say. It's the same with racial attitudes. Our communications system points out how stupid they are, how unthinking some of these prejudices are, so these people I work around seek to excuse themselves. What they're really saying to you is, "I feel this way, but it's not because I'm prejudiced."

The white guys talk about discrimination in reverse. But when it happens, when a black man gets a job because he's black, it's only because eight or ten white people before him got the job, or a similar job, because they were white.

It bothers my friend Oscar to have people call police

[1] What follows is a transcript of Ronald Popham's side of a conversation with us—unedited, except for brevity.

"pigs." He says it dehumanizes them. Oscar says the Nazis took some of the edge off by calling the Jews swines and now, he says, the Panthers are doing that too. If a word can cause a given reaction, just the word, and somebody knows that, they can just use your mind like it's got a steering wheel. William Buckley did it a lot. When a guy starts thinking about the word, he can't effectively refute what the other guy is saying. So many times you see people talking about law and order. Then you spend an hour on the two *words*, then you'll add justice, and then you won't get anything done on the real argument. I try not to let any word do me that way. When a guy finds it out, then he's in command. It used to happen to me with "nigger." People would say "nigger" and I'd get mad. Then I found out they were doing it to me on purpose. There'd be fifteen or twenty people there and we'd be talking about open housing, and somebody would throw "nigger" in there and I'd go into a tirade about why you shouldn't use that word. Then the lunch period would be over and I wouldn't get to say what I *wanted* to say.

They had a straw vote in the plant and 86 percent were for Wallace. My father and my family and my wife's family voted for Wallace. Wallace drove me out of my mind. I wrote seven or eight letters to the newspapers. They were going to get the local to endorse Wallace at the union meeting. I could get only one guy to go with me to try to stop it. When I ran for committeeman, my dad told me he talked to at least fifty guys who said they can't vote for you because you're a nigger lover. I told them I don't care. I don't want their vote. I lost a lot of votes.

People told me to run because I'd done something they liked. The company had air guns for spraying that were hanging down and hitting us in the head. These guns were low, the plant was new, and they hadn't made arrangements to get them down. Everybody in the plant was cry-

ing. They said you got to get 'em up there, they're beating
us to death. But they wouldn't get them up there, for four
months. They told us you have to move the whole super-
structure—you can't just move the gun up. I took it for
about four months. So one morning I wore my football
helmet in, and one of the big bosses said, "Put your safety
glasses on." I said, "I can't get them on because of this
helmet." He says, "I know that. Take the helmet off." I
said, "No, if you want the helmet off, you take it off of me.
I'm not going to take it off until you move those guns."
So he said, "Git up front, go to the office." "Good," I says,
"I've been wanting to talk to someone that had some sense.
I've been talking with *you* and you haven't done anything."
So I went up front with my helmet on, and they asked me,
"Are you kidding?" I said, "No, I'm not kidding. I'm not
going to take this helmet off till you move the guns." So he
says, "If I promise you to move the guns, will you take the
helmet off now?" "Yeah, but if you don't have them up
tomorrow morning, I'll put my whole uniform on. I'll wear
shoulder pads and everything." I went back to work, and
they started moving the guns before I got there.

Then all those guys in the plant said, "That's all right.
Why don't you become a committeeman?" When I do that
kind of thing *now,* they say, "You're crazy." It would scare
them. They don't want to back me. I've done some pretty
outlandish things, but they've worked so far. As a result
it doesn't matter to them that I don't like Wallace.

There's a million reasons I don't like Wallace. Like I
said in one of those letters I wrote, Wallace says that he
doesn't have a racist attitude, but there's a preponderance
of evidence to the contrary. But, accepting his statement
as fact—just for discussion—if he doesn't have that attitude
he still has that image, and having that image will tell a lot
of people all over the world what *our* attitude is. We elect
his image. You'd have to throw out the Declaration of In-

dependence, and the Statue of Liberty would be a joke. Radio Free Europe would be laughed out of existence.

They all had to have an excuse to support Wallace. They couldn't say, "I want to segregate niggers. I want to beat these people up." They had to say things like, "He's right. There's not a dime's worth of difference between the Republican and Democratic party." Or they'd say, "It's time for a change. Johnson's got us in such a mess and Nixon can't get us out. We need somebody strong." When they'd talk to me they'd always talk about foreign policy, they'd get off race.

Wallace had a lot of pamphlets about supporting unions. But I did a lot of research and found he supported right-to-work laws. He was the only governor recently to send in state troopers and violently break up a picket line. That was in '65. He had a lot of backing from big business. You couldn't get him to talk about oil depletion allowance. They didn't even keep it a secret that H. L. Hunt supported him and gave him money.

I guess I'm different from everybody I know. I guess the reason is that it was kind of a traumatic thing for me to find out that the black people weren't really, for example, dirty. I knew all my *life* that black people were dirty. There just wasn't any doubt because I was told by everybody. When I went into service I found they had lied to me about that. I was sort of looking into other things. See, I hadn't had any contact with black people.

We had one black kid in the school I went to. In '57 they started putting in one or two black kids into the whole school and that was the first contact I'd ever had with anybody. They were picking on him in the playground and I went in there to stop it, but not because I thought he was my equal or anything. All the things I had been told about black people—I still retained all of that, but I just didn't like to see anybody picked on. I went in to stop it and an-

other guy said something. Anyway we got into a fight and
they took me into the principal's office. They called my
dad. The principal talked to him, and I told my side—that
they were picking on this guy and pushing him around.
The attitude of the principal was that I shouldn't have,
that I was a troublemaker. When we were on the way
home, my dad told me—and my dad's pretty intelligent—
but when he starts on race he stops thinking. He just re-
acts. He said, "You know, you're right. Nobody should be
mistreated. But you don't know—when they put that kid
in your class, he's going to hold the whole class back, because black people have skulls that are real thick and the
brain's real small, and they just can't learn. It's nothing
against them, we shouldn't hate them for it or anything,
but they just can't learn as well as we can."

I questioned that because we had the track system. You
took a test and only 200 kids got into the school—out of
3,000 who took the test—and when they got in to it, they
were split up into classes by their ability. Obviously if he
were that stupid, he couldn't hold the class back. He'd be
in a class where he belonged—or he wouldn't even be in
the school if he were really stupid.

When I went into the service I found a few *little* things
that weren't true, and then I started really looking into it
and found that *none* of it was true. For example, we always
got the story when I was a kid that all a black man wants
is a car and a jug of wine and a woman, and he's happy.
That's enough. He's content to live in a shack as long as
he drives a shiny car, and I accepted that because everything I'd seen supported that. They *did* live in shacks, and
they *did* have shiny cars. But after I started thinking about
it, I decided, You've never seen a segregated car lot and
you've never seen a segregated liquor store. That's just
what they *will* sell you. A black man can't buy a shiny home
because they won't let him have one.

You can give a man $2,000 a week, but if you won't let him spend it, it's just paper, it's no good to him. It's good to have equal employment opportunity and all that, but as long as you restrict the use of the money, you really haven't accomplished anything. If you can restrict him to a particular neighborhood, he hasn't gained anything by having the money. The major purchase any family makes is their home. In our town you're forced to live down by the river . . . even affluent blacks—doctors, dentists. Martin Luther King's brother A. D. King has a fine home—but it's down on the river. He has beautiful furniture and everything. They have a section for all the rich black people, and then the street, and across the street is this plant. I don't know what it is but the smell is constant, it's sickening. And they live with it all the time, that smell. It's the only really nice black neighborhood in the city. They built the houses first, and then they built the plant across the street.

My wife's father brought her up to respect Negroes and call them "sir," but he voted for Wallace. He knows very few blacks. He's watched Stokely Carmichael. The thing is, the black man he taught her to respect doesn't exist any more. The black man he liked was the Uncle Tom that shuffled and scratched his head and said, "Yes, boss" and all that. There are some of those left, but not many. They ceased to exist in the sixties, and that alienated him. The fact is he never *was* liberal. He was happy with black people because they'd stay in their place.

A lot of things are bothering people in the shop. One is the system of easy credit. They get tied up in that. They spend and then they work their fingers to the bone to get out of debt. We've always been an acquisitive people. It's always been gimme gimme, but never before have we had such a choice. So many things today are necessities that were luxuries ten years ago. Television has a lot to do with that. You see all these things on television. Through motivational research they find ways to convince you you *have* to have this stuff. We make it hard for ourselves to even get the necessities because of all the luxuries. It's the sense of values. It's like conditioned response, like Pavlov's dog. They condition you, and you just react.

I see up here in Michigan something I never saw at home—these snowmobiles. Do people really *need* these? You see them on television seven or eight times a night, every night. People have those and have holes in their socks, or they're riding around on that thing cold because they don't have a coat. They spent all their money on the snowmobile.

General Motors came out with this big thing about how lucky you are to work for GM, how well you're doing. Just about everybody could see through that, they could see they weren't doing as well. Another thing is keeping up with the Joneses. It puts you in a bind.

We have four cars, they're all old, only one of them runs. They call it Popham's used-car lot. I have all these good intentions of fixing these up. What happens is: I have a car, then I get another one. I know I can't get what I want out of a trade-in, so I keep it. The kids play in them, they use one as a backstop for their baseball game. They just sit in our yard.

People in the shop see themselves in relation to people around them. Another thing Wallace did—he said we in the South went through a depression and we didn't riot and loot. That's specious because when everybody around you is bitten by the same dog, it's not so hard to take. It's when you're kept out of the mainstream. You see everybody around you doing well. At least they put on a show— so they do have two cars, air conditioning and all that. You're driven to that, not because of the convenience of having two cars, but because other people have it. If nobody had it, you wouldn't feel bad.

One guy worked with me in this little booth. There were

only two people in the booth. His wife worked for the University of Louisville medical research center. I went to his house one day. It was out of this world. It was about a thirty- or forty-thousand-dollar home, and he had a car and a color television and a pool table and a fireplace downstairs, and a trilevel house. I asked him how he did it. He said one of the tricks was to do things yourself and then charge yourself for them. He built the bar. He got a price on it—the guy wanted $500 to build it. He did it himself, and charged himself $500, and put it in the bank. When he wants to tune up his car, he charges himself $15. He did the wiring in his house and charged himself union scale. He built the house himself. He's been frugal all his life. Even before they were married, he took his wife's money and saved it. Combined they'd have about $14,000 a year. They have two cars and a boat. He bought just the hull and he built the boat himself, and got it all for something like $20. It's got a motor on it, but he rebuilt it himself. He can do most anything with his hands and he does extra work and makes money for it. He pays cash for everything.

He's very unique. I don't know anybody else like him. Everybody else is struggling. My brother works on the line in the plant. He's young, hasn't been married long. He handles money real well, but he's struggling. He's trying to get a house, but the interest rates are out of this world, and the cost is something like $14 a square foot now—maybe about $21,000 for a livable house.

I only went through the ninth grade. I was always a problem in school. I did real well in things I was interested in. In high school I had a 98 percent for the year—in geometry. I failed history and English. That's why I like this school here.[2] Every time somebody talks, you learn

[2] The UAW's Walter and May Reuther Family Center at Black Lake, Michigan.

from them. But in school, you might dwell on the same thing three or four days.

You'd get on the Civil War and who was most responsible for the victory of the North. We had a debate. Some people took Lincoln, some took Grant, some Sumter. But I said McCormick was more responsible than anybody—because of logistics. If they hadn't had the food—if they couldn't feed these people—Grant couldn't lead them, and Lincoln couldn't deploy them. So I thought that was the main thing the North had over the South—logistics. They also had the railroad, to move food and ammunition. Everybody listened and that debate was fun.

I liked that part of school, but the teacher would have that maybe once a month and the rest of the time she'd have you memorize dates and facts, like the Gettysburg Address. We spent maybe three days memorizing that and fifty-five people in the class had to stand up and say it, while the others had to listen while *he* says it, and the *next* guy—while *everybody* says the Gettysburg Address. Most of school was like that.

I felt that way about school from the first grade. You weren't learning. You were just wasting time. While I had to be there, I'd occupy myself with something else—maybe some complex problem. I'd try to get different perspectives on it. I'd try to see it from this angle, like I was moving around, and I used to play little games with myself, and then when I'd be called on, I'd wake up like I'd been sleeping. I wouldn't know anything that had gone on. I was so engrossed in what I was doing. It was kind of a defense mechanism, something I used to keep me from going crazy, I think.

In the fourth or fifth grade you'd learn multiplication tables. Each guy had to say the multiplication tables. It *loses* something after the third or fourth person does it, you know. That's why I had to find something else. . . . I never have, since I've been here at Black Lake, had to do that . . . It's like I told Oscar, until I came here I had certain ideas. I knew I was right, I just knew. After I got here I found I wasn't right always. You hear there are no absolutes. I'm not sure of that, but I know that so far as being right, being absolutely right, I can't say that any more. The weight of the argument may be on your side, but I'm just finding out that there's merit to the other side, too. Everybody has good ideas. We need a meaningful dialogue. Since we're just a product of our environment and since we have so many diverse environments here, we should hear from everyone. Our mind is something like a computer. We can only respond to the program that's put in it. All of our experiences determine what perspective we see. For example, in a speech, this guy is saying the same thing to a hundred-fifty people—at least they're hearing the same words, but no two of them are getting the same thing from it, and it's because of their background. Everybody here has a different background. If a person is an intellectual bully and controls everything, you're only getting the benefit of *his* background.

In school we spent all our time learning facts—and really irrelevant facts. I don't think it really makes a lot of difference that the Emancipation Proclamation was signed on January 1, 1863. I think it makes a difference that it was signed, and the content. It's not a really great document—it didn't really do anything at all. But we didn't find that out in school. We didn't get an in-depth study—not just of that document, but any document. It didn't come alive because there were so many dull, dry facts attached to it.

That doesn't *happen* here. Here, if you have a contract, it comes alive, it takes on meaning. If you just told them: "This part of the contract was won in 1958 and it got us $2.50 . . ." If you just said those things, like they do in school, you wouldn't have anything. The way they do it

here, you're a part of that contract and you really understand it. It's not some superficial knowledge about it. You
start to feeling that you can understand what motivated
the people who drew it up, in bargaining, and from both
sides. I don't think there's another educational experience
like it.

How'd I like the Marine Corps? Well, I played football,[3]
and then I worked in the gym in the off-season, or I would
get a job like in the brig, just taking prisoners to lunch,
then I'd have the rest of the day off. It looked good to me.
I would have stayed in it, if I had thought I could stay in
special services the rest of my life. But when you get thirty
or thirty-two they don't need you any more. You can't do
as much on the football field as you could when you were
twenty-two, so they send you to an outfit somewhere. They
ask you, "Where'd you come from?" You'd say, "Well, I
played football at Quantico." Oh, well, they don't say anything. They know right then that you're probably a dimwit. They give you some *de*tail. Then another thing, you
can't make rank in special services, very little. They don't
have a quota for rank like the other parts of the Marine
Corps, so when you come out of there you're just starting
in the rank structure. Then you have to try to make it, but
with that background you can't.

I had a chance to go to prep school for Annapolis when
I was in the Marine Corps. Out of 3,500 people, they had a
quota of two—two people. There were 1,500 applied, and
they had screening boards. First you talked to the captain,
then you talked to the colonel, then you talked to a board
of maybe three people, then you talked to a general and
some colonels. It ended up you talked to about twelve
officers. They sit in a semicircle and you sit in the middle.
It got down to two, the last two people. I didn't have any

[3] He played football with the Quantico Marines, a team that com-
petes at the intercollegiate level.

idea I'd get all the way through. I never did have any intention of going. I asked to be taken off the program. The reason I gave was that the outfit was going on a cruise. The real reason was that I didn't want to get into that again. I knew what school had always been to me. It'd be the same thing, even worse—regimentation, you know. Be more of what I'd joined the Marine Corps to get away from.

It looks to me like the students are protesting being programmed, being told, "You come in here and we'll tell you what you need to do." They're not helping to equip themselves to take on the outside world. They feel if you leave college and come across something you haven't been programmed for, then you have to go back and find out how it's supposed to be done. It's that computer thing. A computer can't deal with anything it hasn't been programmed for. The answers have to be fed to it before it can give them back. I think the kids are saying, "We want something that's more relevant. We want a say-so in what we're taught."

Then, they have a valid protest against the war. All these people that say, "No, we have to protect ourselves"—invariably they're beyond the age when they'll have to fight the war. You never hear anybody who's subject to that say such things; they're never hawks.

I've seen graffiti that say, "Kill a commie for Christ." It tells a lot, it tells a story. The attitude is prevalent among these kids that it's not like it was in the Second World War. We'd like to think that our boys are going off to fight for mom and apple pie and the girl back home and all of that, but it's not true. In World War II, if they hadn't known they'd be cheered and revered and all that, it would have been a whole lot harder to get them to go. The whole country was behind them—there was the whole aura of heroism. These kids today don't have any of that. They

have to go over there and risk their lives, then come home
and be called murderers. If it were for something they
believed in, maybe they could take it. But they feel maybe
we shouldn't be there anyway. I think I'd feel that way if I
were eligible for the service now. I doubt that I could talk
my way into supporting this war. The young guys in the
shop are against the war altogether because they know they
could be next. In our whole local union, it's about fifty–
fifty, with the younger ones usually against, and the older
ones usually for. There's no majority either way.

Most of the young guys in the shop buy the stereotype
about students. Most are against the student movement.
Every time the paper carries a picture of a campus disorder, they'll run to me and put me in a position . . . well,
sometimes you *don't* agree either, but you have to defend it
anyhow. You know that if you started to say, "Now this is
only one thing," you'd lose a lot—they'd put you on the
defensive, they'd just attack.

On the integration thing, every time something came up
that involved a black person, they'd come to me and demand that I defend it. They didn't ask me if I agreed or
anything, they'd just say, "Now, defend this." There's a lot
of people in the plant who won't commit themselves at all,
and if they do their language is ambiguous. You can get
into a conversation by saying, "There's two schools of
thought on everything"—but you can get *out* of one that
way too.

They object to the violence and the destruction on campus. Like a little shack that the ROTC had at Kent State—
they didn't see too much wrong with killing these people,
but the destruction of property just tore them up. They've
been conditioned by their elders to feel this way about
students. A guy in the plant who's twenty now was maybe
fourteen when he first heard about student protests. He
was living at home, and his parents conditioned him to be

against them. He doesn't think for himself enough, he doesn't look into it. That's the way I was about black people. I didn't question it, because I was raised that way.

Working on the line, I've had a number of jobs. One was building up springs for trucks, one was greasing trucks. You can work a job in the plant *your* way. You can make it a good or a bad job. So many people don't realize that. Assembly line work is so monotonous. Most of our grievances in the plant have to do with failure to perform assigned work. You become almost like an automaton, a robot. You work this job a certain way—you make the same moves all the time. If anything changes, well, then you miss it. A lot of people say you should change—you shouldn't make a guy do one boring job all day. But would you give him *ten* boring jobs? It'd be a little better, maybe, but not a whole lot better. I don't like to talk about things I don't have any solution for. I don't know what can be done to break up the monotony.

I always seek jobs that are the most monotonous . . . You see, what I *really* liked was repair. When you repair a truck it's just like being a mechanic. But I couldn't get a repair job—I had a bad record, because of my mouth. So I couldn't get that job. The other extreme was the real monotonous job, doing the same motions. I'd get on that job, and I could do it and still play those little games I'd play in school. I'd take a problem, a complex problem, and I'd lose myself in it, and then I really wouldn't be in the Ford plant. In school I had to pay attention or get into trouble. In the plant I don't have to mind what I'm doing.

Now I get into trouble when I *am* paying attention. Like, one morning I came in with the paper. A.D. Williams King had told the City Council or somebody that he had 2,000 poor people in Louisville from the Poor People's March and he wanted $8,000 to get them out. If you don't give it to me, I'll leave them here. I came into the plant

with the newspaper story about King and I started screaming, "That's extortion, that's blackmail!" The real reason
I was screaming wasn't that I hated what he was doing. It
was that I knew what was going to happen to all the colored
guys in the building. When everybody read that story—
about King's extortion—these guys were going to have hell
for a day, two days. I knew they'd come down on me too.
So I thought I'd take the initiative; I'd do it first.

I had had other problems, so one of the foremen took
me into the office, and they had a labor relations hearing.
They charged me with creating a disturbance. They said
to me, "Did you call A.D. Williams King a son of a bitch?"
And I said, "I don't doubt that I did, I called him a lot of
things." They said, "You don't have to get smart, you just
answer the question." So I said, "Okay, I guess I said that."
They said, "This is just an investigation. You go home for
the day." That was a whole day. "We'll have a hearing tomorrow morning at eight o'clock." So I went home and I
went to A.D. King's house and I talked to him for about
two and a half hours, and I talked to Martin Luther King's
wife for a half-hour. Anyway, I got this letter from them,
on SCLC paper and signed by them, saying, "We believe
in freedom of speech, and this guy doesn't have to agree
with us. We don't have anything against him. We'd appreciate it if you didn't persecute him."

So I had that letter in my pocket, and I went into the
plant in the morning. I went to the hearing and they said,
"Did you call A.D. King a son of a bitch?" And I said,
"Yes." They said, "Okay, in view of that and in view of
your past record, and the fact that you've been warned,
we're going to give you two weeks off." And I said, "Well,
can I say anything?" They said, "Oh, certainly." I said, "I
was talking to A.D. King last night. I went to his house,
and he gave this letter." Their eyes bugged out. They said,
"We're going to suspend this hearing for a few minutes

and we'll be right back." They were gone an hour and a half. There were people coming down from upstairs, all the big shots. They put all their brains together and worked it out. They came back in, and this time there were five labor relations people. One of them said, "Did you push George Turner a couple of weeks ago?" I said, "Yeah, I pushed him away from my cigarettes." They said, "All right, we'll give you two weeks off for that." I said, "It's probably this haircut that makes me look that stupid, but I'm not stupid and I'm not going to take that. I don't care if I have to take it to Earl Warren, or L.B.J. or G.O.D. or where I have to go, I'm not going to take that."

I went down to city hall. I wanted to see the mayor, but everybody I talked to gave me the runaround. So finally I told one guy, "I'll tell you what you do, you just go on with your business. I don't want to hold you up or anything. You get everything done and you all go on home and feed the kids and watch television and go to bed, and when you come back I'll just be right here in this hall—until *somebody* helps me." They were convinced that I was convinced, so they took me to the Human Relations Commissioner, and he said, "Look, I could help you. I could call that plant and tell them to bring you back to work. And that would be it. But they'll be *after* you." I went wild, and I said, "Man, if they weren't *after* me already—that's why I'm here. Everybody else, in an election year, is talking about Wallace and Johnson and everybody, and A.D. King's not even that big a public official and I get two weeks off—so how much more could they be after me?" So he said, "Well, you got a point."

So he called them and told them, "I have a report that you sent this guy home, and I want him taken back to work. I don't want anything done to him. I don't want any repercussions."

So I went home and the baby-sitter said, "You've had a

dozen phone calls in the last half hour." Before I got a chance to call, he called again. It was the personnel manager. He said, "Can you come in now?" I said, "No, I already sent the baby-sitter home." He said, "Well, be in my office at six in the morning." I said, "You don't come to work till nine." He said, "That's all right, just be here."

I went in the next morning and they said, "We've done some further investigation and we found this wasn't entirely your fault, so we're going to give you a break and let you go out to work." I wanted to say, "You phoney——" but I didn't. I went ahead and took my job back. So they waited to get me. They took me into labor relations about a week later. I forget what the charge was. So I told this guy, "Look, the last time you tried to railroad me I was the one that got the Human Relations Commission to call. But not only them. I had the NAACP, and even the Ku Klux Klan wanted to test the question of why this could happen to a white guy when no black man's ever been sent home for saying something bad about Wallace." It was all a lie, but I told them all this. "I had about ten irons in the fire and I dropped every one of them when you brought me back to work. It's not going to happen again. Next time you pull something like this, I'll be in Detroit or Washington, wherever is necessary, before you finish filling out the papers to send me home. So what I'm trying to tell you is you'd better get off my back. You'd better never ever again bother me until you've got something concrete. You better make sure you catch me drinking while I'm stealing something. You better have both charges on me before you try to get me again, and I mean it." So the guy said, "I don't know who you think you are, talking like that." I said, "I *have* been talking to you like that, and if you don't think I'd talk to the superintendent that way, just bring him up here." He said, "That won't be necessary." I said, "Can I go back to work?" "Yeah," he said, "I'll call you

back." That was in May of '68. I had twenty-one r and w's
[reprimands and warnings] before that. In these two and a
half years I haven't had *one*. I've never been called into
labor relations.

But they *do* that. If they want to call you on one thing,
and you're in the right, they get you on something else. My
whole trouble started when I marched for open housing in
Louisville. One guy said, "Why don't you just sleep with
the black bastards?" And I said—I knew this would gag
him and there were a lot of people—so I said, "Sonny,
really the only reason in the world is because they won't
let me."

They all had it in for me when I was marching. There
was a lot of hatred, but I weighed two hundred-thirty and
they weren't sure how to go about getting me. No one of
them was going to confront me, so they just did it in little
roundabout ways. I got twenty-one r and w's out of it. But
one night I was leaving the plant with this guy that I ride
with, and about twelve guys got around us because of
something I had said. That afternoon this guy had said to
me, "Would you want your daughter to marry a nigger?"
And I said, "Well, if it came between her marrying any of
the black people I know and *you,* I'd rather she'd marry
any of them." And I told him why. He was mad and the
people around him were mad. So when I came out of the
plant, they were around us. Their obvious intention was
to do me in. I was scared. My legs were shaking and everything. I knew that if I said, "Please leave me alone and let
me go to my car," that would have been the end of it. So I
told them, "If all of you want to beat me up, or do whatever you want, go ahead. You know I can't stop you. But
you'd better kill me, or I'll see each one of you. Another
thing about you beating me up, you could go home and tell
your kids that you beat up a nigger-lover and you might be
a hero—if *they're* as stupid as *you* are . . . or if you go home

and tell them that two of you beat up two of us, that'd be all right. But if you go home and tell them that you and eleven other guys beat up a nigger-lover, even your kids will see through that." They didn't like that—"even your kids." So they said, "Look, we're not bothering you and we're not going to talk to you. You just stay away from our table at lunch." I said, "You just stay away from mine." The next day I sat down in my usual place, and they all moved away.

In this incident, Popham tangled with some of the most extreme racists in the plant. Though belligerent and conspicuous, such extremists are actually a small minority in the Southern working class. Most of Popham's fellow workers, though disturbed about black militancy, are less violent. Despite Popham's strong and outspoken views on race, he was chosen by this silent majority of about five hundred workers in his district of the plant to represent them as their union committeeman. He was chosen because other issues were far more basic to them than race.

We would not pretend that Ronnie Popham is an ordinary worker, but he is much closer to the center of working-class life than the stereotypical "hard-hat" who is represented in the mass media and in the film "Joe."

II : Victims

5

War and Casualties

The average man lives closer to death than do the rich and affluent. He is more likely to die before his time. Death comes slowly, through neglected health and neglected despair. It comes swiftly in war and on the job.

We all know what war is like. The average man knows it as well as others—better, because he suffers more from it. As in other matters, however, he tends to acquiesce— he obeys the law of the land, protecting it with his life against its presumed enemies. Others protest; he stands by helplessly while his sons are being drafted. Then, when he sees that there *is* a real enemy out there who is trying to kill his son, he joins the battle cry. It would be too painful for him to allow himself to believe that his son fights and dies in a pointless war. When the draft-exempt sons of the affluent call his son a murderer, his rage is compounded. He feels that his son is only performing the same dangerous but essential duty that others performed in World War II and Korea.

Through Edward Kennedy, the authors made an inquiry about the availability of information on the social and ethnic background of Vietnam casualties. The Defense Department supplied the following statement.

"There are no current records compiled within this department which segregate casualty lists by social or ethnic background as well as by geographical location. It would be impracticable to attempt to extract and prepare a meaningful casualty list containing the information requested. With the rate of rotation of military personnel to and from Southeast Asia approaching one half million per year, it would be manifestly impossible to segregate casualty rosters by both ethnic background and state of origin. In addition, a number of other variables are involved. For example, while the personal record of a serviceman lists his home of record by state, this is not necessarily the state in which the man's next of kin resides. In many instances, it merely reflects the state in which he enlisted or the state in which he resided at the time of enlistment or reenlistment."

So speaks a Brigadier General: we have no information about the background of war casualties. The Defense Department is able to hit one computerized missile with another one, but it cannot put its computer to work on the child's task of determining the social and ethnic backgrounds of those who have suffered wounds or death in combat.

Obviously what is at issue here is a serious "identity

crisis," one that receives far less public notice than the notorious crisis of identity among college freshmen.

A clue to the operation of the "equality of sacrifice principle" in Vietnam comes from Joseph Alsop. According to his information, during the entire Vietnam war, only one student from the three great Ivy League schools—Harvard, Princeton, Yale—has been killed in combat.

We may get some clues about Vietnam from the Korean war, a rather similar conflict. Much after the fact, we have learned a few things—not about the identity of casualties (for that apparently stretches military curiosity too far)— but about the men who served in the armed forces. The research was commissioned by the Department of Defense and carried out by social scientists. Access to a large sample of officers and enlisted men was given the researchers.[1]

According to this study, about three out of four men who were high-school graduates served in Korea. Only about half of the college graduates served. If a white man had no college and was the son of a blue-collar worker, he had an 87 percent chance of serving. Since so many fit that description, the "common soldier" was typically white, a high-school graduate, the son of a blue-collar family, and a Northern city dweller. (The city boy was far more vulnerable than the small-town or farm boy, and if he lived in the North he was somewhat more vulnerable than if he lived elsewhere.) This average soldier, mainly because he had no college education, had virtually no chance of becoming a commissioned officer, but an excellent chance of being sent into infantry combat.

About half of all college graduates who entered the service became officers or candidates. Only about 5 percent

[1] *Military Service in American Life Since World War II: An Overview*, Sept., 1966, Report No. 117, by Albert D. Klassen, Jr., National Opinion Research Center, NORC, University of Chicago.

of those who had only "some college" became officers. Among those who did not go to college at all, the number was almost zero. (According to common observation, even the college men who didn't become officers were less likely than others to be sent into combat. Usually they became technicians, clerks, etc., and were put in noncombat units.)

The sons of professionals, managers, and white-collar workers were far more likely to become officers than the sons of blue-collar workers. Men from a high socioeconomic background were about five times more likely to become officers than those from a lower socioeconomic background.

As any serviceman knows, life in uniform is very different if you're an officer. It is easier, better paid—and a hell of a lot safer. Casualties are far lower among officers—and it is the casualty list that really counts. The rest will pass away.

During the Korean period, about 66 percent of whites and 50 percent of blacks eligible to serve, actually did serve in the military. Such is not the case in Vietnam, where the racial proportions are practically reversed. Still, because whites are ten times more numerous in our population than blacks, even in Vietnam they vastly outnumber black soldiers. The middle American who is told that this is a black war, that it is blacks who are making the largest sacrifice, is legitimately resentful that his own sacrifices are so glibly overlooked.

More of the truly poor have served in Vietnam than in Korea. They are better able now than before to meet educational requirements and, where they can't, the military has helped them with "special service" programs. The college educated, the sons of the rich and the affluent, have served less than in Korea. The wholesale exemption of boys whose fathers can afford college is reminiscent of times when men legally bought their way out of military service. Such privileged exemptions have caused the burden to continue to be borne very much by middle America and blue-collar workers of low and moderate means, even with increasing numbers of soldiers coming from the poor. Although the Brigadier General is unable to identify his fighting men in Vietnam, we may draw certain inferences from one sociologist's interviews with combat squads:

"The 34 soldiers had the following civilian backgrounds prior to entering the service: ten were high-school dropouts, 21 were high-school graduates, six directly entering the service after finishing school; and three were college dropouts. None were college graduates. Eighteen of the 34 men had full-time employment before entering the service, 12 in blue-collar jobs and six in white-collar employment. About two-thirds of the soldiers were from working-class backgrounds with the remainder being from the lower middle class.

"As for other social background characteristics: eight were black; one was a Navajo; another was from Guam; the other 20 men were white including three Mexican-Americans and one Puerto Rican. Twenty of the men were draftees and 14 were Regular Army volunteers." [2]

Even in 1969, after the draft law was changed, of 283,000 men drafted, only 28,500 were college men—10 percent, in a country where 40 percent of youth are now *said* to go to college.[3]

One other note, not simply a passing one, on the victims of war. Military service is actually "slave labor" of a kind, endured only under duress by most citizens. Men are compelled to serve and are jailed for refusing. For their service they are provided the most wretched and dangerous living and working conditions, and wages that are only a fraction

[2] Charles C. Moskos, Jr., "Why Men Fight," *Trans-action*, Nov. 1969, p. 17.
[3] Ward Just, "Soldiers," *Atlantic Monthly*, Oct. 1970.

of their civilian pay. The soldier's sacrifice involves more than his life. The loss in wages and education (to qualify for jobs with even greater wage potential) is a burden on middle America that has not yet been tabulated.

Contrary to the general impression, the working class has, from the beginning, been more against the war than the classes above it. Intervention in the war was more opposed by blue-collar than by middle- and upper-middle-class people.[4] This pattern has been sustained during the course of the war. Blue-collar workers continue to be more dovish than high-status people, as measured by occupation, education and income.

A national survey in 1964 showed that 53 percent of college graduates wanted to put more American soldiers into Vietnam, even at the risk of war with China, compared with one-third of people with only a grade-school education.[5] Total troop withdrawal was opposed by three-fourths of the former and only 38 percent of the latter.

Another survey after the 1964 elections showed that the major support for escalation of the war came from people in professional and managerial occupations, the college educated, those earning more than $10,000 a year. At the same time, the greatest approval for troop withdrawal came from those who had not finished high school, from blue-collar workers, and from those with annual incomes below $5,000.

2

Next to battlefields and highways, the most blood-soaked place is the factory and the industrial plant. Ac-

[4] R. F. Hamilton, "A Research Note on the Mass Support for 'Tough' Military Initiatives," *American Sociological Review,* June 1969, pp. 439–445.

[5] Martin Patchen, "Social Class and Foreign Policy Attitudes," paper presented to American Sociological Association, San Francisco, Sept. 1969.

cording to Ralph Nader, the industrial safety problem is far more serious than crime in the streets. In some blue-collar neighborhoods he has found many people without arms, fingers, or legs. "It's like Dusseldorf after the war," Nader says. Virtually all industrial and work accidents are suffered by blue-collar workers, the typical mid-Americans. A clerk may get a splinter in his finger or a teacher may fall down the up staircase, but such accidents are generally minor and occur infrequently.

In 1968, a total of 14,300 people died in industrial accidents in our country—almost exactly the same as the number of American servicemen who died in Vietnam that year. Between the beginning of 1961 and the end of 1969, about 46,000 Americans were killed in Vietnam. During that same period, 126,000 American workers were killed in industrial accidents. The toll was almost three times greater on the job than in Vietnam. Moreover, according to Ralph Nader, companies vastly understate the number of accidents in order to win Safety Council awards.

Those workers who are not killed, but are seriously injured on the job make up a huge army of their own. In 1968, 90,000 workers suffered *permanent impairment* from industrial accidents, and a total of 2,100,000 suffered total but temporary disability.

The Wall Street Journal quotes one company executive: "When you come right down to it, a lot of our safety decisions are really cost decisions. We give our workers safety glasses because they cost just $3.50. Safety shoes, which they also need, cost $14.00, so they aren't compulsory and the men have to buy them themselves." [6]

Wars are not always totally avoidable. But industrial accidents *are*—almost completely. Required are: spending for safety devices, education, research and its applications, stiff laws and penalties for infringements. Also required are the reduction of fatiguing compulsory overtime hours,

[6] *The Wall Street Journal,* Aug. 5, 1969, p. 1.

and special protection of new workers, who suffer about half of all accidents.

Millions of workers are exposed to dangerous pollutants without being aware of it, and even when they do know it, are unable to protect themselves. In 1969, these exposures caused one million new cases of occupational disease. Among the casualties were 3,600 dead and over 800,000 cases of burns, lung and eye damage, dermatitis and brain damage.

Damage comes from organic chemicals, of which there are over 100,000 in the work place. The effects of many of them on humans are unknown. Some, like beta napthlya-mine, a textile dye, are known to cause high cancer rates in workers who are exposed. Over six hundred new chemicals are added to the work place each year without any knowledge of their effects on humans. All 900,000 chemical and plastic workers, and the 460,000 rubber workers are exposed to these chemicals—and many other toxic substances.

Damage comes from exposure to toxic and lethal gases, of which there are over four hundred in the work place. These cause death, cancer, corrosion of lungs and eyes, severe brain damage. Garage workers and warehouse men are exposed to carbon monoxide, which can be lethal in a half hour, without the protection of an enforced law. A federal study found that in plants employing some 2,000 beryllium workers, over 50 percent of the air samples were not within the safety limit. Chlorine gas has cumulative effects on the worker's lungs. Some gases are not painful when inhaled, as fumes of chromium compounds are, and workers in glass, metal, cement, etc. are unaware when they are in danger.

Damage is caused by inhaling air particles, including mineral dusts such as silica, quartz, asbestos, mica, soap-stone, Portland cement, metal particles. These cause emphysema and general lung deterioration. They are usually invisible to the naked eye, and are usually retained in the lung once inhaled. Their effect is cumulative and delayed. Miners are ravaged by "black lung," a type of silicosis caused by inhaling coal dust. Over 2,000 cotton workers suffer from "white lung," from inhaling cotton fibers. Asbestos workers have a lung cancer rate seven times that of others.

6

Crime

The middle American is caught between two criminal elements. On one side there is the much-publicized crime of the poor. Petty theft, robbery, riots, violence. The average man—white or black—who lives near the city (as most blue-collar workers do) lives in fear of damage to himself or his property. Such fears are general and powerful enough to unseat governments.

On the other side, the average man is victimized by a far more sophisticated element—the truly rich and powerful and those they control in government. To judge by who fills our jails, the government pursues and prosecutes the crimes of the poor and ignores or encourages the crimes of the rich and powerful.

Because the news media tend to underplay "white-collar crime" because it is, in their view, not newsworthy or not quite criminal enough, the attention of middle America and its anger about crime is directed mainly at blacks and youth.

The average man is a natural victim, placed, as he is, like a bull's-eye between the criminal rich and the criminal poor. He is a common victim of the poor man's thefts. These are usually petty, but they are always annoying and often dangerous. He is also a victim of the predatory and exploitive behavior of those shrewd enough to stay within the law: he is cheated and persauded out of his earnings by the myriad shysters who thrive in the mercantile world and the "serving" professions. The predators are usually beyond the grasp of the law. Often they *are* the law. Government agencies, lawmakers and enforcers are everywhere more responsive to the wishes of profit makers than to those of the average citizen. Since they must jail *someone* to show they are prosecuting crime, they fill their jails with the poor.

Certainly the most distressingly criminal element among us is not the Mafia or the angry poor. It is those who are powerful enough to manipulate law and justice to their own advantage and the disadvantage of others. The average man's greatest loss is not as a target of crime, but as a victim of injustice. As such, he is cheated out of more than money spent on consumer goods and services. He is cheated out of rights and shares given him by those political principles that presumably inspire the law.

It is possible to distinguish at least three types of crimes. The first is those that are prosecuted in the courts and for which the defendants, usually the poor, are sent to jail. The second is the marginally legal acts and those that stay within or go beyond the grasp of the law. The third is crimes against the nature and rights of man. This latter variety touches virtually every aspect of our social life.

Indeed, our society, like most others, is built on exploitation of the weaker by the stronger, and on the manipulation of power and social institutions and the environment to benefit a few at the expense of the majority. It is built, in other words, on social injustice. This is the massive base on which other types of crime rest. The ultimate weapon used in this third category of crimes is legal violence. Property is protected and dissent suppressed by armed police, national guards, armies.

Muggings, assault, murder are not the only forms of violence. Violence can also be seen as hungry and sick people in a rich nation. It is an act of violence to poison the air, water, food, for profit and useless productivity. The violence and injustice of the law afflicts the average man as it does the poor—in the form of inadequate housing, education, health care, goods and services; in monotonous and unrewarding labor; in the form of war and economic insecurity; in the strains of living in a hostile and lethal environment; in the lack of good public transit; in tax and income inequities and the misappropriation of public funds; in the thwarting of the public will by big-money interests; and in the absence of means by which citizens can participate in the society and share power in their communities.

It is generally agreed that the worst crime on the books is murder. Many murders are committed by the poor. But people die in many needless ways other than by the mugger's knife. Responsibility for many of these deaths can be traced to the most respectable among us, who are neither accused, nor judged, nor punished for these crimes.

Among those whose victims vastly outnumber the 12,000 or so who are murdered each year are:

Those in the American Medical Association and their collaborators who indirectly cause the deaths of tens of thousands of people each year. Those dead of neglected ailments are not all indigent. Most are average people who simply cannot afford the high cost of good health care imposed by the AMA.

Those who put cars on the road that are unsafe at any speed, and oppose safer forms of mass transit in favor of highways. The slain number more than 50,000 each year.

Those who cause the deaths each year of more than 14,000 workers, dead of preventable industrial accidents. Added to the list are those thousands of workers who die less violently from such preventable afflictions as black lung, silicosis and other occupational ailments.

Those in the National Rifle Association and their supporters who oppose gun control and limitation of the 22,000 yearly gun deaths.

The New York Times is less likely than most papers to report crimes of the poor, and somewhat more likely to report crimes of the rich. In one rather typical day's news, the *Times* reported the following: [1]

—Price Fixing: The U.S. Department of Justice files an antitrust suit to prevent local real estate boards from enforcing uniform sales commissions. Such price fixing is illegal and subversive of "free enterprise." It is also very costly to consumers, involving millions of dollars in artificially inflated fees. The government asked no penalty, only that the boards desist.

—Perjury: A company vice-president is indicted for lying to a federal grand jury about possible graft paid the New York City agency that handles Medicaid funds. The company does business with the agency. A company employee was also indicted for stealing about $220,000 in welfare checks from the agency. Also indicted was the state senator who chairs the senate committee on Medicaid legislation—on charges of receiving cash payments from the company.

—"Overcharges" of the poor: Unscrupulous practices by hospitals, nursing homes, doctors, dentists and pharmacists

[1] *The New York Times,* Dec. 19, 1969.

are said to cost New York State Medicaid $60 million yearly (in a $1 billion-a-year program). Losses come from falsification and padding of bills, unnecessary referrals to specialists, unneeded tests, cheating by druggists on prescriptions. The state has in no instance prosecuted professionals or institutions involved in such practices.

—Carting firms are accused of defrauding the city of Yonkers of $1 million a year. The Republican chairman of Yonkers is accused of giving public contracts to high bidders so they would kick back to the party, and of permitting them to use the city incinerator to dump garbage, while the city itself had to pay to use the county dump.

—Federal grand jury indicts the mayor of Newark and fourteen others for extortion and income-tax evasion; for taking about $253,000 from companies doing business with the city.

—The physician who called the nation's attention to hunger and malnutrition in the South is sent to jail in South Carolina for allegedly dispensing drugs without a prescription. Justice at last!

These items are only a few in an inexhaustible list of crimes that afflict the man in the middle. None of them are among the big game—the crimes involving subversion of the economic system itself.

Closer to the big time was the federal case against General Electric and twenty-eight other electric firms for conspiring to rig prices and prevent free competition. In the end, seven executives went to jail (including four vice-presidents), and fines totaling about $2 million were levied. This penalty—the largest ever imposed under the Sherman Antitrust Law—was only a small toll to this gigantic industry. Sales of electric equipment by these firms reached almost $2 billion a year. The companies paid the fines, and after the executives came out of jail, most of them went back to their old jobs again.

Since it does not involve familiar misdeeds such as rob-

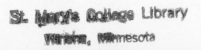

bery or short-changing, the average man may be puzzled by such high-level crime. Still, he probably suffered greater loss from this one conspiracy alone than from all the ordinary theft he is subject to in his life.

Just before the indictment, the President of General Electric had told the Senate antitrust committee: "The contrast between East Berlin and West Berlin, one a regulated economy and the other a free economy, is a vivid demonstration of what happens to the consumer when the competitive incentive of a free market is replaced by the restrictions of a regulated economy."

This is the same GE that vigorously and successfully opposed the unionization of its workers for many years; the same GE whose top executives testified in a court trial in 1957 that they had supplied call girls to their last company convention, that they thought such posh pimping was a part of their job, and that they believed their activities had sold seven carloads of appliances.

The electric conspiracy was not unique. It was simply one of the most dramatic attempts by big business to subvert its own system. The only news was that executives went to jail. Throughout the years the Justice Department and the Federal Trade Commission have had a full docket of similar conspiracy cases. In 1965, for example, eight steel companies were found guilty of conspiring to fix prices of carbon sheet steel. The companies were fined $50,000 each. Their annual business is about $3.6 billion. Their rigged prices have probably robbed consumers of steel products of tens of millions of dollars throughout the years. The worst crimes against consumers are the work of the biggest merchants, not the fly-by-night operators and the corner grocer. Again, the victims are mainly average and poor men.

Even the stock exchange, the heart of the "capitalist system," was charged with being rigged early in the sixties, by a Securities and Exchange Commission investigation of the American Stock Exchange. Under pressure of the examination, the president of the American Exchange resigned. The problem centered around a small group of specialists who were said to control the exchange.

Medieval Christianity regarded usury, the charging of interest on money, as sinful. A good Christian did not lend money for profit—perhaps because the Church wanted to keep control of capital in its own hands. Protestantism and capitalism changed all that, beginning with sixteenth-century English law that allowed limited interest rates and brought moneylending into moral repute.

Now most moneylenders are free to charge all the market will bear. Recently interest rates on small loans reached as high as 3½ percent a month, or an annual rate of about 42 percent.

Truth-in-lending laws, vigorously opposed by money-lenders, will make it more difficult to extract flesh from borrowers, simply by requiring that the true annual interest rates on any loan or extension of credit be made known. Some states have also put reasonable limits on interest rates. Organized labor in Washington, for example, won a state referendum to limit interest on consumer credit to a true 12 percent a year, the lowest state rate in the nation.

A close relative of the usurer is the credit merchant. This fellow has persuaded Americans to put themselves into about $95 billion worth of credit debt (not counting mortgages) on which they pay about $13 billion a year in interest—only about a billion less than the yearly interest on the national debt. Installment credit can be useful to those consumers who want to mortgage their future for some comforts now, but it becomes a national pathology when it reaches its present swollen dimensions.

As many as one in ten families is in debt over its head. Millions of average families succumb to the tricks of credit merchants—such as the popular revolving credit plans that enable merchants to repossess purchases that have already been paid for when payments due on more recent purchases have not been met. This sinks families deeper in debt. Millions of others are badly shaken.

The law (state law, which is traditionally the merchant's guardian) deals liberally with the creditor in most cases and harshly with the debtor. In most states, a man may default on only one payment of an installment debt and find his pay check garnisheed without even a court order. In some states, garnishments require a court judgment, but the easy-credit man can still get his victim to sign, at the time of purchase, a "confession of judgment" that waives his rights to a court judgment.

Many states permit creditors both to seize merchandise when payments lapse and insist on payment in full. The consumer then has nothing, neither his money nor his purchases. They also permit the creditors to "add on" to previous credit, making it also possible to repossess previously purchased goods. Millions of garnishments are made each year. They are the main cause of the dramatic rise during the past decade in consumer bankruptcies—to about 200,000 in a recent year. Perhaps half of those garnisheed are hooked not for their own debt but as co-signers for the debts of others. The middle American is the most frequent victim of the moneylenders and credit merchants.

2

Consumer abuses have become conspicuous enough to generate an incipient consumer movement. Ralph Nader, the advocate of the vulnerable middle man, has become a household hero.

One of his earliest and most publicized inquiries dealt

with auto safety. Since then a Nader study group has reported on the "chemical feast" and the Food and Drug Administration. The failure of federal regulation, Nader says, "to insure safe, pure, and nutritious food in the world's largest breadbasket has been in step with each new ingenious technique for manipulating the content of food products as dictated by corporate greed and irresponsibility. Making food appear what it is not is an integral part of the $125 billion food industry." [2]

Chemical food additives and the decline of nutrients in our food, unchecked by the FDA, have brought us to the point where, according to the Department of Agriculture, the nutritional value of the American family diet has actually declined. The food industry puts some 16 to 18 percent of its gross revenues into advertising, but virtually nothing into research that might improve the quality and nutrition of food.

The FDA, the report concludes, finds its meager efforts neutralized by powerful interests that include the large and wealthy Washington law firms, giant trade associations (made up of some 50,000 food-producing firms), and a group of "scientists" who routinely support marketing decisions. In short, the FDA is unable, even when willing, to influence a $125 billion industry, one that is six times larger than GM.

The regulatory agencies cannot cope with corporate power. Officials are wooed or intimidated. "I have never seen a bureaucrat take a strong principled stand without being retaliated against for it," said Julius Cohn, chief counsel to a Senate committee investigating the FDA.

The most important lesson of the Nader Summer Study of the FDA, the report concludes, was the futility of trying to treat the FDA as an isolated organization. In effect, a

[2] James S. Turner, *The Chemical Feast*, New York: Grossman, 1970, p.v.

vigilant consumer movement is required, which will generate action and enforcement in every part of public life. In addition, Nader proposes competition from cooperatives and public "yardstick" industries.

The Interstate Commerce Commission is the federal agency charged with regulating surface transportation—railroads, highways, trucking, house moving, etc. It is the oldest independent federal regulatory agency, and it has, says Nader, set longevity records in its systematic failure to protect or further the public interest in surface transportation.

In 1892, shortly after the ICC was established, Attorney General Richard Olney sent a letter to a railroad president, which read:

"The Commission, as its functions have now been limited by the courts, is, or can be made of great use to the railroads. It satisfies the popular clamor for a government supervision of railroads, at the same time that the supervision is almost entirely nominal. Further, the older such a commission gets to be, the more inclined it will be found to take the business and railroad view of things. It thus becomes a sort of barrier between the railroad corporations and the people, and a sort of protection against hasty and crude legislation hostile to railroad interests . . . The part of wisdom is not to destroy the Commission but to utilize it."

The Nader study group came to the following conclusions about the commission. The ICC is mainly a forum for settling disputes among transportation interests. It has not created any mechanism for representing the public interest. Its upper staff has a "collective personality of extreme conservatism," which makes policy within a framework of conditions that existed in the 1930's. Its relationship with industry is "intimate." It has numerous advisory groups to help set policy, but not one consumer representative is included. Its staff members frequently leave the ICC to take jobs in industries being "regulated." Its policy is unaffected by Congressional hearings. Its relations with the public are nonexistent—and "there is evidence of deep corruption at the ICC, beyond 'politics' and favoritism." [3]

Specific recommendations made by this group as a result of its investigation include: "The ICC should be abolished in its present form. A transportation regulatory agency should be created from the ground up." The new agency should concentrate on encouraging competition within the various modes of transportation, and policing rates where monopoly power exists.

Nader study groups have also reported on the Federal Trade Commission and on its love affair with the very people it is supposed to eye with suspicion. With such watchdogs guarding his interests, the average man becomes a fair mark for every cheat, price fixer, and product peddler in the commercial world. [4]

To protect consumers against products that are shoddy, unsafe, overpriced, and built for obsolesence, Nader proposes that a federal agency be set up to develop prototype products for the market. These prototypes will show manufacturers and consumers what good products can be like. Such proposals are not especially popular with business. One spokesman for the Better Business Bureau (its president) declared that Nader advocates socialistic proposals and appears bent on destroying the business system. [5]

So strong is business antagonism to consumer protection

[3] Robert Fellmeth, *The Interstate Commerce Omission,* New York: Grossman, 1970, pp. 311–313.

[4] Among the other federal regulatory agencies are the Federal Communications Commission (electronic communications—radio, TV, telephones); the Atomic Energy Commission (atomic power); the Federal Power Commission (hydroelectric plants and navigable waters and, reluctantly, natural gas); the Securities and Exchange Commission (securities markets on Wall Street and elsewhere).

[5] Ralph Smathers, *Miami Herald,* Feb. 12, 1970, p. 29-A.

that even Nixon's Secretary of Commerce warned that we must decide "whether we are going to let the wave of consumerism move too far and destroy the freedom of choice of consumers." [6]

In answer to consumer demands for effective regulation, business has turned to the "consumer education" ruse. Instead of protecting consumers, business wants to "educate" them. Most business organizations—the U.S. Chamber of Commerce, the National Association of Manufacturers, etc.—have launched such education programs. These same organizations have vigorously opposed all attempts to put real teeth into consumer regulation. They offer education but oppose the labeling of products. Nothing can educate consumers better than knowledge about what it is they are buying—what's in the soup they eat, the aspirin they swallow, etc.

Large business lobbies in Washington have successfully blocked most consumer proposals. About 80 percent of all people attending congressional or agency hearings on consumer issues, it is reported, are lobbyists of corporations or trade associations. About 5 percent are from consumer groups.

When legislation does slip through these committees somehow, the appropriations committee often undercuts it by starving the regulatory agency of enforcement funds. The regulations serve no end if they are unenforceable. The truth-in-lending law, for example, was passed after long and bitter debate. Yet only five government technicians were assigned to work with industry on the staggering enforcement job of establishing some uniformity in package sizes.

In some cases, the courts have come through where the regulators have failed to protect the average consumer against corporate predators. Class action suits, for example,

[6] Maurice H. Stans, *The New York Times*, Sept. 24, 1969, p. 18.

have recently been permitted. Previously only the individual consumer could use the courts. Consumers can now pool their complaints to make legal action feasible. And a government agency or consumer organization can go to court for consumers even when the agency is not directly involved itself. The collective sums involved in these cases are often substantial. In one court action, for instance, state and local governments and individual retailers and consumers won $100 million from drug companies for overcharges on tetracycline drugs.

The process of government-business collusion in regulatory agencies against the interests of the average consumer is described by *Business Week* in a moment of unusual candor.[7] What happens is more subtle than a commissioner's resolve to be "liberal" or "conservative," according to the article. Instead, he is absorbed by the industry he regulates, the process starting even before his appointment.

The White House usually begins by asking industry for nominees for a commission vacancy. When the industry has been a heavy campaign giver, its views are given special attention. Even when the industry is not asked for nominees, it can influence the choice behind the scenes before the time for Senate confirmation arrives.

On the job, the commissioner is promptly visited by industry representatives—to "get acquainted." They offer to help the commissioner understand complex issues and announce they are ready to talk with him at any time. The commissioner is invited to address the industry's conventions. At cocktail parties, the industry reps are very attentive to the new man. Then come invitations to join the rich social life of the Washington lobbyist. Weekends at the sea, hunting trips, summer jobs for the children, bottles of booze at Christmas, invitations to country clubs. A whole new social world opens up to the commissioner's wife.

[7] *Business Week,* Feb. 28, 1970, p. 64.

Then there is the prospect of a good job in the industry being regulated, after the commissioner leaves his job. The most attentive treatment is given to those aides who have the most influence over the agency's work. In no time everyone is good pals, and the absorption is complete.

One insider calls the system the agency subgovernment— an informal governing body composed of a trade association and a trade publication, lawyers who practice often before the commission, the agency itself, one or more of the agency's staff bureaus, and a handful of Congressmen and congressional committee staff men. The people involved give their loyalty to the subgovernment, rather than to the organizations that formally hired them.

According to Nader, the action is at the bottom of the agency, where it's cheaper and easier to buy off staff members. Bank loans and stock tips are given. The agents relax their inquiries. Meat inspectors, for example, are bought off with overtime paid for by the meat-packing companies.

3

So it is that the average man languishes, a victim of predatory profit makers, while the watchdog is off licking the burglar's hand. Some agencies, of course, are better than others, and virtually all do some good deeds. But all of them are grossly inadequate to the function they are charged with—protecting the average citizen against business crimes and activity that should be regarded as criminal.

Those who give us our news have spotlighted the crimes of the poor and minimized the crimes of the rich. The latter are certainly newsworthy, even when they involve no violence. Indeed, nowadays mugging is hardly news at all, while high-level conspiracy to restrain trade, if treated, would be hot news and high drama. Clearly such top-drawer crime deserves much more coverage than it usually gets, which is, at most, a mention in the financial section of the newspapers.

Though the mid-American is alarmed about crime in the streets, there is no definite evidence that people are more criminal now than in the past. The most crime-prone age group (eighteen to twenty-four) has swollen as a proportion of the total population; this may account for part of the rise in crime statistics. Crime has risen in the city because more of the poor live there now. Also, the massive migration of the poor into the cities has come mainly from the South, the highest crime region in the nation. Moreover, reported crime increases as our police force increases, and there are more people around to report crime.

The crimes of the poor that afflict us can be traced, through a not very circuitous route, to the crimes of the rich. Poverty and discrimination generate crime among the poor. These in turn are generated by national policies that produce joblessness, low wages, unfair taxes, and neglect of public need in health, housing, education, welfare and wholesome environments.

7

The Curses: Sickness, Insecurity, Hard Labor

Other "curses" victimize the average man, including many ancient but still lively ones: sickness, insecurity and hard labor.

Good physical and mental health are the foundation of the good life. Yet the availability and distribution of health care in the nation are notoriously bad. Quite simply, we Americans have religiously turned over our health, as we have most other things, to private enterprise and profit makers—that is, to the AMA and the system of private fee-for-service medicine.[1]

---

[1] Some 75 percent of all our citizens, it is claimed, are covered by some form of health insurance. These plans, however, cover only

Virtually every European nation has a national health care program.[2] The British system of "socialized medicine" —to the dismay of those who predicted disaster—works. It is not too costly, and it is enormously popular with patients and even with doctors. It is, in fact, generally viewed as one of the outstanding achievements of British domestic history. Even the Tories in power will not reverse this Labor party creation, as they reversed a previous nationalization of steel.

Though Sweden spends only 5 percent of its GNP on health care, it is ahead of the United States on virtually every index of good health—including life expectancy, disease rates, nutrition.

In seventeen countries, men live longer than they do in the United States; women, in ten countries. At birth an American male can expect to live sixty-seven years (as of 1964).

In Israel, Denmark, Iceland or Switzerland a man can expect to live seventy years, and in Sweden, Norway and the Netherlands, seventy-one years. The death rate of American males between forty-five and fifty-five (the years of their peak powers) is double that of Sweden and is higher than the rate in any other Western country. We rank behind thirteen other countries in infant mortality. In the United States (as of 1967) twenty-two infants under one year of age died per thousand live births—in Sweden and the Netherlands only thirteen died; in Finland and Norway only fourteen; in Japan, fifteen; Denmark and Switzerland, seventeen.

---

about one-third of the costs of health care—and the costs have zoomed since federal programs (under pressure from the medical profession) gave doctors and hospitals a carte blanche on charges. Since 1966, medical charges (for the same service) have risen at an average annual rate of 7 percent.

[2] America spent 6.7 percent of its Gross National Product on medical care—more than any other nation.

The neglect of health care in the United States is especially poignant for the mid-American. Again, he is caught right in the middle. The affluent can afford good health care. The poor, in some places, have access to Medicaid and other public health programs—although they too are seriously victimized. The average man can play neither end of the field: he cannot afford good care, nor can he get it free.

As for psychiatric care and treatment for mental illness, they are far out of the reach of the average man, even though research indicates that he is more victimized by mental illness than his affluent boss.

The quality of our medical care, never mind the cost, is revealed in a summary report made by the National Advisory Commission on Health Manpower (1967): 25 percent of reported laboratory results on known samples were erroneous; 70 percent of operations resulting in castration or sterility were unjustified; only 57 percent of hospital patients and 31 percent of general medical cases received "optimal" care.

Consistently and successfully over the last decades, the American Medical Association has opposed voluntary prepaid group practice plans—plans in which doctors work on salary. It harassed doctors who entered these plans, until the practice was recently outlawed, excluding them from AMA membership, and thereby from the hospitals that require such membership. In some seventeen states, it has won the passage of laws that forbid prepaid group practice.

The AMA has opposed the expansion of medical schools and the admission of a sufficient number of doctors into the profession. It has blocked every federal effort to finance health care. Only in the past few years, as it has seen the inevitability of some form of federal program, has it gone along with Medicare (for the aged) and Medicaid (for some of the poor, and other groups). Both programs operate on a fee-for-service basis: that is, they permit doctors and hospitals to do what they please and charge what they please. Neither would have passed if any public controls had been imposed. Between 1964 and 1969, the reported median earnings of doctors rose from $28,000 a year to $40,000.

The federal government in 1968 spent about 30 percent of the total of $53 billion that was spent on health care in the nation as a whole. The average man got virtually nothing from his tax money for health care, except a steep rise in medical charges.

The medical profession is aided by other profit makers in undermining the health of the average American. It is aided by those who pour pollutants into our air—industry, auto makers, producers of noxious fuels. It is aided by cigarette manufacturers, their advertising agencies and other supporters, and by those who pollute the water we swim in, fish in, drink. It is aided by the food manufacturers who contaminate our food and rob it of nutrition; by those who sell harmful chemicals and drugs. It is aided by those institutions (schools, work organizations) that create a sense of worthlessness, powerlessness and insecurity in the average person, laying the groundwork for emotional illness. It is aided by those who impose grinding labor on millions, while depriving them of recreational outlets to keep physically and mentally fit.

The average American, particularly the manual worker, is victimized by overwork and overweight. The fatigued worker, ending his eight-hour shift, is hardly fit for the tennis courts. Instead—a heavy dinner, a few hours of TV, and bed are the evening's routine. Because he is overweight, overworked and under-cared-for, according to a study at American Telephone and Telegraph, he is more prone to heart attacks than is the executive or professional man, and to a variety of other ailments that flow from neglect and abuse of the body.

2

Next to good health, what most people seem to crave most is security. Employment waxes and wanes unpredictably. Sometimes it's up and sometimes it's way down, into depression and recession. People with steady and secure jobs may regard these dips as inevitable or even desirable. Some even say that a small depression would be good for the country because we are all getting too affluent. The Nixon Administration, indeed, has adopted this perverted idea as its basic economic policy. The people who are most *affected* by these dips, however, have a far less cavalier attitude toward them.

Unemployment rates are lifeless statistics, abstractions without much body to them. A rise in unemployment of only 1 percent may seem modest enough. In human terms, a rise of 1 percent means that about 800,000 people have lost their jobs and that, including their families, about three million people have been directly affected. When unemployment goes as high as 6 percent, it means that nearly five million working people are out of jobs; this affects families with about fifteen million people in them. These figures do not even include the millions of people who are not in the work force because there aren't enough jobs, but who are nonetheless unemployed. Moreover, unemployment has a contagious effect. A jobless worker will buy less, thus putting others out of work or reducing their incomes.

From a secure perch in the professional world, the observer may regard an unemployment rate of 5 percent as a successful conquest of joblessness. The worker without a job has a different view. When a plant closes down or cuts back for good, the worker loses his lifetime seniority and other accumulated job rights. It is possible that he will not find another decent job. When his unemployment compensation expires after six months at the most, he may have to uproot himself and start again, a stranger in a new place. Those most likely to be hurt by recessions are the least likely to have skills or savings to tide them over the bad times.

Professionals, managers and white-collar workers are seldom laid off. The blue-collar worker is the one who is vulnerable. When unemployment rates stand at 4 percent nationally, unemployment among blue-collar workers will probably be over 10 percent.

Along with the blue-collar worker, the black teen-ager is among those hardest hit by layoffs, though society can least afford to drop these young blacks from the job market. As the newest members of the American work force, brought in often only through expensive job-training programs, they are the first to be let go. Unemployed, they often add to what is already a swollen and angry society of street-corner youth.

A college professor or other New Classman would find it intolerable to be laid off because of an employer's monetary whim. With tenure, the professor is almost impervious to layoff or firing. The worker finds layoffs just as intolerable, but there is very little he can do about it. Most cannot last more than a month or two on their life's savings. Unemployment compensation is his only cushion.

The Japanese system of industrial relations is hardly admirable, depending as it does on employer paternalism, yet it has at least demonstrated that a society can be enormously productive and still guarantee job security to workers. The Japanese worker is never laid off, and rarely fired. He has a permanent job with his employer if he wants it. Employers arrange schedules so that there are few slack periods, and carry workers on the payroll who would be laid off here. The Japanese blue-collar worker is as secure as is the executive and white-collar worker in the United States.

Another cause of massive insecurity is low income. In this respect the middle American suffers along with the impoverished worker. A family with a small income and small savings is uncertain about each day. It cannot feel much certainty about the future. Such insecurity accounts for much mental distress among low-income earners. A related form of insecurity is the fears and uncertainties attendant on growing old. As we have seen in previous data, most families simply do not have the resources—in savings, income, pension plans, health insurance—to deal with the ravages of old age.

3

The average man is also victimized by hard, monotonous and unrewarding labor. Among the routine sources of happiness, which the New Class takes for granted in a job, are a good chance to move up, flexible working conditions and satisfying work. In his white- and blue-collar job, the middle American gets little of the pleasure, purpose or freedom that are essential to job satisfaction. His rewards are a more-or-less regular pay check and associations with other workers.

The worker (blue-collar and clerical) is Marx's original "alienated man." It was the estrangement of the industrial worker from the product of his labor which, Marx predicted, would generate the revolution and topple the capitalist class. While this has not come to pass in the United States, the nature of industrial work remains a source of massive discontent.

Involved in the discontent are: *Fatigue*—the work is often physically exhausting; the hours are long and rest periods few; on assembly jobs, the speed of "the line" is fast and, even worse, inexorable. *Boredom*—the work is monotonous, uncreative, unrewarding. *Pollution*—the shop is noisy, dirty, ugly; the air is polluted with smoke, dust, chemicals. *Discomfort*—there are usually no decent eating places, nor comfortable rest rooms, nor enough safe parking lots. *Dead end*—there is no way to get out, no future, no purpose in the work. *Lack of freedom*—there is no freedom of choice, no coming and going from the job at the worker's choice; the discipline and chain of command are like those in the military—the worker must do what he is told, when he is told, on penalty of immediate discipline. *Lack of power and participation*—the worker participates in few decisions concerning the product, process, or nature of his work, and has little control over the conditions of his labor.

This job alienation is not limited to blue-collar workers. Except for the dirt and noise, the white-collar worker is in much the same boat. Many others who work for organizations, unless they identify closely with them, are also in that boat, from junior executives to elevator operators. As the size and power of organizations grow, so does the volume of discontent with work. The most aggrieved are the young. They usually enter the organization at the bottom, where there is least freedom, participation, rewards.

Once men found their identity in their labor. They even took the names of their trades (Taylor, Sexton, Weaver, Goldsmith). It is hard to imagine a worker wanting to take the name of General Motors or Libby-Owens.

One national study found that most men say they would work even if they had enough money to satisfy all their needs.[3] In the working class, however, two-thirds of those studied said they did *not* want to continue in their "pres-

[3] Robert L. Kahn, "The Meaning of Work," *The Worker in the New Industrial Environment,* Foundation for Research on Human Behavior, Ann Arbor, Michigan.

ent" job. Among professionals, the opposite was the case: two-thirds of professionals said they wanted to continue in the same work. (Many dissatisfied workers wanted to set up a small business of their own.)

Another study found that professionals, technicians, managers and proprietors were far more likely than unskilled and semiskilled workers to report ego satisfactions from their job.[4] These satisfactions derived from the nature of their work—its value, variety, the skill involved, interpersonal relations, responsibility and independence.

The industrial worker's job is not a happy one. He usually must start his shift at seven A.M. He is probably up at 5:30 A.M., when it is still dark. He is at work while the New Class is still asleep. Frequently he will have to use public transit to get to work. This means a walk to the bus stop, perhaps a fifteen minute wait for the bus—often in the dark, rain or cold—and then a jerky trip to work. Or if he drives, he will have to cope with plant traffic and the parking problem.

His arrival at the plant is controlled by the time clock. If he is five minutes late, he will be docked on pay day—he has no margin of error or comfort. From then on, his movements are usually lock-step. If he is on an assembly line, he will face the ultimate in automatic control. The movement of the line is inexorable. The worker cannot stop it, slow it down, influence its flow. If his particular task is not done exactly when it should be, it will be detected immediately down the line. He can no more escape the line's insistent demands for instant gratification than he can the time clock's. Both are exacting and tyrannical masters, with no human sympathy. The worker is a servant and time is his master.

Typically, he works steadily and swiftly during the time

4 Gerald Gurin, "Work Satisfactions," *ibid,* p. 7.

he is on the job. If his job is to tighten a nut, his work may be time-studied at, say, five jobs a minute. Such a speed will require him to repeat his job three hundred times in an hour, or 2,400 times during the course of a day, or 12,000 times a week. Typically, he will get a half-hour for lunch, a ten-minute break in the morning, and another ten minutes in the afternoon. Aside from these brief respites, he is tied to the line. Even if he does not work "on the line," his production will be rigidly controlled. He will be only somewhat freer to make his own breaks and set his own pace.

At lunchtime, while the executives go to their private dining room and the clerks to their clean cafeteria, the worker will often be assigned to a table and bench near his work where, only a step removed from the line, he takes out his sandwiches and thermos jug and dines. Sometimes there will not even be benches and tables, so that he must either run out to the local greasy spoon or simply squat on a box or on the oily floor near his work to eat. If he doesn't bring his lunch, he may have to buy it off the coffee wagon, a grimy mobile cart serving up unpotable coffee and unappetizing food. Dining under such conditions is degrading beyond the empathetic capacity of those professors who spend a leisurely lunch hour—or two or three—at the faculty club, where they talk casually about worker affluence.

The work environment is usually as loathsome and unhealthy as the lunchtime environment. Indeed, they are often one and the same—except that during the lunch period the awful noise and air pollution stop briefly.

In most plants the noise reaches a deafening volume, literally, permanently impairing the hearing of many workers. Some of these workers have successfully presented claims for compensation as a result of this deafening. Researchers have recently tried to study the effect of loud music on the hearing of adolescents, but workers have not yet received such solicitous attention. Not only hearing, but the entire nervous system, all aesthetic sensitivities, and all communications among people are impaired. Most workers, unless inured by overexposure, report that the noise in the shop is almost as fatiguing as the work itself. It is constant, cacaphonous, uncontrollable, nerve-jarring.

Employer response to worker complaints about noise is, at best, to issue earplugs. Tuned out with earplugs, the worker is a deaf-mute—shut off from the world around him and from communication with his one source of pleasure, his fellow workers.

In the plants there are fumes from chemicals and machines and smoke from the factory chimneys. The atmosphere is soaked with them. The air is foul with odors—grease, oil, hot metal, machine shavings, leather, detergents, ammonia, paint spray, sawdust, and so forth. In calculating the costs of pollution, as we have seen, we must also figure in the thousands of workers who are crippled and killed each year by industrial pollution—the black lung of the mine, the silicosis of the plant, etc.

When the worker confronts the time-clock at the end of his shift, he is usually exhausted, physically and psychically. Despite the fatigue of the workers, the plant empties instantly, so great is the desire to escape. Given this description of a typical worker's day, it seems ludicrous to go on as some do about the creative uses of leisure in middle America. The worker has very little leisure to play with. He may get home at four P.M., wash, rest, read the evening paper, have dinner at six o'clock, talk to his family and watch TV for a while, clean up and go to bed. Because he rises at 5:30, he goes to bed around ten. By that time he is ready to sleep; in fact, he has probably been dozing at the TV long before that.

A union committeeman we know, who works in an auto

shop, puts it this way: "These guys on production, I don't know how they can do it—thirty years, six days a week. They press the button, the press comes down, they pick up the fender and put it to the side—push the button, pick up the fender . . . Do you know how many times those guys do that each day? Three thousand three hundred times. Three thousand three hundred times each day. They make about thirty-eight dollars a day for it—on piece work—or around $10,000 a year for a full year. They get a ten-minute break in the morning, a thirty-minute lunch hour, and a ten-minute break in the afternoon. Other than that, they work straight through, not a minute's rest. Sometimes the presses leak, and oil is dripping down on their backs from the press. You ask the company to fix it, and you keep asking them. You file a grievance. They laugh at you. The only thing that works is when you show them you mean business. You take guys off the job and shut down the production. Then they take you seriously. You can't get young guys to work on those jobs. They take them and then ten minutes later they've got a bellyache and they go to the hospital, and they're finished. Then the noise is so great. In the press room there are ninety presses, all working at one time. The noise will crack your eardrums. They can't even get skilled guys to go in there."

One student, lucky enough to get a summer job in a Detroit auto plant, working afternoons as a drill and tap man, describes his encounter with industrial work:

"God, the place is huge. It is composed of 11 buildings with more planned. The bewildering maze of complicated machinery, conveyor belts, smoke and steam, is a surrealistic landscape of well-organized insanity, but you don't mind so much because you're being paid well. The cacaphony of roaring, whirring, pounding, whistling noises is painful to your uninitiated ears . . .

"You are led to a small aisle located between six clanking, detergent-spewing 'mechanizers.' The job is simple, you are told. Take a metal cylinder weighing five pounds off the conveyor line as it comes in (there are four such lines). Place the cylinder underneath a device in one of the machines, push a pedal on the floor, press a button to your right. A huge tank will rise out of the machine's main body, enveloping the vibrating cylinder for 30 seconds and spraying it with a powerful, pungent detergent that splatters in your eyes despite your safety glasses. When the cycle is complete, press a pedal releasing the cylinder; return the cylinder to the conveyor line.

"Grab, push, clamp, press, push, remove: grab, push, clamp, press, push, remove: grab, push, clamp . . . The parts begin to pile up. There's nowhere to stack them. The sweat trickles into your eyes; the hot water from the machines burns your hands. You grit your teeth and laugh at yourself out of desperation.

"At last it's lunch time. Twenty minutes to eat, 10 of which you spend either in the restroom or hunting for the cafeteria. Your ears ring. Two men are engaged in a conversation only five feet away, but your barely hear them. You gulp down a hot dog . . .

"Money is important. Your newly acquired position is exactly what the hordes of unemployed are clamoring for, although this fact may be hard to believe. No wonder every fourth word spoken by a Detroiter is profane. No wonder the factory worker's range of conversation is limited to the Tigers, the weather, cars and management versus labor.

"You return home and take a shower, fall into bed and dream. Your dream consists of grab, push, press, clamp, push, remove." [5]

[5] James R. Amos, sophomore at Oakland University, *Detroit Magazine, Detroit Free Press,* Aug. 30, 1970.

For many of us, work is the mainspring of our lives, our purpose, satisfaction, the object of our creative efforts. Work, and preparing for and getting to work, consume more than half of our waking lives and much of our vital resources. To be alienated from work is, in a sense, to be alienated from life.

Students who protest—as they should—about lack of control, participation and power in *their* institutions have real grievances. Yet they are modest compared with those of the average worker. Workers have not been complacent about these grievances; they have simply confronted authorities that are far more powerful and far less benign than university administrators. They have also—like students—confronted a public that is usually quite unwilling to listen to their grievances or sympathize with their strikes and protests.

For all this, the industrial worker is better off than many workers—the miner, the slaughterhouse worker, the longshoreman, the long-haul truck driver, the construction laborer who must climb high and do risky work, the laundry and restaurant worker, who do tough and dirty work for next to nothing.

The choices that students have are far too limited. But, even so, they have many more options open to them than workers do. Students may come late to class or absent themselves occasionally without penalty. They may choose their own curricula and the classes they will take each term. From among the readings and activities in each course, they may usually select what interests them most. They may decide to take classes at eight in the morning or nine at night. They may choose, if they wish, to take all their classes on one or two days, and knock off the rest. They may choose their own teacher or adviser. They can influence school policy to some extent through their councils. They are not servants to time-clocks, machines or lock-step routines. They are usually not troubled by noise, dirt or discomfort. They are not subject to hard (or even easy) physical work. The conditions of their labor are hardly comparable to those of workers.

Students have many *other* legitimate grievances—the meaninglessness of work that should be exciting, the hierarchy of authority, the rigidity of bureaucracies, the lack of opportunity to participate and make decisions affecting their lives. Students have, at last, opened real issues here and may in the end make schooling more tolerable for those who succeed them. But workers have *also* had these same grievances, only worse, and they have almost always protested them, openly, vigorously—and, on the whole, fruitlessly.

Why do workers put up with it at all? Simply enough, they have been conditioned to accept no other of the few alternatives available to them. "Dropping out" entails an abrogation of the responsibilities they must meet to maintain satisfactory self-images. Unemployment is stigmatic. Although concessions must be and have been made to them, industry bargains from the very strong position of knowledge that the worker must work.

III : Equity and Alienation

8

Equality

Probably the middle American would be more concerned about equality if he understood more about the nature of his own grievances. As he sees it, those who cry for equality are demanding a share of his own small holdings. As a result, egalitarian slogans shouted by those who feel excluded from the benefits of society arouse resentment in the average man, when they should be clarifying his own discontent. The question that is still unasked by mid-America is: Why can't the sharing start at the top, where the great wealth is piled, and move down so we can all have more? The answer to this unformed question will unlock the discussion of equality and perhaps give middle America a new perspective on its political future.

It is said that equality no longer excites much public passion, that it is an old and dead issue compared to such lively new ones as love and participation. Maybe.

Though history may seem—while we are making it—to be controlled by fashion, it has a certain rhythm and persistence over time. Themes which lie as deep in the hearts of men as equality does cannot be discarded as easily as miniskirts and the twist.

In the "advanced" nations like America, the idea of equality does not currently arouse the revolutionary ardor it once did, or that it now does in the Third World. Only the most excluded among us are eager to overthrow the existing system in order to enter a new one on a more equal footing. The rest of us have fallen under a conservative spell in the last decades, a spell cast as much by the failures of egalitarianism in the USSR as by its neglect at home. We like equality, but are without the enthusiasm necessary to help bring it about. Or else we are afraid that the ideal may become the Frankenstein of the Stalinist state once it is off the drawing boards. We tend to regard equality of opportunity as one of our most cherished and yet somehow dangerous social ideals.

But this conservative calm that has prevailed among us has recently been shaken by succeeding waves of protests over inequality—the civil-rights demonstrations, the war on poverty, the student movement, women's lib.

The hunger for equality in the average man can be pacified to some extent by material progress. He will be less disturbed about the great fortunes of others if his own are doing fairly well. However, the average American can not be satisfied with just this. His needs and grievances are many and his appetite grows.

Traditionally, we have tried to satisfy his appetite for more of what others have by simply enlarging the national pie. That way, each of us can have a larger slice, without

any sharing of portions. Such an enlargement of total resources takes a lot of time. People want their share now.
They get impatient. They can't wait until economic growth
engulfs them too. Those at the bottom turn for their share
to those who, in a literal and metaphoric sense, live next
door to them—the middle Americans. And the latter re-
lieve their frustrations on those restless and disorderly
people down below.

Envy requires proximity. One may covet the new color
TV or the promotion of the man next door, while ignoring
the man in the next suburb who has a color TV in each of
his ten bedrooms. People usually seek equality with neighbors and with those they come into contact with. The men
at the top are far away and out of sight. One cannot yearn,
after all, for what one does not know exists. For most of us,
the rich and the super-rich are only legendary—the closest
we come is through vicarious glimpses we get into the
dream world of Jackie Kennedy Onassis and the Jet Set.

Not since the Depression have people known or cared
much about the holders of great wealth and power. In the
sweatshops, during the Depression, and at early grim
stages of our industrialization, an ardent hatred of the
rich was quite naturally aroused because industrialization
made the poor aware, in a new way, of the power of wealth.
Many wanted to throw out the rich oppressors and set up
their own communal styles of life, whereby wealth and
authority would be a shared function of the community.
Desperation, more than envy or abstract ideology, spurred
these sentiments. The average man was less enraged about
conspicuous wealth and power than about his own sorry
condition. Yet he was not slow to connect the two, to see
that his desperation was ignored because others had cornered too much power and wealth; nor was he slow to
organize against the rich.

Usually it takes a cataclysm such as depression or war to

arouse the average person against a system that gives rich rewards to some and poor ones to others. Even then, one or another demagogue usually succeeds in changing the trajectory of the general discontent by projecting it onto a handy scapegoat. Any minority or outsider may become such a target. In Germany, and elsewhere, it was Jews. In this country, it was one immigrant group after another, and now it has become blacks, students, dissenters, hard hats. All are victims rather than creators of the inequities under which they chafe.

When the average man feels he is making any kind of progress, however minimal, he will usually resist an upheaval in the social system. Who knows, after all, what nightmares may be conjured up by the new fellows? In his experience, even small gains are hard to win, and personal disaster may be only a step away. He takes a firm grip on what is in hand, and tries to pull himself up slowly.

This tendency to choose the bird-in-hand usually increases when he feels that his society, and his safety, security and values, are being threatened from outside. The attack may come from "foreign enemies," or from strangers in his own community who say they loathe everything he loves. Like any animal, he will defend himself when cornered. He may even end up stoutly defending a system from which he himself would otherwise feel estranged.

The average man is sorely troubled when he himself is the target of the assault—especially when he is hit from below by blows that should be aimed at people higher up. By definition the middle American is usually in the middle. When dissenters—blacks, students, left, right—attack the system, the average man is usually standing in the direct line of fire, taking shots from all directions. This cannot make him very happy about dissent—even when it is in the name of so venerable a cause as equality.

Another obstacle to achieving greater social equity is the amazing lack of data about basic inequalities. This may surprise some people who think sociologists and their kindred do nothing but study equality. The opposite is the case. They have only the sketchiest knowledge about the infinite varieties of inequality that infect this and other societies. The middle American cannot be expected to be very concerned about inequities, when men of knowledge know—and apparently care—so little. Usually social research goes where the money is. In this it resembles other resources in the society. There is simply no money available to study inequalities, nor, for that matter, to study workers, unions, middle Americans. The private foundations have not, until recently, been willing to fund any research into the subject, and federal agencies have been equally aloof. Similarly, it has been all but impossible to get financing for studies of the very rich and the economic and political empires they govern.

When we speak of equality, money is one of the first subjects that come to mind. Money, as the songs go, can't buy you happiness, but it can buy you a lot of pleasure, comfort and prestige. It can't buy love and health either, but it has a certain value even in these areas. Moreover, money offers freedom and options, a chance to come and go as we please, work and play as we please, buy what we please. Its value is rather hard to underappraise. For this reason, most of us would much rather have it than not.

In considering its relation to equality, we will deal with two forms of money: income and wealth. The two are obviously related, even inseparable: wealth is the total assets we own, and income is the increment of wealth each year. Today, in the United States, income and wealth are no more equally distributed than thirty-five years ago.

As for income (as distinct from wealth), in 1968 the top

10 percent of families (with a mean income of $26,740) received almost 30 percent of total personal income.[1] In effect, they received about three times more than their equal share. These figures, remarkably enough, do not include income from capital gains (realized or unrealized), the many income substitutes (such as expense accounts), or other specially treated income. With these included, the share of the top 10 percent would be significantly greater than 30 percent.

The top 20 percent (income of $14,300 or over) received 44 percent of total income in that year—or more than twice their equal share. The top two-fifths received 65 percent of all family income. The bottom 40 percent, on the other hand, received only 15 percent of total income— much less than half their equal share.[2] In fact, the share of the bottom 40 percent was about the same as the share of the top 5 percent. The bottom fifth received only 5 percent of total income.

At the top, families with incomes of $25,000 or more make about five times more than their equal share of total income, as indicated in the following: [3]

[1] Survey Research Center, University of Michigan, *The Distribution of Family Income in 1968* (including one-person units), Economic Behavior Program, Statistical Report I.

[2] Survey Research Center, University of Michigan, *Survey of Consumer Finances, 1968*, G. Katona, et al.

[3] *Ibid.* The figures for 1968 are comparable and indicate that, while only 36.1 percent of families earn $10,000 a year or more, they receive 64 percent—almost two-thirds—of all personal income in the nation.

Income Before Taxes, 1967	Proportion of Families	Share of Total National Personal Income
$10,000–14,999	21.6%	30%
15,000–19,000	6.4	12
20,000–24,999	2.1	6
25,000 or more	2.5	12
All four income groups	32.6	60

If anything, inequality has increased.[4] (Those with large incomes need not fear looking back; they are not being followed.) Even between 1913 and 1930, including a war period, there was little change in income sharing.[5] The only significant shift during the century occurred in the late thirties, after the New Deal had reduced the shares of the very wealthy and passed along the gain mainly to the next-highest income fifth. The start of World War II began the present period of stability in income distribution.

In 1929 the top fifth received 54 percent of all personal income, and in 1962 it received only 46 percent—an 8 percent relative loss in more than thirty years. Half of this relative loss was picked up by the second-highest income fifth.

Among the top 5 percent of family-income recipients, Kuznets' study revealed that professionals, managers and owners are greatly overrepresented. They make up 69 percent of income receivers in the top 5 percent ($17,307 and over, in 1964, the last year for which these figures are available) but only 29 percent of the total work force.

The professional and managerial class has risen in numbers and income. This is the most rapidly growing of all occupational groups. Between 1950 and 1964 the relative size of this group almost doubled, from 7 percent to 13 percent of the work force. (Most of the growth was in salaried rather than self-employed people.) All other groups, except one, either grew or held fairly steady as a proportion of the total. The exception, the only group that declined dramatically, was "farmers and farm managers." What farmers lost, professionals gained.

[4] Between 1960 and 1968, the shares of low-income families (the second and third tenths) grew by 29 and 25 percent, respectively. The top earners—those in the ninth and highest tenths—grew by 51 and 46 percent, respectively.

[5] S. Kuznets, "Economic Growth and Income Inequality," *American Economic Review*, March 1955.

The New Class of professionals and managers—the highly educated and highly paid—should not be mistaken for the really wealthy. The Big Fortunes are in a class by themselves—an Old Class of owners of immense wealth. Most families in the top 5 percent of income recipients are simply affluent, with incomes spent as fast as they are made.

2

It is axiomatic that money tends to rise to the top, and that the higher it rises the more likely it is to be concealed from public and revenue observers. The means of concealment can be legal, devious or downright illegal.

Most income figures are not refined enough to tell us how much the rich really get. Too many hiding places are provided for the concealment of big incomes. Wealth is a far better index to equality than income. The problem with using it as an index is that neither scholars nor government agencies bother to keep systematic records of the ownership of wealth in our country. We tax income, not wealth, so we let the latter slip by us without recording it or exacting a toll.

For data on wealth we must turn back to old studies, most of them laboriously compiled from other sources. A study by Robert Lampman, for example, shows that wealth (real estate, stocks, bonds, insurance, cash, retirement funds, mortgages) is more inequitably distributed than income.[6]

About $2 trillion were held in personal wealth in 1961. In that year, the richest 1 percent of adults held 28 percent of this wealth. The accumulation of wealth at

[6] Robert J. Lampman, *The Share of Top Wealth Holders in National Wealth*, Princeton, N.J.: Princeton University Press, 1962.

the top grows; in 1949, the richest 1 percent held only 21 percent of all wealth.

The concentration of wealth is actually far greater than these figures show. The rich form powerful family units. The figures, however, do not combine the wealth of individual family members, or show, for example, how much a wealthy wife adds to her husband's wealth. In most rich families, even children have fortunes of their own. None of this family wealth enters the reported figures.

According to Lampman, the top 10 percent of the adult population in 1953 held *more than half* (52 percent) of all national personal wealth. The top 1 percent of adults held *more than a quarter* of all wealth. By contrast, the lower 50 percent of adults held only 8 percent of wealth. The average "estate" of this half of the population was a pittance: $1,800.

A later study by the Federal Reserve Board reported that wealth was even more concentrated than Lampman had found it:

WEALTH HOLDING

Percent of consumers	Percent of wealth
Bottom fifth	Less than 0.5
Three middle fifths	23.0
Top fifth	77.0
Top 5 percent	53.0
Top 1 percent	33.0

The top fifth of the population holds 77 percent of all wealth, according to this study, but reports only 40 percent of total income. The top 5 percent owns 53 percent of the wealth, but reports only 15 percent of income. The top 1 percent owns 33 percent of the wealth, but reports only 8 percent of the income.

The wealth of our nation is so concentrated among the

rich that it seems almost absurd to talk about equality in the distribution of assets. In an alarmingly real sense, our national wealth is virtually a private treasury of the truly rich, passed from one generation to the next.

As for the types of assets, a study by Internal Revenue officials James Smith and Staunton Calvert found that the top 1 percent of wealth owners in 1958 held 76 percent of all state and local bonds, 71 percent of all corporate stock and 16 percent of all real estate.[7]

Stock ownership is reputed to be widely dispersed. Indeed, the Survey Research Center found that 23 percent of all families owned some common stock in 1967. But "some stock" does not say much. Most holdings are imperceptibly small. Only 6 percent of families, for instance, owned stock worth $10,000 or more. Among middle Americans—those earning near the median income—only 7 percent held shares worth $5,000 or more. About 41 percent of all people with large stock holdings ($25,000 or more) inherited either all or part of them from deceased relatives.[8]

The average American's liquid holdings can only jokingly be called assets. The median liquid asset of the American family is, unbelievably enough, a mere $660. An emergency, a special event, a birth, a wedding, an accident will instantly drain this tiny kitty. The only asset left for most people in such emergencies is equity in a home.

Others are even less fortunate. Almost one in five American families has no liquid assets at all. Another 15 percent have less than $200 in liquid assets. Another 12 percent have less than $500.

Two-thirds of the liquid assets of American families are held in savings accounts. Such accounts yield very low

[7] Survey Research Center, University of Michigan, *Survey of Consumer Finances, 1967.*
[8] *Ibid.,* 1968.

interest rates. Other liquid assets of the average American are held in U.S. savings bonds, which also yield low interest rates. The average man either does not (because he doesn't know of the alternatives) or cannot (because of his small assets) put his cash where he can earn enough to keep up with inflation. About one in four middle Americans does not even have a checking account.

Liquid assets, however, account for only 13 percent of total wealth. Home equity, investment assets, business— all account for a large share. The most common equity, held by 57 percent of American families, is in home ownership.[9] The median amount of wealth held by Americans— including liquid assets and equity in homes and autos—is a mere $6,721.

It appears, the Survey Research Center concludes modestly, "that financial assets and especially increases in financial assets are concentrated among a relatively small proportion of the population." This conclusion applies to total wealth as well, with one exception: the ownership of one-family homes.

In spite of the overwhelming evidence to the contrary, a surprising number of people will still deny that there is any financial inequality among us. We can all be rich if we want to be, they will say. We have equal opportunity, an equal chance to make it: if a man has ability and drive he can get his million, just like anyone else. These sanguine, smug folks who think that a son of a black sharecropper, the son of an Irish lathe operator, and the son of a Pierre Du Pont are all born with an equal chance to get rich, should be referred to the field or the lathe for their next reincarnation.

[9] *Survey of Financial Characteristics of Consumers,* Dorothy S. Projector and Gertrude S. Weiss, August 1966.

Some degree of inequality may be inevitable, even in the best of systems. But we have, in our system, far exceeded the limits of tolerability. Gross inequality and the concentration of wealth and power in the hands of a few degrades the poor and the average man. It glorifies materialism, makes flunkies out of the merely affluent and robs everyone of a sense of true community, participation and brotherhood. It fosters an idle and unproductive upper class, sets people against each other and diverts their purpose from the common good. Many prefer to drop out rather than play the game by the present rules. Far from making people more productive and aspiring, such tremendous inequality makes many of us despondent, resistant, hostile and lazy.

9

Taxes

Taxes are the chief device for distributing or equalizing wealth in our society. We could, of course, distribute wealth in other ways. The USSR, for example, has almost no redistributive income tax. Instead, wealth is allocated by controls over wages, salaries and prices. In the United States, except during national emergencies, we shrink from such controls, so we must rely on tax and fiscal policy as a means of re-allocating money.

Most Americans think they are overtaxed. In fact, we pay only about 28 percent of our Gross National Product in taxes, as compared with the 35 to 40 percent paid in Ger-

many, France, Scandinavia and the Netherlands. Unfortunately, the major part of our taxes goes into defense rather
than public service.

Few public acts arouse greater corporate vigilance than
tax legislation. Perhaps only federal regulation of business
penetrates deeper into the corporate skin. When the tax
reform bill of 1969 (the biggest reform effort of two decades) was before Congress, brigades of corporate lobbyists
descended on our lawmakers. A total of 656 lobbyists registered during that session, more than one in five expressing
specific interest in the tax bill. With only a few exceptions,
the 141 organizations present were corporations and foundations. Many of the corporate lobbyists came from leading
law firms. Many had once held important political offices
themselves, in such strategic spots as the Treasury Department and the Internal Revenue Service. Among the organizations lobbying for corporate tax interests were: American
Bankers Association, American Smelting and Refining,
Cities Service Co., Corporate Fiduciaries of Chicago,
Owens-Illinois, Standard Oil of Indiana, Xerox Corp.

Registered for Owens-Illinois, for example, was the law
firm of Clark Clifford, former Secretary of Defense. Other
members of Clifford's firm had held such influential public
posts as Assistant Secretary of Defense, special assistant to
the Attorney General, counsel to the Senate Finance Committee, staff members of the Justice Department Antitrust
Division.

With such powerful lobbyists, little wealth redistribu-
tion through tax reform can be expected. Only the Arctic
Slope Nature Association and the United Auto Workers'
Union were registered as representatives of the lower- and
middle-income groups.

The official Washington lobby helps keep taxes low for
the wealthy. Such influence has been even more successful
at local and state levels, where inequitable taxes still pro-

vide the bulk of revenues. At the federal level, failure, during the New Deal, to block the increased progressiveness of the income and corporate taxes led these influential groups to create loopholes and other special provisions that destroyed the impact of the progressive tax rate on big wealth.

Some taxes hit the poor and the average man harder than the rich. Most local sales taxes are examples of regressive taxes.

Such inequitable taxes have the startling effect of taxing the poor and average citizen at a higher rate than the affluent and rich. Families with incomes under $3,000 paid 34 percent of their income in taxes (city, state and federal combined) in 1965. Families with incomes of $5,000 to $7,000 paid 33 percent, and those with $7,000 to $10,000 paid 32 percent of their income. Families making $15,000 or more, however, paid only 28 percent of their income in taxes.[1]

While the income-tax bite into the poor has been somewhat eased by the reforms of 1969 (by removing many from the tax rolls), the average citizen continues to pay a relatively high tax rate, compared to that paid by the affluent and the rich.

Moreover, according to Gabriel Kolko, the rich conceal large sums of taxable income. Only 91 percent of personal money income was reported on individual income tax returns in 1957.[2] The missing sum included: 3 percent ($7.1 billion) of wages and salaries paid; 14 percent ($1.6 billion)

[1] Includes federal and state income taxes, Social Security payroll taxes, sales, property, and all other taxes.

Basic data: U.S. Departments of Commerce, Labor, Treasury, and Health, Education and Welfare; Federal Housing Administration; Tax Foundation and other private sources. Summarized in *U.S. News and World Report,* Dec. 9, 1968, pp. 66, 67.

[2] Gabriel Kolko, *Wealth and Power in America,* New York: Praeger, 1962.

of distributed dividends; 58 percent ($5.5 billion) of interest; 27 percent ($10.8 billion) of entrepreneurial income (nonsalary profits, unincorporated businesses and income from farming). Doctors, lawyers, businessmen and others who receive cash payments are notorious for under-reporting income. The fortunes that lie in unidentified Swiss bank accounts suggest that the very wealthy also have large concealed assets on the accumulation of which they have probably paid no taxes.

The rich and their advisers are notoriously artful at tax dodging. Some of the richest people pay no taxes at all. We do not know them by name, since their identities are concealed by the IRS, but sometimes, off the record, the identities do come through. David Rockefeller, for example, president of Chase Manhattan Bank, revealed in Congressional testimony on another subject that he paid practically no income tax at all—only a "token" amount. Many others in the Rockefeller class also carry off this artful dodge and do what is beyond the legal talent of the average man— pay no tax at all.

In 1968 there were twenty-one people with incomes over $1 million who paid no tax. (A few years ago, one man with an income of $20 million paid no taxes on it.) Also in 1968, 381 people with incomes in excess of $100,000 paid no taxes whatsoever. In the last dozen or so years, untaxed incomes of a million or more have become five times more numerous, and untaxed incomes more than $200,000 have become seven times more numerous—far exceeding the proportion of these income groups in the population.

The top income group (over $5 million income) paid half as much taxes, proportionately, as those who made only one-tenth this much. Most taxpayers in the $500,000 to $1 million group pay the same rate as those with incomes only one-twentieth as large.

It is a cherished misconception that income tax rates on

the rich are nearly confiscatory. In fact, some people even believe that the rich pay more in income tax than they keep for themselves—which is hardly the case.

While the official tax schedule has called for those with incomes of over $1 million to pay about 65 percent of their income in taxes, in fact more than two-thirds of those in this group traditionally pay less than 30 percent.

Another common misconception is that though the rich can't take it with them, they can't leave it behind either. Theoretically inheritances are heavily taxed. In reality, great fortunes are frequently hereditary. The effective tax rate on inheritances, according to the best calculations, is less than 10 percent, and the tax on gifts made to members of the family amounts to even less. In the end, only about 2 percent of our total federal revenue comes from this source.

The inheritance of vast fortunes, and the power that is transmitted with these fortunes, conflicts with all our national standards of public morality. We glorify the self-made man. Our Protestant Ethic insists that the life of struggle and austerity—starting poor and making it rich— is good both for the soul and the society. We assert in our revered political and religious documents that each man should begin his life with the same chance of success as everyone else. What we get instead is a plutocracy of inherited wealth, a large class of scions who have no special monetary incentive to work or innovate and a system that flagrantly violates our sacred trust in equal opportunity.

Not only do the rich stay rich, but the effective tax rates on them have actually declined in the last decades. During World War II, income tax increases, guided by a demand for "equality of sacrifice," were highly progressive. But the tax cuts between 1945 and 1963 moved in the other direction.

According to economist Leon Keyserling, these cuts increased by only 5.2 percent the disposable income (income after taxes) of those making $3,000. The increase was only 6.7 percent for those making $10,000. The increase was 17.2 percent for those making $25,000, 26.7 percent for those with $50,000, 36.9 percent for those with $100,000, and 47.2 percent for those with $200,000.[3] The 1964 tax cuts moved even further in this direction, according to Keyserling. The cuts increased the after-tax income of middle America by only about 2 percent—and those at the top (over $200,000 income) by 16 percent.

Subsequent to the tax cuts of 1962–1965, says Keyserling, "it was almost universally recognized by economists and others that these tax cuts had glaringly neglected the moral mandate of seeking equity and fairness in the tax structure. And so the promise was widely made that, when another opportunity came for a 'fiscal dividend' in the form of still further tax cuts, or alternatively when the need came for tax increases to fight inflation, the pursuit of equity and fairness would be resumed. But nothing like that happened. When a stiff 10 percent surcharge was imposed 'to fight inflation,' it totally ignored that a 10 percent increase in taxes across-the-board was extremely unfair and inequitable."[4]

Continuing the trend that Keyserling noted, by 1967 the top 1 percent of income receivers ($43,000 and over) were paying only 26 percent of their reported income to Internal Revenue.[5] In 1952 they had paid an effective rate of 33 percent and in 1963, 27 percent. So, the rich get richer and middle America pays the bill.

[3] Leon H. Keyserling, *Taxation of Whom and for What*, Conference on Economic Progress, Dec. 1969.

[4] *Ibid.*, p. 9.

[5] Statistics of Income. Total income is the sum of adjusted gross income and excluded capital gains, dividends, and sick pay.

2

The major tax loopholes, taken together, cost the public about $20 billion each year. Virtually all these billions come from the pockets of mid-America and are a gift to the wealthy.

One of the most glaring inequities in the tax law is the "capital gain." This gaping hole, in effect, taxes money made from the sale of capital (real estate, stocks, etc.) at a much lower rate than it taxes money made in wages, salaries, etc. Thus *earned* income (from wages, salaries) is more heavily taxed than income made simply by telling an agent to sell capital assets.

According to the capital gains law, only half of all profits made on the sale of capital assets is taxable; the other half is tax free. Moreover, the tax rate cannot exceed 25 percent of the total profit. The big asset owners benefit most from the capital gains loophole.

In all, the staggering sum of $8.5 billion is lost to the federal treasury each year in capital gains exemption (including gains not taxed at death). Almost all of these billions go to the wealthy. Tax reform in 1969 barely touched this golden calf; it merely increased from 25 to 30 percent the maximum tax rate on capital gains over $50,000.

Oil depletion allowances are among the most infamous of tax loopholes.[6] While the standard tax rate on corporations was 48 percent in 1964, the five biggest oil producers, because of depletion allowances, paid the following rates: Gulf, 8.0 percent; Socony-Mobil, 5.9; Standard of California, 2.1; Standard of New Jersey, 1.7; Texaco, 0.8 percent.

[6] The oil man pays no tax at all on the first 27½ percent of gross income from his wells (as long as it does not exceed 50 percent of net income).

About 87 percent of all tax-exempt bonds are owned by the top 1½ percent of income recipients. The rich own them because they pay off handsomely in tax savings. The average man usually has nothing at all to gain from putting his small savings into such bonds. They are a tax haven only for the rich.

Countless other loopholes exist.[7] Even though some are less limited to the rich than those noted above, the rich still benefit more than others do. Income splitting is one example. Wives are far more "valuable" to the rich than to the middle American. A man with an income of $1 million can save vastly more money if he assigns half that income to his wife than can the man who makes only $10,000. The higher the income, the more saved on income splitting. This provision of the law, enacted in 1948, reduces total tax revenues by about $10 billion each year.

In addition, there is the whole failure to tax increases in wealth that do not derive from the *sale* of something. The capital gains tax is based on the difference in the value of capital assets at the time of purchase and at the time of sale. Many people, however, own stock and other property, and accumulate vast fortunes, but do not sell what they own. The value of these holdings may well increase each year, but the increase will not be taxed at all.

People with incomes in excess of $100,000 increased their wealth by a total of $31.8 billion in 1967. About half that sum (over $15 billion) was derived from capital assets that were *not sold* and might never be. No tax at all was paid on that $15 billion of acquired wealth. We might ask, "So what?" If the wealthy do not sell their assets, they cannot very well spend the profit. But the value of wealth

[7] Among other major loopholes have been excess depreciation (on property)—which cost the nation $4.1 billion; investment credit (buying new machinery, etc.)—$2.3 billion; tax-free bonds—$1.8 billion; oil depletion—$1.6 billion; miscellaneous—$1.6 billion.

cannot always be measured by consumer standards. Even gains which have not been realized, so-called paper gains, represent economic power. An example of this economic power is the collateral value of unrealized capital gains which can be used to acquire income, generating wealth. Unlike the average man, the rich man does not think of wealth in terms of what he can "spend."

What the increased wealth gives him is more power, greater economic leverage, more influence and prestige, the ability to borrow money as a means to make more money. Moreover, all this increase in wealth and power can be passed along the hereditary line. So skewed are the tax laws, in fact, that those who inherit these "unrealized" capital gains can then *sell* them, "realize" a gain on them, yet pay no capital gains tax at all on what they make.

3

In recent years, tax exemptions have been a major form of public policy. Instead of spending public money on health programs, for example, the law permits tax deductions for medical expenses. Instead of spending public money on construction, the law allows rapid depreciations on commercial property.

Henry Aaron of the Brookings Institute insists that tax exemptions are the same, in their net effect on public treasuries and public policy, as spending on public programs.[8] He calls these exemptions "tax expenditures."

[8] Henry Aaron, "Tax Exemptions—The Artful Dodge," *Transaction*, March 1969.

Some of the largest "tax expenditures" are: $5.2 billion on Housing and Community Development (deduction for mortgage interest and property taxes); $9.7 billion on Commerce and Transportation (investment tax credit, accelerated depreciation on buildings, etc.);

They cost the public money, he says, in the same way that regular "budget expenditures" cost money. The cost of all these "tax expenditures" combined exceeds that of any item in the national budget except that of the Defense Department. While regular "budget expenditures" are given close examination by the President, Congress and the public, similar programs, financed instead by "tax expenditures," are given minimal public scrutiny and are slipped through Congress with almost no fanfare. Tax programs are rarely reviewed and revised. When an exemption gets into tax law, it is likely to stay for a long time. On the contrary, budget expenditures are reviewed annually and are always in imminent danger of being scrapped.

"Tax expenditures" are far more likely to benefit the rich than are regular "budget expenditures."

A good example is tax exemptions on Social Security income, which have been part of our tax system for many years. These exemptions (or "tax expenditures"), Aaron points out, give the largest "benefits" (in the form of exemptions)—$70 per month—to aged couples with a real income of $200,000 or more a year. The smallest "benefits" ($14 per month) go to couples with incomes between $1,600 and $2,600. No "benefits" at all go to those with very low incomes.

If such an old-age program were a "budget" rather than a "tax" expenditure and if the nation were given a chance to weigh alternative programs and scrutinize their costs and effects, the program as it is now set up would have no chance of passing, Aaron concludes.

$8.5 billion capital gains; $19.5 billion on Health, Labor, and Welfare (deduction of medical expenses, contributions to charity, etc.); $1.7 billion on Natural Resources (depletion allowances, etc.); $4.6 billion on Direct Aid to State and Local Governments (exemption of interest on state and local bonds, deduction of state and local taxes, etc.).

4

The 1969 tax bill was the most serious effort at reform since the adoption of the income tax in 1913. The statement of the Secretary of the Treasury to Congress, on introducing the reform, was remarkable for its candor:

"As believers in justice and fairness we can only deplore circumstances like these:

"Under present law, 2.2 million families with incomes below the poverty level are required to pay Federal income taxes. These persons of all our taxpayers are least able to pay taxes.

"On the other hand, there are a sizable number of individuals with very high incomes who pay little or no income tax. Indeed, although the Federal income tax is designed and understood to be progressive, the fact is that many persons with incomes of $1 million or more actually pay the same effective rate of tax as do persons with incomes only one-fiftieth as large.

"There are many billions of untaxed capital gains income included in the assets owned by persons who die each year—in 1966 about $15 billion. Simply because the owners found it neither necessary nor desirable to sell the assets during one's lifetime, these gains are not and will never be subject to income tax under present law, unlike other wealth accumulated during their lifetime in the form of taxed income, such as wages.

"There are a number of large business organizations, with millions of dollars of wealth subject to overall common control, which pay tax almost entirely at the special rate designed for small businesses—not at the substantially higher rate applicable to large corporations—by organizing their businesses in the form of a chain of small corporate units, and claiming multiple exemptions from the corporate surtax rates. An enterprise with total assets of many millions can divide itself into hundreds of separate corporations with the aim of achieving an annual tax saving of millions of dollars.

"Some tax-exempt private foundations are being used to accumulate assets and wealth. Over a period of years, such foundations do not realize any appreciable amount of income and consequently do not distribute any significant percentage of their resources to charity. Thus such foundations accumulate wealth, and thereby deprive charitable activities of funds which the tax-exempt status accorded the foundation (and contributions to it) was designed to accomplish. This abuse is compounded when the motivation of the accumulation is to further personal or business purposes of the donors of the foundations and their families.

"Many of these special benefits and devices are intricate, subtle, and difficult for the average person to understand. But all of them flaw our tax system and undermine the standards of justice and fairness which should prevail. There is no comfort to be found in the view that, after all, no tax system is perfect. The flaws are too severe, too widespread, and—in some cases—too notorious for that." [9]

[9] "Statement of the Honorable Henry H. Fowler, Secretary of the Treasury, for the Congress of the U.S., on the Tax Reform Program," Washington, D.C.: U.S. Govt. Printing Office, 1969.

The tax reform program was, in the Secretary's words, a minimal one, designed for passage, not for comprehensiveness. What got through was indeed minimal: people below the poverty line were exempt from federal taxes. At the same time, a maximum tax rate of 50 percent was applied to the earned income of the rich. Capital gains, oil depletion allowances, charitable contributions, special low tax rates on financial institutions—all were tightened somewhat. Real estate depreciation was tightened a lot. The 7 percent tax credit for business investment was eliminated. The personal exemption for all families was increased. Most other inequities, such as exemption of state and local bonds and the inheritance of capital property, were not touched at all.

While federal tax rates (but not revenues) have been declining, state and local rates are rising rapidly. As a result, inequitable sales and property taxes greatly over-burden the working man. Between 1951 and 1968, state and local tax revenues rose from 7.1 percent of the Gross National Product to 11.9 percent. To produce this increase in revenues, the tax rates must have gone up by 68 percent. At the same time, the federal rates stood still or declined slightly.

5

The tax revolt of middle America is evident in the widespread rejection of school tax increases in those communities where citizens vote on school taxes. The property tax on home ownership has been one of the most inequitable and burdensome of all taxes, especially in the cities. Property is often unfairly assessed, and rates vary wildly from place to place.

The mid-American, looking for a home, finds it harder each year to buy one, in the face of ascending tax rates. Asked to vote on increases—as he is *not* with other taxes—he often rejects them even at the cost of good schools.

The tax frustration extends to the sales tax, the most egregiously inequitable of all taxes. As millions of people have begun to itemize their tax returns, it extends to the growing complications of the federal and state income tax forms. Since the income ceiling on this form has failed to keep up with inflation, many people with modest incomes can no longer fill out short forms. It extends also—perhaps most of all—to the growing inequities of our principal revenue-raiser, the personal income tax.

State and local governments cannot pay for needed public programs out of present sources of revenue—they are deeply in debt as it is. Between 1947 and 1967, the federal debt increased at an average rate of 1.1 percent a year, compared to 12.6 percent for state and 9.1 percent for local governments.

Only the federal government can fund the programs needed by middle America. Only the federal government can move toward the equalization of wealth. The federal income tax is more equitable than state and local taxes and its revenues automatically increase as the economy grows. And yet even this last hope for funding the programs needed by middle America—the federal income tax —has become increasingly inequitable.

10

Climbing Up

Even though the material condition of the middle American's life is not satisfactory now, the thought of future prospects at least sustains him. He continues to hope that he will move up, through luck or hard work, or at least that his children will. Part of the American creed is the belief that the average citizen has the same chance for success as anyone else. It is this belief that inspires personal ambition and fuels the whole society. Moving up is the game, the source of gratification—or frustration. This "upward mobility," or the belief in it, de Tocqueville observed, accounts for the great political stability of a society that is essentially volatile and restless.

Unfortunately, we know very little either about how Americans feel about their prospects for moving up, or what their chances are in fact. The studies on the subject are puzzling, to say the least.

"There is much upward mobility in the United States," concludes one of the most optimistic interpretations of the American success story, "but most of it involves relatively short social distances. Men are much more likely to experience upward than downward mobility because of expanding salaried jobs and contracting farm jobs." [1]

Sociologists Reinhart Bendix and Seymour Martin Lipset found, however, that three other countries had higher rates of movement than that of the United States from the middle class into the elite class—Sweden, Italy and West Germany.[2] They found almost no difference in mobility rates among nine other industrial nations. Their data, however, are contested by other sociologists who assert that Americans are more mobile than people in other industrial nations.

The Blau and Duncan study found that only four factors alone account for 50 percent of a man's chances for moving up in the job world. These are: education, first job held, occupation of father, education of father. The calculation does not take into account the numerous other background factors that affect mobility, and over which the individual has no control (education and occupation of mother, family income, size of family of origin, quality of education, race and ethnicity, etc.).

Much "upward mobility," however, comes simply from people leaving the farm and going to the city. Financially

---

[1] P. Blau and O. Duncan, *American Occupational Structure,* New York: John Wiley & Sons, Inc., 1967.

[2] S. M. Lipset and R. Bendix, *Social Mobility in Industrial Society,* Berkeley: University of California Press, 1960.

speaking, the best move Americans have made is from farm to city. Socially speaking, the benefits are more ambiguous.

More than ever, the way up is through education. In the new industrial state, Galbraith says, one should expect, from past experience, to find a shift of power in the society and the industrial enterprise from capital to organized intelligence. Increasingly it is the university that screens out this "intelligence."

But in what way does education really bring about "upward mobility" in America?

Though effective training is obviously needed in almost every field, countless hours of busy work are usually piled on top of the necessary learning time in order to drive out aspirants, restrict supply, increase demand and thus artificially ensure status and rewards for the lucky survivors.

A rise in social status and economic position is determined by acceptance by one or another in-group. Status and rewards are distributed according to the scarcity principle. Skill, learning, knowledge and ability have much less to do with the rewards, both financial and social, people receive for their work, than does membership in an organization with the power and desire to restrict the number admitted, elected, or licensed to practice.

Access to almost any desirable work position is limited by requirements for irrelevant training, artificially-concocted entrance standards, or discrimination along lines of race, culture, class or sex. Any one of us who has a piece of occupational turf will defend it. By hook or crook we move up the job pyramid and, because space is more restricted at each higher level, as we rise, we turn to step on the fingers of others coming up from behind.

Craft unions are notorious for restricting their numbers —through artifice, subterfuge, racial discrimination. Their sins have been widely publicized. Most literate people know that the earnings of plumbers are sometimes set at high levels because organized plumbers have conspired to restrict apprenticeship programs to a favored few, thus imposing upon the market an artificial scarcity which makes the bidding for their services sharply competitive.

But of what craft or profession can't the same be said? Physicians are notoriously overtrained, especially those who expect to go into anything resembling general practice. In most states, lawyers must now earn an undergraduate degree before entering law school, whereas in the past, aspirants—like Lincoln—could read for the law in an apprentice relationship with an established attorney. In these and other cases, increasing the years of training reduces the numbers of those who can become licensed to practice. It also raises the cost of training, generally ensuring that entrance will be open only to those who can afford these higher costs.

The cry for "professionalism" is often a cover for the drive to restrict the numbers in a given craft or profession. Thousands must earn advanced degrees in recreation, communications, group work and countless other disciplines, although many feel that the skills these courses attempt to impart cannot be taught in a classroom. Teachers win their advanced degrees, higher salaries, and higher status, not by demonstrating their skill in teaching, but by putting in time, taking courses, studying irrelevant texts.

The liberal arts professors who criticize the "Mickey Mouse" courses imposed on teachers are themselves part of an occupational Mafia that restricts the Ph.D.s in their fields by imposing the same kind of empty requirements. The irrelevance of it all often drives the most competent students out of the field of college teaching altogether.

Beginning with the first grade, we start weeding out— through ability groupings and track systems—those who will be disqualified from competition for good jobs. We drive thousands of competitors out of the "professional job market" by dumping children of workers and the poor into so-called vocational schools when they are about age fourteen. Entrance to these dumping grounds seals the fate of all but the most tenacious and competent of these children.

It is now well known that when occupational entrance requirements are inflated, the first to suffer are the disadvantaged. University students have forcefully called our attention to the fact that young blacks have long been virtually excluded from professional training.

Just as well known, and almost as callously neglected, is the fact that educational discrimination has doomed the children of blue-collar workers to dead-end jobs. The public schools these children attend may not be as bad as many of those attended by black and Latin children, but they are vastly inferior to those attended by the affluent.[3]

In big cities, the kids who are accepted by the prestige universities are drawn from a few elite public and private high schools. The children of workers attend a clutter of usually mediocre schools, often poorly equipped and understaffed, from which only a lucky few make it to the prestige colleges. The working-class schools are starved by the political manipulations of those powerful groups whose children go to well-financed schools in fancy suburbs.

Even the student who graduates with the highest honors from a working-class high school will have trouble getting into and financing his way through a good college. Yet the B-minus student from a fancy suburb will go off to a university. Even if the worker's son does get into a state teacher's college, for example, when he emerges, he may qualify for admission to only a low-level master's program, and then a low-level doctoral program—if he's lucky. He will even have trouble competing for admission to a grad-

[3] For a fuller examination of these inequalities, see Patricia Sexton, *Education and Income*, New York: Viking, 1961.

uate school of social work, with the suburbanites who are now applying. When he enters the job market, personnel men will assume at a glance that as the top student at Wabeek State Teachers, he is not the equal of the young man from a prestige school who may have graduated at the bottom of his class.

Though many middle-class people seem to think that workers don't notice or care, the class bias of schools is obvious to workers.. However accepting they may appear, working-class people are not that dense. Much of their bitterness about students may be traced directly to this awareness of school bias.

2

Professor Galbraith hopes that all of us will join the New Class—go to college, find status jobs, enjoy our work and leisure, wear sort-of-sloppy clothes, and forget about material things. It would be nice. Certainly, the average man would be the last to dispute the point. Yet he might wonder: how do I get into this club? And we might all wonder: who is going to do all the real work when the average man moves up to the reflective heights of the leisured class?

The mainland Chinese have solved the same problem to some extent by demoting their leisure class to at least part-time manual and productive labors. They have sent hundreds of thousands, if not millions, of their intellectuals (the educated and government officials) into the fields and factories, where they receive work-ideology therapy. "We must be resolute," the official declaration states, "to do away with bureaucratic, apathetic, arrogant and finicky airs, go into the midst of workers, peasants and soldiers, throw ourselves into the revolutionary movements of class struggle, the struggle for production and the struggle for scientific experiment, persist in taking part in productive labor, criticize and repudiate the bourgeoisie, and remold our world outlook."

That is one way to do it. We in America, on the other hand, operate on the push-up rather than the pull-down theory of equalization. As long as the push-up system persists, however, the average man will want to push himself up. What are his chances of doing so?

A typical blue- or white-collar worker can raise his income by working overtime or putting his wife to work, but however hard he works, his job leads to an occupational dead-end. He can rarely advance. He may break out by setting up a small business, but his chances of failure at it far exceed his chances of success.

The road to the New Class, obviously, leads through the schools and comes to a main fork at high school graduation. College and graduate school are one fork; they continue the movement to the New Class. The other road leads to occupational oblivion. A college man has a clearer line of advancement and a chance to move from employer to employer, based on competitive bids for his service—he has greater prospects for the future. He can play the game until late in life. High school and grade school graduates reach their earning peak at ages forty-five to fifty-four, thereafter declining in earning capacity; but college graduates do not reach their peak until ages fifty-five to sixty-four.[4] After retirement, the college man may have a business or profession which he can practice part-time. He has "leisure"—the working man has "idleness."

In 1969 the median income of people with *some* high school was $7,260. Those with a high school diploma

---

[4] Consumer Income, Income in 1967 of families in the United States, Series P-60, No. 59, April 18, 1969, Bureau of the Census, U.S. Dept. of Commerce.

earned $8,940. Those with *some* college got less than $600 more—but those with a college degree earned $11,240, and those with an advanced degree, $13,120.[5]

The more education, the more income. If we weeded out the less lucrative professions (nursing, teaching, etc.) from the calculations, reported incomes for those with college diplomas would be substantially higher.

Calculated over a lifetime, these income differences are substantial. The lifetime earnings of a person with only *some* high school will be about $284,000; of a college graduate, about $508,000—a difference of $224,000.[6]

At the very top, among family heads with incomes of $100,000 a year and over, more than half had had five years or more of higher education. Only 16 percent had not gone to college at all, and of these almost all were high school graduates.

An inquiry into college opportunities in England found that the proportion of working-class boys at the university was no different in 1960 than it had been from the late twenties to the late forties.[7] In fact, it was slightly lower. According to the English educator Brian Jackson, the welfare state has been largely a public subsidy to the salaried and professional class. After the "liberal" Butler Act of 1944, he says, this class took most of the new free grammar school places. Members of this class, more than others, claimed the free medical service, as they claimed most of the places in the new universities. With some mod-

[5] Survey Research Center, University of Michigan, *Survey of Consumer Finances, 1969,* Statistical Report I.

[6] Current Population Reports, Consumer Income, Series P-60, No. 56, Aug. 14, 1968, U.S. Dept. of Commerce, Bureau of the Census, p. 9, 1966 income, age 18 to death.

[7] The Robbins Report, 1963.

ification, these observations about schools might be applied as aptly to the condition of middle America.

Despite the initiation of new educational programs, the increase in school years completed in the United States has been modest. In the period of sixteen years from 1950 to 1967, the median years of school completed by people from ages twenty-five to twenty-nine increased from 12.1 to 12.5, a total growth of less than half a year during sixteen of our most prosperous years.[8]

By contrast, the World War II years did produce a dramatic leap forward in schooling. In 1940, median school years was 10.4 years. By 1950 it had increased to 12.1, or almost two years in one decade.

Strange assumptions are frequently made about the availability of a college education. On this point, the sketchy data kept by federal sources are puzzling and inadequate. The U.S. Office of Education estimates that 40 percent of our youth now go to college (400 of every 1,000 entering the fifth grade in 1959 went to college nine years later, in 1968).

This 40-percent figure is based on, first, the number of students entering the fifth grade in 1959; second, the number of first-time college enrollments in 1968. The rub is this: not all students entering college for the first time in 1968 were in the fifth grade in 1959. People of all ages enter college for the first time each year. The proportion of those who are not of the "class of 1959" is apparently unknown, but it is probably a significant part of the whole. Excluding these might significantly reduce the popular 40-percent figure.

Data on college entrance are absurd from another point of view. Entering college does not mean much in itself.

[8] U.S. Dept. of Commerce, Bureau of the Census, "Current Population Reports," Series P-20, Nos. 99 and 158.

What is meaningful is how long students *stay* and what *kind* of college they enter. Many people enter college, take one or two courses, and drop out.

More than half of all students who enter college drop out before graduation. The dropouts are more often from middle than upper America, and more often from blue-collar than from professional families. As we have seen, it is the college *degree* that really counts in the world of work and income. Anything less than a degree is not much better than high school graduation. Students enter colleges that are as different from one another as geese from swans. In the range are the Negro junior college of Natchez, say, and Harvard. Again: in the world of work and income, the difference is huge.

First-time enrollments in all institutions of higher education were 1,453,000 in 1965. Of these, 402,000 were in junior colleges, and 156,000 in independent professional schools (mainly teachers' colleges). The others went to regular four-year liberal arts schools. In all, then, 38.4 percent of first-time students entered schools with a reputation, earned or not, for being . . . shall we say, less than first-rate?

Most of the benefits of college, the costs of which come mainly from the public treasury, flow to the sons and daughters of the New Class. In 1966 about $15 billion was spent on higher education. This was about half the expenditure on all elementary and secondary education in which enrollments were about nine times greater than in higher education.

In 1969 it cost an average of $1,740 to attend a public college, and $2,640 to attend a private college for the year. Such costs soar far over the heads of the middle American. Sending even one child to a public college, at that rate, would cost at least one-fifth of the total family income.

High cost, high admission standards, the need to work—all conspire to keep the sons of middle America on the assembly line or war front and out of college. Seldom will they enter a first-rate university, except on an athletic scholarship. At best, they may make it to a junior college or perhaps even a state college. (Public subsidies to students at junior colleges are less than half what they are at state universities.)

Middle Americans are more often part-time students than are the affluent. Many must work their way through school and limit their college work to an occasional course in the evening.

Even when he goes to the same school as the affluent, the middle American is more likely to enter a course of study that has a low pay-off in the job market—such as teaching, social work, nursing, etc.

The blue-collar worker's chance of sending his child to graduate school are not good. Only 7 percent of graduate students in 1965 had fathers who were semiskilled operatives, though this group represents about 20 percent of the total male work force.[9] While professionals were only 12 percent of the male work force, their children were 39 percent of all graduate students. Managers and proprietors were 13 percent of the male work force, but their children were 18 percent of graduate students.

The worker's child who becomes a graduate student is, ironically, less likely than others to get a student tuition stipend. In 1965, 37 percent of the sons of semiskilled operatives who were graduate students received stipends, compared to 47 percent of the sons of managers and proprietors, and 56 percent of the sons of professionals.

Nationally, only about one in four boys who rank in the top 30 percent of their high school classes go to college.

[9] "The Academic and Financial Status of Graduate Students, Spring 1965," U.S. Dept. of Health, Education and Welfare, Office of Education. These figures do not include professional schools, such as law, medicine, dentistry.

According to the National Science Foundation, the main reason the other three do not attend is inadequate financial resources.[10]

California has the most generous system of higher education of any state. Students there have a better chance of entering college than students elsewhere. California's vast "multiversity" has branch colleges scattered throughout the state, and there are also numerous four-year colleges and two-year junior colleges.

An inquiry into the costs and benefits of this elaborate system concluded that, while 9 percent of students receive large subsidies (over $5,000), more than half receive less than $750.[11] A student at the University of California for four years gets a total subsidy of $7,140; at the state colleges, $5,800; at the junior colleges (two years), $1,440. Attrition is highest by far at the junior colleges, somewhat lower at the state colleges, and lowest at the University of California. The higher the family income, the more likely students are to go to the university. Middle-income students were most likely to go to junior colleges and least likely to go to the university. Families making $14,000 or more a year were 12.3 percent of the total in California but their children were almost 40 percent of the enrollments in the university.

Balancing college subsidies against effective tax rates for various income groups showed that net subsidies rose with the family income level.

The researchers concluded that the effect of subsidies

[10] Donald S. Bridgman, *The Duration of Formal Education for High Ability Youth*, National Science Foundation.

[11] "The Distribution of Costs and Direct Benefits of Public Higher Education: The Case of California," W. Lee Hansen and Burton A. Weisbrod, *J. of Human Resources*, Vol. 4, 2, Spring 1969.

on higher education is to "promote greater rather than less inequality among people of various social and economic backgrounds." They suggest that eligibility for public subsidies might be expanded to embrace all young people—not only those going to college but also those who seek apprenticeship, on-the-job or other vocational training.

11

Power

F. Scott Fitzgerald—who should have known—
once said, "The rich are different from us." Ernest Hemingway responded, "Yes, they have more money." They
have a lot more money, and although Hemingway treats
this as the entire difference, the very size of the disparity
makes them very different from the rest of us in many ways.
Even the member of Galbraith's affluent society, who has
more money than the average American, is more cousin
to the worker than to the very rich.

The executive, professor or small business owner who
makes $50,000 a year is prosperous but not really rich. His
income may just meet his expenses, especially if he lives in

New York or another high-cost area where rent, private school tuition, etc., may push his income right up against his costly walls. From his earnings he may save ten or twenty thousand dollars in a lifetime, but that margin of affluence cannot be called riches—not compared to the holdings of the really rich.

No arbitrary line can be drawn to divide the affluent from the rich. It is not enough to say that the rich are those who can buy virtually anything or anyone without having to worry about the price. Their wealth far exceeds savings and investments acquired from previous income. There are no more than a few hundred families in this one class but they exercise a power and influence far surpassing that of their more numerous counterparts.

For purposes of our present discussion, then, we have a four-class society: the poor, the middle American, the affluent and the rich. Each has an identity and a social role. These large categories can, of course, be further subdivided; none of them forms a homogeneous population. For our purposes, however, the four categories will do.

Who are the rich? How did they make their fortunes? Most fortunes are inherited from previous generations. Most of the present holders of great wealth did not earn their fortunes. They were simply standing in the hereditary line when previous owners passed away.

Even in their origins, most great American fortunes were not "earned" in any ordinary sense. They did not come out of the sale of goods and services in a competitive market. Most derived from monopolies and the manipulation of financial or consumer markets, or from the exploitation of natural resources, or from phenomenal increases in land values or from outright theft.

Many of the largest fortunes come from the extraction

of minerals from the earth. The Rockefeller, Harkness, Getty, Whitney, Hunt, Pew fortunes, among many others, were floated on oil. The Mellon fortune came from mining as well as oil.

The Du Pont fortune, the biggest of them all, came principally from the manufacture of munitions. The Astor and Kennedy fortunes, and many others, derived from the ownership of land.

One of the most significant and concealed aspects of American economic life is that the great fortunes, and the great power derived from them, belong almost entirely to white Anglo-Saxon Protestants. With the exception of one Catholic (Kennedy) and several Jewish families, all of the greatest fortunes (the top fifty) belong to white Protestants. Blacks and the "ethnic" groups (Italians, Poles, Irish, Slavs, Spanish, Asians) all are missing from the very top.

These white Protestants, moreover, dominated the public as well as the private domain. Every President and Vice-President (except Kennedy) has been a WASP, as have the vast majority of Congressmen and other high public officials. Blacks, Asians, Indians and non-Anglo–Saxon Europeans have this in common: they have not entered the elite club where the really rich and powerful gather. Some status and income gains for all these outsiders are perceptible, but they are slight compared with the distance to be traveled.

The Du Ponts have come to personify great American wealth. Because their wealth, power, and diversity of holdings are so great, they have been called the Krupps of American industry. The Du Ponts are the wealthiest of all American families, and are unusual in that they were not WASP in their early origins. But neither were they immigrant "ethnic." Originally they were French Protestant; by now they have become, through marriage and assimilation, thoroughly WASP.

The combined wealth of only four of the leading Du Ponts is estimated to run as high as $1.2 billion. The total family fortunes, including those of the 250 richest Du Ponts and the hundreds of lesser Du Ponts, are vastly greater than that. The total is estimated to run well over $7.5 billion.

General Motors has been, in a sense, a captive of Du Pont, an outlet for the sale of Du Pont auto finishes, fabrics, tires and other products, a situation that gives Du Pont an unfair advantage over competitors. Though the Christiana Corporation, an E. I. Du Pont de Nemours holding company, was ordered by the Supreme Court to sell its 63 million shares of General Motors common stock (a controlling interest of 23 percent), the stock was passed on to individuals in the family. The Du Ponts hold (with an estimated 17 percent of shares) the largest known block of stock (more than 40 million shares!) in the world's largest manufacturing corporation.

The Du Pont family controls the United States Rubber Company, E. I. Du Pont de Nemours, and has major interests in such companies as Phillips Petroleum, Remington Arms, United Fruit, American Sugar Refining, Mid-Continent Petroleum. It owns banks, a brokerage house, holding companies, large tracts of valuable land and a variety of major financial institutions. Its biggest holdings are in chemicals, automobiles, oil and rubber. The manufacture of munitions, in which the fortune was originally made, is a rewarding specialty it has dominated since the War of 1812. During World War I, the family's fortunes rose on dynamite and explosives.

The Du Ponts have established at least eighteen tax-free foundations. The largest of these, with assets of more than $122 million, spends its tax-exempt funds on the maintenance of former Du Pont estates as public museums.

The Du Pont story is roughly duplicated by other families and individuals. These great fortunes provide much more for this class than simple purchasing power as we know it. The presence of this class among us is not significant simply becaues its members can easily afford any extravagance. That there is this opulence side by side with starvation is remarkable enough in a society that prides itself on equal opportunity. What is far more significant, however, is the influence of this class on our economy, politics, culture and way of life.

Its influence on economic institutions is obvious. A relatively small group of people own the controlling stock in most of our major corporations. Sumner T. Pike, chairman of the Securities and Exchange Commission, summarized on September 24, 1940, one of the most thorough reports on corporate control ever undertaken: "In the case of about 40 percent of these 200 largest corporations, one family, or a small number of families, exercise either absolute control, by virtue of ownership of a majority of voting securities, or working control through ownership of a substantial minority of the voting stock. About 60 of the corporations, or an additional 30 percent, are controlled by one or more other corporations. Thus, a small group of dominant security holders is not in evidence in only 30 percent of the 200 large corporations."

The twenty largest shareholders in each of these two hundred corporations account for an average of "nearly one-third of the total value of all outstanding stock. In the average corporation the majority of the voting power is concentrated in the hands of not much over one percent of the stockholders."

It was also found that a total of only thirteen family groups owned over 8 percent of the stock in the two hundred largest nonfinancial corporations. The situation has not changed appreciably since that report was made. These giant corporations form the backbone of our present economic system, and make most of our major economic decisions—about the type of goods and services produced, and their price and quality. Such decisions are, in turn, influenced—if not ultimately controlled—by the dominant shareholders. It was the Du Ponts, for example, who laid down GM's iron law that auto prices shall be set to yield a 20 percent profit on capitalization, no matter what market conditions may be, even where it meant firing and laying off workers in order to hold that rate of profit.

Ours is, of course, a private economy. That is to say, it is owned by *some* people rather than by *all* people. Somehow we have come to attach great virtue and public morality to that fact. Strangely, we do not attach comparable immorality or vice to the fact that schools, colleges, post offices, some transit systems and power plants are publicly owned. We do not denounce the teacher or the postman as a communist or tool of communist managers because he works for the public. Indeed, in all of our political and religious manifestoes we declare our devotion to the principles of brotherhood, equality, community. Judging by such declarations, it is surprising that we do not identify morality with public ownership, and sin with the greed of private acquisition. But we do not.

Many people believe that it is less a matter of virtue than of efficiency that our economy should be privately owned. Such may indeed be the case. Individual greed and the acquisitive impulse may lead to greater efficiency and productivity. Certainly our economic system, in times of prosperity, has proved itself ably competitive with other systems. However, the mixed economies (such as Sweden, whose cars compete with ours) and the publicly owned economies (such as the USSR, whose armaments compete with ours) have done an astonishing job of producing goods and services. We may or may not like what they produce, or their political and social life, but we cannot deny that such economies are giving us a run for our money as far as sheer productivity is concerned. An economic system that is entirely publicly owned, as in the USSR, can be lethargic, oppressive, unresponsive to public demand—but then so can a system which is effectively owned by a relatively small elite of individuals and families, as ours is. And the existence of great wealth extorts an even greater price politically for the nonwealthy American. We are proud of the fact that our political system is a democratic one—a government of, by, and for the people, devoted to the principle of "one man, one vote." If each citizen has an equal vote, then presumably each has equal power to determine what public policy will be. The inordinate influence of wealth and corporate power on political affairs often borders on, or leans well into, subversion of the democratic process. Much is for sale in public life. On the list are public officials, public employees, leaders of citizens' organizations, purveyors of information in the mass media. Most do not have a cash selling price and are not, wittingly, for sale at all. They are simply awed by the wealthy and powerful, or are subject to their influence or favors. Many, however, *do* have a cash price. What the middle American has most to pride himself on is his right to vote to influence government. But the power of concentrated wealth steadily and quietly erodes even that treasured possession.

Generally, the wealth-holding class is politically conservative and strongly Republican in its partisan preferences. The spectrum of conservatism runs from the moderate to the most extreme reaction. There are a few exceptions (mainly the "ethnic rich," Jewish and Irish) who are Democrats and give funds to the Democratic candidates. To that extent, neither party completely escapes the direct financial influence of the rich. Campaigns cost too much to pass up big contributors. Overwhelmingly, however, the will of this class is felt through the Republican party and its operating coalition: the rich themselves, those executives and others who serve the rich, small-town businessmen and the anti-city votes they control and the Southern racist vote. Conservative voters are largely WASP both in the North and in the South, with some recent entries from backlashing ethnic votes.

Organizationally, conservatives try to turn public authority (on social issues at least) away from the federal and back to state governments. State legislatures are safe. They have no authority to regulate business or make national decisions. They are much easier to control and manipulate than the federal government, being less visible, narrower in perspective, and greatly influenced by business. Similarly, conservative policy tries to limit the authority and taxing power of local governments because they are far more responsive than the states to liberal interests.

In general, conservative policy tries to lighten taxes on the rich, permit uncontrolled rises in profits, prices, interest; limit federal programs in health, education, welfare; control the power of trade unions, provide government subsidies (in the form of direct grants and purchases) to business and industry, hold down wages, keep a slack labor market and a relatively high level of unemployment, eliminate federal regulation of business, de-emphasize the needs of the poor and of minorities, limit funds going into urban and other social problems, use force and suppression in dealing with troublesome dissent.

Ironically, the very wealthy (especially the old wealth) and their chief executives are often the most enlightened in the conservative coalition—which is not saying a lot. They are less narrow and bigoted. They have a better view of the larger scene, nationally and internationally, and can better grasp the need for concessions to avoid the collapse of their system and their own perch in it. Still, they are not above manipulating and supporting extreme reaction when it suits their purposes. Some of the key members of the Du Pont family, for example, are far out on the reactionary right.

The impression that liberal mavericks abound among the very rich may spring from the examples of Franklin Roosevelt and the Kennedy brothers. These were, in fact, rare specimens, despised by their own class as traitors and reds. No doubt the politically liberal rich are most numerous in the East. The old wealth of the East is certainly more moderate in its politics than the new wealth of Texas and elsewhere, and is more tempered by the liberal ethnic groups of the big Eastern cities.

Nelson Rockefeller may be regarded as an example of "liberal" Republican wealth. As the rich go, he is certainly liberal, but his attitudes toward the Latin American "colonies" and his persistent coolness as Governor of New York to the poor and the desperate needs of the city certainly do not place him anywhere left of center in the total political spectrum. His fabulous wealth disengages him from all the mundane problems of the average New Yorker. He commutes by helicopter and need not contend with the state's clogged highways. He is not bothered by the housing shortage, rats, cockroaches, recessions, failing schools, and other minor irritants. As "businesslike" as his attitudes are toward public problems, he is still shunned by his rich Republican brethren who much prefer men like Barry Goldwater.

What is best in some of the old wealth, as far as the public is concerned, is its "enlightened self-interest," both short- and long-term. Rockefeller, for example, created a state university system in New York after protracted failure of Republican legislatures to do so. His enlightened interest was the desire to compete with California and other states in offering university-trained personnel to business. He also has a personal stake in New York's future, namely his own fabled interests in real estate and banks. Then too, as one of the richest of a rich class, he has a long-term interest in the survival of the society which provides his privileges.

Henry Ford II is a very conspicuous member of the rich class, and one of its richest. He is remarkable for taking an interest in some social problems and for supporting Lyndon Johnson against Barry Goldwater. Though his liberalism is limited to only a few noneconomic issues, he too (a Protestant turned Catholic) is a pariah in his own class.

The public may look at highly visible figures like Ford and Rockefeller and conclude that the rich are on the side of the poor. The conclusion is, of course, absurd. The rich whom we do not see, behind their heavy curtain of privacy, are the very people who create poverty. Their domination of public policy generates inequality and permits the poor, the unemployed and the marginal middle American to live in our midst.

Among the chief associates of the rich over the years have been the Southern "Dixiecrats," the nominal Democrats who have persuaded many average Southern citizens to fear black men more than their cruel employers. They have used Southern prejudice, fed it, and collaborated with it on states' rights and other key issues. In this way the Republican-Dixiecrats coalition has worked in Congress throughout the years to thwart liberal legislation. Now the coalition has apparently swung a majority of white citizens of the South into the Republican party.

The rich use the small-town vote in equally "enlightened" ways. Most small towns are run much like company towns or baronies. Usually a few leading citizens pretty much control opinion and town policy. These leaders often operate a dealer's franchise from a large corporation. They may sell cars, tractors, agricultural equipment, household appliances, insurance, bank service. Since these are lucrative businesses, those who run them are often the richest

men in town. Like feudal barons, these men are beholden
to their liege, on whose favor their position depends. The
small-town GM dealer is an arm of GM; the household
appliance dealer may be an arm of General Electric—and
so it goes.

These leading citizens are part of the corporate structure. They reflect corporate policy and depend for their
own prosperity on the continuing approval of the corporate
hierarchy. They think and act like the corporation. Usually
they are somewhat less enlightened, even though more
folksy, than the parent body, because they live in a smaller
world.

The farmer, the really rural man, is something else. He
is more likely to be his own man and a populist by natural
inclination. Yet even he usually falls under the influence,
and the debt, of the town tractor dealer or banker.

One need only scan a typical small-town newspaper or
tune in a typical radio station to see into the depths of
small-town conservatism. These media are part of the business clique that links the average citizen in small towns,
and in the South, to the conservative interests of the giant
corporations, thereby cutting his ties of mutual interest
with other average citizens in cities and in the North.

The very rich and those who emulate them may seem
more civilized than they are. Their manner is a façade
that covers many barbaric political sentiments. They do
not flinch at sending armed men to break strikes, and
break up student demonstrations. They manufacture na-
palm, bombers, guns and other weapons of political murder. Yet, in their personal deportment they are well-bred
ladies and gentlemen. They do not slurp their soup, slop
it on their clothes, or rush through doors ahead of old
women. Except for the eccentric *grande dame* who is permitted every incivility, they rarely speak their minds
to the point of insult. They prefer the "finer" things to

popular vulgarities. They are warm, hospitable, friendly to strangers. Their style is part of a family secret handed down by the British upper class to their kin in the new world: a cool and refined exterior covering the calculating and rapacious inner man.

2

Institutional wealth and power are even more concentrated than personal wealth, and are growing at an even more ominous rate.

"In unprecedented fashion," the Federal Trade Commission concluded in its 1969 *Economic Report on Corporate Mergers,* "the current merger movement is centralizing and consolidating corporate control and decision-making among a relatively few vast companies."

Early in 1969, the two hundred industrial corporations controlled over 60 percent of the total assets of all manufacturing corporations. The share of such assets held by the hundred largest corporations was greater than the share held by the two hundred largest corporations in 1950. The two hundred largest manufacturing corporations control a share of assets equal to that held by the thousand largest in 1941, when the most probing study of monopoly was made.[1]

The size and power of these corporations is so great that the layman may have difficulty comprehending the enormity of such corporate concentration.

The new conglomerates are not quite like the old trusts and monopolies. An oil company no longer swallows up other oil companies or buys up firms it does business with

[1] Federal Trade Commission, *Economic Report on Corporate Mergers,* Hearings before the subcommittee on antitrust and monopoly of the Committee on the Judiciary, U.S. Senate, Part 8A, p. 3, 1969.

in order to create monopolies. Instead, it buys companies operating in other fields—perhaps fertilizer or coal companies.

Defenders of conglomeration say there is no danger of unfair competition or price fixing, but a Federal Trade Commission study concludes:

"The current merger movement has done more than merely increase the concentration of industrial assets in a relatively few multimarket corporations. There is evidence of important and increasing connecting links between this growing centralization of industrial resources in a few hundred vast corporations and the performance of competition in particular markets.

"These interrelated developments pose a serious threat to America's democratic and social institutions by creating a degree of centralized private decision-making that is incompatible with a free enterprise system, a system relying upon market forces to discipline private economic power." [2]

The two hundred largest manufacturing companies acquired more than two thousand concerns, with combined assets of $17.5 billion, between 1950 and 1964. If this rate of acquisition continues, by 1977 the hundred largest manufacturing corporations will control more than two-thirds of the nation's manufacturing assets, Dr. Willard Mueller of the Federal Trade Commission predicts.

Profits tell us even more about the corporate giants. The top fifty corporations made 40 percent of all industrial profits in 1965. The five hundred largest industrial corporations made 72 percent of all industrial profits in 1965. Yet these five hundred corporations are only *one-fourth of one percent* of all industrial corporations in the country.

[2] *Ibid.,* p. 5.

Even after taxes, General Motors profits alone exceeded the tax revenues of every state except New York and California in 1965, and were greater than the combined revenues of eighteen states. General Motors sales run about $23 billion a year, while the second biggest salesman, Standard Oil of New Jersey, sells about $14 billion.

12

Alienation

Among the alienated who have come most recently to our glazed attention are youth, students, the poor, blacks, women. These now visible and vocal groups protest that they are not partners or real participants in the society. Those on the lower end of the economic ladder (the poor, the blacks) feel like outsiders but want to get inside; many of those at the top (the affluent youth and students) feel alienated and want to get further outside.

A hidden assumption in all the talk about alienation and participation is that there is a massive and homogeneous body in the middle of America that is content with its lot. The satisfied are undoubtedly common in all social groups, even students, blacks, and the poor. They are perhaps most numerous in middle America. But alienation is also common there—deep, festering and unattended.

We have already examined some of the sources of this discontent—the sense of being victimized by war, crime, work, insecurity, low wages, sickness, ethnic discrimination, shoddy merchandise, inert institutions, inequality. The symptoms of the alienation are found in voting behavior, work habits, absenteeism on the job, strikes, hard-hat disturbances, backlash, antagonism to students, and feelings of distrust and impotence. As with students and blacks, the alienation does not touch everyone in this class, but it does seriously afflict a sizable minority.

The very term "alienation," as we have seen, came out of the Marxian concept that industrial workers became alienated from their work as they lost control of it and the product of their labor, as they lost their skills to the assembly line, and as they gave up their independence and went to work for others. Thus the worker no longer controlled his own labor and product (as the peasant and craftsman to a greater extent did) but worked for others—machines, employers. Workers became alienated not only from the product of the labor but from the whole process. Unions could to some extent control the speed of the line and the worker's "production quota," but the job itself, the nature of work was out of the worker's control. These decisions were management prerogatives.

Such alienation did not, as Marx predicted it would, lead to world revolution, but it did result in massive discontent with work. In America, the discontent is seen today in the increase in strikes—up from 19 million man-hours lost in 1960 to 42 million in 1968. It is seen in heavy labor turnover and in absenteeism. At Ford, for example, the quit rate was 25.2 percent in one recent year. Many new workers walk away at mid-shift and don't come back for their pay. Absenteeism has doubled in most places over the last ten years. It is seen in the fact that, according to the Survey Research Center, two in three working men say they have dead-end jobs.

But underlying the alienation from one's work that Marx predicted is the ancient affliction troubling mankind—the problem of genesis, of existence, of place. Who am I? Where did I come from? What am I doing here? It is said by many sage sociologists, and it may be true, that modern man is uprooted and anonymous, relative to his rural forebears. In the transition from farm to city, he abandoned those communal bonds which previously gave him an intimate sense of sharing and belonging. He became a stranger, frequently neither known to nor knowing his neighbors. This new "anomie," said the French sociologist Emile Durkheim, is responsible for most of modern man's distress.

Perhaps the most seriously afflicted by anomie are the young. Their roots in the past do not always nourish them through the fast transition of generations. So they speak of love, community, participation, identity. They wish to find in each other, by huddling together, the community bond, the comfort blanket that many have lost.

The middle American may not be the most afflicted by the anomic condition, but he is certainly touched by the contagion. The migrant worker from Kentucky knows he will be laughed at for his accent and will be generally regarded as a redneck, a dimwit, an "alien," when he comes up North. Unless he is an accepted member of a closely knit family or ethnic group (or a religious, social, or neighborhood community), the average American too may lose his way and his sense of rootedness.

Though the average citizen is often a church member, nominally at least, he is, according to every sociological survey of the subject, far less likely than the rich and affluent to belong to social and recreational groups and clubs. He often works too hard and long to have time left for the gratifications of intimate group relations. Nor does he have the money to become a joiner. Given such enforced isolation, he is, at the end of his life, after retirement, often alone.

Most average citizens presumably find their closest attachments in their immediate families. An astonishing proportion of marriages, however, are not particularly happy. The average citizen is more tied by the marriage vows than classes above him. Decorum, religion, and the high cost of divorce keep him bonded to disagreeable marriages. Even the poor can more casually get out of unhappy marriages.

Most tragically, the long history of unresolved conflict among disadvantaged ethnic and racial groups makes it very difficult for the average man to form bonds across ethnic lines. The very people who should share his community—because they occupy the same general class station in life—become instead his adversaries. He fights rather than joins them.

Similarly, the fragmentation and neglect of urban communities keeps the average man who dwells in a city from joining with neighbors in programs of community action and civic betterment. As a result, the individual and his class become increasingly anomic.

2

Perhaps the worker does not display his discontent and alienation as openly as youth and the poor because he works very hard for a living, and has little time or energy for parades and protest during or after work hours.

His only chances for real protest are in strikes and in the voting booth.

Middle America is politically alienated far beyond what those of us who speculate about the passive majority suspect. It is not a new phenomenon, either.

Several sociologists, exploring one community's political attitudes in 1957, found that alienation varied with socioeconomic status. The lower the status, the greater the alienation.[1]

About half of all respondents in the middle socioeconomic status (compared with 38 percent in the upper) were found to be "alienated," that is, distrustful of public officials and convinced that the little man's interests don't count to these officials. The young and the very old were the most alienated. Among occupational groups, blue-collar workers were the most alienated—68 percent compared to 33 percent of managers and officials. Similarly, almost twice as many high school as college graduates were alienated.

The authors' own analysis of data from a national survey done in 1968 indicated serious political alienation among a majority of Americans. Such alienation varied with income level. The higher the income, the less the alienation. Relatively the middle American was less alienated than the poor. Still, on most issues, a majority in the middle group expressed alienated sentiments.

Among white middle Americans, 80 percent felt that politics and government sometimes seemed so complicated that they couldn't understand what was going on; 74 percent felt that "people like me" didn't have much say about what the government does; 72 percent said that political parties usually did what they wanted after the election, rather than keeping campaign promises; 59 per-

[1] Wayne E. Thompson and John E. Horton, "Political Alienation as a Force in Political Action," *Social Forces*, 1960, v. 38, pp. 190–195.

cent felt that government wasted a lot of tax money. More than half felt that the only way they could affect government policy was by voting.

3

Yet the political alienation of middle America is consistently expressed in the failure to vote. In 1968 about 38 percent of eligible civilians failed to vote in the Presidential election, and about 44 percent in the congressional election. The higher the family income and education levels are, the more likely people are to vote. The average man is more likely to vote than the poor and the uneducated, but much less likely to vote than the affluent and the college educated. Among family heads making $5,000 to $7,500 in 1968, for example, more than 34 percent failed to vote; among those making $10,000 and over, only 19 percent failed to vote. To be sure, the proportion of eligible voters who go to the polls has risen steadily since 1920, when about 57 percent failed to vote, but the record is still poor.[2] Many people stay away from the polls because they feel their vote doesn't matter, that they can't affect government, that politicians "are all crooks anyway." They also stay away because it is made so difficult and troublesome for people to register and vote. Buried among these nonvoters is a "hidden majority" for economic liberalism.

In 1968, political alienation in middle America was registered in votes for Wallace and in the rise to na-

[2] In 1920 many voters lived in rural areas and did not own cars to get to the polls easily. Blacks in the South were effectively denied the vote. The rise in participation may be explained by these factors rather than by a decline in alienation.

tional popularity of Wallace's American Independence Party. The Wallace vote (about 13.5 percent of the total) exceeded that given to any other third-party candidate during this century.

More than ever before, voters in 1968 divided themselves along racial lines. Blacks voted overwhelmingly Democratic—97 percent. Only about 36 percent of whites voted Democratic. The Jewish vote was 84 percent Democratic; the Catholic, 54 percent; and the white Protestant, only 25 percent. Among these groups, Nixon won a majority only among white Protestants—58 percent. White Protestants, mainly in the South, were also Wallace's chief support. In the South, 46 percent of Protestant voters were Wallace *sympathizers,* compared to only 29 percent of Catholics.

While race and ethnicity were obviously related to voting behavior, social class and income were not. Class lines were everywhere blurred. Blacks voted their ethnic and economic interests, but a majority of whites, in the lower- and middle-income groups, apparently voted only what they regarded as their ethnic interest. The Republican vote cut into all income groups, gaining 49 percent of the votes of whites with incomes of $4,000 or below; 49 percent with incomes of $4,000 to $8,000; 50 percent of those with incomes of $8,000 to $12,000; and 55 percent of those with incomes of $12,000 and up. Whites with incomes of $25,000 and over voted 74.3 percent for Nixon. They, at least, did not lose sight of what they regarded as their economic interest.

Furthermore, Republicans won a larger proportion of the white vote in metropolitan areas than in the more conservative small towns and cities. Many of these white urban votes undoubtedly came from racial backlash. In the South, backlash was so great that whites gave as large a percentage of their votes to Wallace as to Humphrey (27 percent), despite the solid Democratic tradition of the South. Half of all Wallace votes came from the South, and in the North, Southern migrants voted twice as heavily for Wallace as did Northern whites.

Wallace *sympathizers* were far more common among manual than among nonmanual workers, but in the final vote, there was not that much difference. In the North, 10 percent of nonmanual workers and 22 percent of manual workers were Wallace sympathizers; in the South, 36 percent of nonmanual and 59 percent of manual. In the actual vote, however, most of these manual workers switched away from Wallace to Nixon. In the final vote, 9 percent of professionals and managers voted for Wallace nationally, 11 percent of other white-collar workers, 15 percent of skilled and semiskilled workers, and 13 percent of the unskilled.

In the North, 9 percent of both union and non-union manual workers voted for Wallace. In the South, the unionized manual worker was much *less* likely than the non-union worker to vote for Wallace (40 percent and 58 percent respectively). In the North, the union worker was much less likely than the non-union worker to vote for Nixon (34 percent and 52 percent respectively).

While workers, in the end, voted more liberally than they threatened to, the prevalence of Wallace sympathizers and the switch to Nixon suggests a massive discontent among manual workers.

The anomie in middle America is also expressed in a sense of personal alienation and impotence. Our further analysis of reponses from the Survey Research Center showed that, among white middle Americans, 21 percent felt that the problems of life were sometimes too big for them (compared with 6 percent of the affluent); 42 percent felt that most people cannot be trusted (compared with 33 percent of the affluent); 44 percent felt that most of the time people are just looking out for themselves (compared with 24 percent of the affluent); 45 percent felt they usually could not carry out their plans (compared with 24 percent of the affluent). The middle American is less likely than the affluent to say that his life is completely satisfying, that people can be trusted, that most people try to be helpful, that life will work out the way he wants it.

IV : People
and Policy

13

Blacks and Ethnics

The deepest rift in the liberal alliance is an ancient one—the division within the ranks of labor. In other generations it was among the many European groups that made up the working class—the polyglot army of immigrants who, until this generation, populated the ranks of labor, had little in common except suspicion, antagonism and low status on the job totem pole. They spoke different languages—Italian, Polish, Russian, German— lived in separate worlds, and eagerly protected their own kind and excluded outsiders. Perhaps no other working class in the Western world faced such forbidding obstacles to mutual aid, organization and class solidarity, or has been, for that reason, slower to organize itself and create a genuine labor movement. Today most discord is between black and white workers. Race has always split American labor, but less seriously in the past than now. Only in the last three decades have blacks, entering massively into the industrial labor market, competed seriously for the jobs of ethnics or replaced them in their jobs and neighborhoods when they moved up.

Racial cleavages are wider than the old ethnic ones because the migration of blacks has been so massive, sudden and concentrated in the cities. Hardly more than one in fifty Americans is first- or second-generation Italian (the largest recent immigrant group); one out of nine Americans is Negro. Race differences are greater because they are more visible than ethnic ones, and because they extend to prejudices that are deeper than language and culture.

In the South, race conflict has kept labor from organizing and unionizing. Average men, black and white, who share the same economic status and grievances, instead of throwing their lot together, have wasted their energies and the considerable collective influence they have, in racial discord. Whites have joined political alliances with economic conservatives in exchange for votes to "keep the colored down." Blacks, by themselves, have been relatively impotent at the polls and in union campaigns.

While many of the early craft unions were as close to lily-white as they could get, historically the industrial unions were the first major organizations to bring whites and blacks together into effective working-class action. Yet even the early days of industrial organization were torn by race conflict, much of it created by employers to forestall unionization. The Ford Motor Company, for example, the last of the auto makers to be organized, used Negro churches as hiring agencies and Negro ministers as purveyors of anti-union gospel. By hiring many anti-union Negroes and keeping them at odds with whites, the union was kept out of Ford long after the time for unionization had come.

"To further hurt the C.I.O.," one historian writes, "industrial management often cultivated relations with black community leaders. By means of financial contributions to local Negro organizations, management gained their allegiance and increased their dependence upon local industry. The black church became the focal point of this support, and the most sophisticated practitioner of the policy was the Ford Motor Company. Ford made financial contributions to selected Negro churches, and then in effect used the ministers as employment agents. Prospective workers were hired, upon presenting a written ministerial recommendation from their minister to company officials. Negro ministers welcomed Ford's assistance because it increased church attendance, helped keep the church financially solvent, and strengthened their community leadership position. Once having secured company approval, a minister was anxious to keep it, and thus willing to follow Ford's anti-CIO position." [1]

Walter White, former leader of the NAACP, charged that the Negro church, the one institution Negroes assumed belonged to them, was actually the property of the white industrialist. When the big 1941 Ford strike came, 1,500 Negro workers refused to strike at the Rouge plant in Dearborn, Michigan. Ford pressured black ministers into condemning the strike and unions, and Walter White wrote that even at the NAACP meeting at which the strike was discussed, the atmosphere was as anti-union as a meeting of the Ford board of directors. Finally, the national leaders of NAACP and others persuaded blacks to join the strike and it was won.

[1] James S. Olson, "Organized Black Leadership and Industrial Unionism: The Racial Response, 1936–1945," *Labor History,* Summer 1969, Vol. 10, No. 3.

After seeing the gains won by the CIO for black workers, the NAACP reported in 1943: "Every attack on labor is an attack on the Negro, for the Negro is largely a worker . . . Organized labor is now our national ally. The CIO has proved that it stands for our people within the unions and outside the unions . . . If labor loses a battle, the Negro loses also.[2]

Black and white workers share identical economic interests. They work at the same jobs, have the same grievances and the same need for better wages, working conditions, hours. Both are hard hit by the military draft. Inflation and recession hurt them in similar ways. Both are discriminated against in schools. Both are poorly housed. Both need real public-health programs, a fairer tax structure, more aid to the cities, and better public transit, schools, pensions and social security—to name only a few shared needs.

Black and white workers still compete and fight with each other over scarce jobs, goods, services, school funds, college places, living space. Instead of voting for better housing and schools, many whites join up with conservatives to drive the blacks back. Instead of settling their grievances with those who cause them (opponents of decent social legislation), black and white workers battle those who are closest to them—their fellow workers.

Despite these strains, open race conflict has diminished. Even the city riots of the mid sixties were not true race riots in the sense that they were not, at least overtly, wars of blacks against whites. The black protest was for greater power and prestige in society.

There are some signs of movement in the schools. College enrollments of blacks increased 85 percent from 1964 to 1968, compared to an increase of 46 percent for all en-

---

[2] "The 1943 Line-up vs. the Negro," *The NAACP Bulletin,* III (Feb. 1943).

rollments. Still, of course, Blacks are only about 6 percent of college students, while they should be, relative to their numbers, about 11 percent.

In 1963 black income was 53 percent of white. By 1967 it had risen to 62 percent. In the North Central states, black income is now more than 75 percent of white. In 1969, outside the South, the average non-white family man in a blue-collar job earned about 86 percent as much as his white counterpart.

About eight years ago, half of all black families were poor. Now less than one in three are. Eight years ago, young black men averaged two years less schooling than whites. Now the gap is less than half a year.

During the sixties, Negro professionals increased 109 percent and Negroes in managerial jobs increased 53 percent—compared with an increase of 41 percent and 12 percent, respectively, for whites.

In 1966 there were over 140 blacks in state legislatures, a number that is almost triple what it was four years earlier.

Blacks themselves think they are doing better. In a national survey, more than half of both blacks and whites said that "a lot" of change has been made in the position of Negroes in the last few years.[3] In another survey, 64 percent said things "are getting better"; 77 percent found great cause for hope in the fact that more blacks are going to college; 70 percent, in the fact that new kinds of jobs are opening up for blacks; and 63 percent, in the rising racial pride of blacks and the increase in black business.[4]

More blacks stressed increased educational opportunity, black ownership of business and black public officials than other avenues of mobility; and 83 percent said they

[3] Survey Research Center, University of Michigan, election survey, 1968.
[4] *Time*, April 6, 1970, p. 29.

favor working more closely with whites who want to help blacks.

A sizable minority of blacks (9 percent, or two million people) count themselves as "revolutionaries" and think that only a readiness to use violence will get them real equality. The vast majority, however, want to work with whites and get along with them.

On all issues, more than three in four blacks prefer integration to separatism. One of the most consistent findings is that overwhelmingly blacks want to live in integrated housing. Yet more than half of all whites think blacks prefer to live by themselves.

Many whites have been convinced by some Black Power advocates that blacks are generally separatist and hostile to whites. In fact, blacks are split into three clear and almost equal categories in their perceptions of whites, according to the *Time* report. A third think most whites are well meaning; about a third think they are clearly hostile and repressive; and about a third think they are indifferent.

Strangely and ominously, for the future, black youth are more strongly separatist than their elders. At the same time, white youth have become more strongly integrationist than their elders.

The major source of discontent, as registered in the *Time* survey, is perception of job discrimination; yet almost four in five think it is possible to get ahead in spite of discrimination. Another major grievance, shared by the vast majority of blacks, is the police. Blacks think the police do not properly enforce the law, that they use unnecessary force and are dishonest.

Only about 5 percent of blacks live in the suburbs, yet almost 80 percent of all new jobs are there. Though about 200,000 blacks move to the suburbs each year, they are largely confined to ghetto neighborhoods. Housing discrimination is outlawed by federal law and the laws of twenty-seven states, but the law is notoriously unenforced. Restrictive zoning in many suburbs put limits on the type of housing, the cost, and acreage of construction—all effective barriers to black residency.

A large majority of whites think that whites are more ambitious than blacks, and that they have higher moral standards. Many believe blacks are careless of property and let their neighborhoods run down. Most whites mistakenly believe that whites are the chief victims of black crime.

The pattern that comes through is that, though white attitudes are not good, they are better than they have been. Many whites still feel put-upon and discriminated against in relation to blacks, and many are afraid of black violence. But while political backlash has been great, the grounds for racial collaboration (if it can occur in time to stem the tide of rising black violence) have perhaps never been greater. Such collaboration depends on a program of action that will unite black and white workers as they move toward shared goals.

What has come of the black revolt is a solidification of blacks as an ethnic group. What may come out of the post-revolt period is the solidification of the working class as an economic group.

Contrary to what was predicted about the "black bourgeoisie," most blacks who have advanced economically still maintain a rather strong identity with blacks as a class. In this, they resemble some other ethnic groups whose rising members have often kept their ethnic identity and voting behavior, even when it seemed to conflict with their new economic interests. While many blacks reveal the ultimate in "bourgeois aspirations" (as symbolized in a zeal for status symbols—expensive dress, cars, fancy home décor, proms, debuts), most show a remarkable tenacity as far as black political, economic and social issues are concerned.

That is to say, they vote with the black working class and the dispossessed. The votes most solidly against Nixon in the '68 election, for example, were the black vote, the Jewish vote, the Polish vote and the urban working-class vote.

While black militancy has greatly increased, there has been no similar popular gain in truly "revolutionary" sentiment. While the Panthers wish literally to overthrow the government, overwhelmingly blacks want only to change the society as quickly as possible so they can become part of it. They aspire to rise in the system, not to overthrow it by force of arms. In the very process of attaining power and status in the system, they will be significantly altering that system for the better; for what has been most wrong with our society is its exclusion of blacks.

2

Figures comparing the status of whites and blacks are misleading on one major point. Most blacks are workers, but the figures do not tell us anything about how blacks compare with other ethnic groups who are mainly working-class.

Italians, for example, a recent and large immigrant group, remain overwhelmingly working-class. Aside from the "lumpen" group at the bottom and the unemployed or derelict in both groups, it is perhaps not outrageous to speculate that urban Italians have roughly the same general status as urban blacks. Italians have been in the cities longer, but they seem to have been, despite this advantage, not much more successful at moving up, going to college, becoming high-level managers and professionals than blacks have been. As we will see later in the chapter, among Italians who are third-generation or later, and who are high-school graduates, only 12 percent hold "prestige" jobs, and only 3 percent earn over $14,000 a year, as of 1968. If high-school *dropouts* were included, the figures would be even lower.

As far as social status goes, New Classmen tend to look down on Italians (as crooks and dummies) even more than on blacks. While it is enlightened and chic to support the black cause, or Mexican "La Causa," Italians do not excite any similar awareness of deprivation.

Italians, to be sure, have not faced the same violent forms of prejudice and discrimination as blacks. On that score, all ethnic groups have been better off. But, like the Irish, Poles, Jews and others, Italians have known most ugly forms of prejudice. They are still underdogs and outsiders. The old ethnic images linger in the public mind, associating Italians with crime, Poles with stupidity, Jews with avarice, and Irish with laziness and belligerence. The labels are grossly unjust, to say the least. The major vice of these groups is that they are not, even yet, 100-percent pure-bred middle-class white Anglo-Saxon Protestants. They are the "minorities"—that now make up a majority of our population.

The ethnics of first-, second-, or third-generation stock alone number about 40 million people. In 1960, almost 20 percent of the white population was foreign-born or second-generation (excluding those from the British Isles). These recent immigrants numbered 31 million people, compared with 19 million Negroes.[5]

These ethnic immigrants came mainly to Northern cities and many, because they did not move up fast in life, tended to remain there. In the Chicago metropolitan area, for

[5] Between 1820 and 1967, 9.4 million immigrants came from Great Britain and Ireland, 6.9 million from Germany, 5.1 million from Italy, 4.3 million from Austria and Hungary, 3.3 million from the USSR, 1.3 million from Sweden, 3.9 million from Canada, 1.5 million from Mexico, and 1.6 million from other Latin American countries.

example, there are still 319,000 people of Polish descent; 250,000, of German; 204,000, of Italian; 116,000, of Russian (most of them Jewish); and 90,000 of Irish descent. About 85 percent of this huge Polish minority, it is estimated, still lives inside the city limits, compared with only 38 percent of Germans. The Russians have the highest income of all these minorities.

These urban ethnics, most of them lacking funds or the inclination to suburbanize, have been jostled a good deal by the massive migration of blacks to the city. They have been required to share their old neighborhoods—or move out; to share their jobs, their schools, their parks—or move out, to places where they feel like the aliens they are, leaving behind the old ties and neighborhoods that held their lives together.

Still, the transition of Northern cities from white to black has been swift and remarkably smooth. The ethnics and other working-class whites resisted in many places but never with much force and only rarely with any violence. In the end most left their homes and their neighborhoods and moved on. Nevertheless, the whites who go to truly integrated schools, live in truly integrated neighborhoods, work on truly integrated jobs—are largely working-class and ethnic.

Besides the "invasion" of their turf, the ethnics have been put off mainly by two things: black crime and violence in the city, and what they think of as black demands for "special privileges."

In crime, the ethnics have a real grievance, of course. But we have already seen that they do not know that crime in the streets afflicts blacks much more than whites, and that far worse crimes—crimes against society—are committed by the rich and affluent whose skin is purest white. Moreover, the ethnics might do well to remember their own past. The most dangerous neighborhoods in New

York City's history were Irish. The Italian involvement in crime is not all myth—even though fabrications about the Mafia Menace are periodically spun out in order to boost FBI appropriations. And some of the most murderous gangs in criminal history (the Purple Gang, Murder, Inc.) were Jewish. Such lawlessness came out of desperation, poverty, uprootedness, discrimination. These people were torn up by the roots, living far from their homeland and culture as outsiders in a hostile land. Often the only way they could make their way in the world was through crime.

On the second point, the ethnics are perhaps even touchier. Blacks want special privileges, they say. They don't want to work their way up "the way we did." They want to start at the top and they want exceptions made for them. *We* never had it so good . . . Nobody gave *us* anything . . . We had to do everything the hard way. Nobody passed laws against discrimination when we were the victims. They never agreed to let *our* kids into college ahead of others, just because we were immigrants. We got no special privileges in hiring, housing, education, promotion or anything else. We were always just wops, dagos, kikes, micks, hunkies, polacks, greasers, spicks. We still are, in fact, and nobody gives a damn.

The point is well-taken. Life for the immigrant has been hard, and has not been softened by the guilt, understanding, sympathy of the privileged—nor, more importantly, by special poverty programs, or court rulings and laws against discrimination.

On the other hand, however despised the immigrants were, they had no history of slavery in this country. They were not regarded as commodities rather than people, or legally segregated into different schools, rest rooms, restaurants. For most immigrants there was a way out, though not an easy one; the door was stuck and it was heavy, but with enough force it could be opened. If they were willing and able to assimilate Anglo culture, values and language, some of them could pass out of their servitude into the world of privilege. Black men could hardly pass in white society with the same cultural disguise.

Then too, when most immigrants came, America was a far more barbarous, more ignorant and poorer country. However insensitive we may now be to human suffering, we are better than we were before. We care more and we can afford more. Much of the improvement, of course, is due to the immigrant himself and to the democratic, humane, and egalitarian institutions and traditions he helped generate in this country. We are more humane to children, animals, criminals and the poor than we used to be. Child labor is forbidden by law. The cruelties of the poor house have been replaced by old-age assistance and welfare. Even criminals are far better off. Chain gangs, the lash, sweat boxes and even capital punishment have been largely abolished. We no longer tar-and-feather or draw-and-quarter the miscreant. Rape, cattle rustling, witchcraft are no longer capital offenses. It may even be called progress. Each generation gets more freedom and attention than the last. We can afford to treat people—even minorities—more humanely.

The real question to be probed is not the simple one raised in some ethnic circles: should we extend special privileges to blacks when we didn't give them to depressed minorities in the past? The question is rather: since most members of most ethnic groups are *still* disadvantaged, should we not *also* extend rights and privileges to *them*? Shouldn't we also attend to their privations and to those of the poor whites, and others who have dropped out of sight in recent years?

Perhaps most conflict between blacks and the ethnics can somehow or other be mediated. Some of it, however,

is inevitable, given the shortage of resources and opportunities. Blacks and ethnics are in an unavoidable conflict
over a number of things—control of schools, college enrollments, jobs in civil service and skilled trades, control of
the Democratic party, to name a few. Public service jobs
are plums that all ethnic groups, in their turn, have sought;
now blacks have come to their turn. New York City alone
employs more than 300,000 people and spends about 60
percent of its $6 billion budget on personnel. Blacks want
their share of these good jobs. They also want their share
of college places in that city's vast university system, places
denied them until recently by a qualification system set up
largely by the ethnics. They want their share in other social
institutions as well.

Though such bargaining and jostling for position will
continue, what should be diminished is the mutual alienation and antagonism. As in a family, sibling rivalry may be
inevitable, but in the long run survival depends on awareness of common interests and progress toward common
goals.

For most Scandinavians, Germans, British, Northern Irish, Scottish, Canadian immigrants (mostly white
Protestants), the United States has been a genuine melt-
ing pot. Most of these Protestants disappeared into the
general population as quickly as they shed their accents,
sometimes sooner. Doors have been open and descendants
of these immigrants, more often than most aliens, have
achieved some status in the society. While large numbers,
especially in the South, may still be found in the working
class and on skid rows, the way up for the white Protestant
was less complicated than for most immigrants.

Jews have faced more barriers than most immigrant
groups, and are still barred from some fancy neighbor-

hoods, social groups, country clubs. Nor have Jews been allowed into the top levels of big industry (General Motors, U.S. Steel, General Electric, Standard Oil, etc.). Among non-Protestant immigrant groups, however, the Jewish population has traveled further than others. Most Jews were literate (however modestly so) when they came to the States, and cherished the Talmudic tradition of scholarship. Their centuries-long history of persecution caused them to build in this country formal and informal systems of mutual aid, through which established Jewish groups (the Germans, for example) assumed responsibility for assisting more recent arrivals. The tightly organized Jewish family enabled Jews to nurse the tiny neighborhood businesses which supported the family and ultimately became schools of commerce for many of the family's members.

Also, ironically, Jews from Eastern Europe probably were helped up by their rather widespread participation in socialist and radical movements, which further encouraged a reverence for education and scholarship. Even without willing it, radical Jewish parents insured success for their children by pushing them to academic achievement and to the professional status that rewards such achievement. Thus Jews, while still facing discrimination and even some persecution, have won a place in American society. Like others who moved up, of course, many of them did it by imitating WASP manners, wearing the Brooks Brothers suit, sending their children to Harvard, and otherwise submerging their own immigrant identity.

European Catholics, in contrast, though they have faced less virulent discrimination than Jews, have not done as well. Italians, Slavs, even the Irish have been slower to catch on, and millions of them continue to live at the economic and cultural margins of American society.

Prejudice against Catholics is still rampant in some sections of the country, and unconscious discrimination remains fairly widespread. Hostility toward Catholics used to be general, and did not really begin to wane until some fifty years ago. Anti-Catholicism is one of our society's guilty secrets, as the underground campaign against Jack Kennedy's Catholicism illustrates.

Perhaps factors inherent in their own culture have also kept Catholics from moving up. Many Catholics do not aspire to act, live, talk like Anglicized Protestants. This disinclination to ape their bosses has barred the upward path of many. In general, Catholic training, education and culture do not produce strivers or even scholars in the modern sense of the term. The parochial schools attended by so many Catholics are often better suited to the production of priests and nuns than businessmen and professionals. Many working-class Catholics still honor manual occupations. In a typical Catholic family, the craftsman, fireman, policeman, minor civil servant will often be regarded as successful. Relatively low economic and social aspirations are usually correlates of Catholic culture and education.

The weakness of Catholic education starts at the top and is passed on down the line, from the Catholic University to the primary school. In higher education, perhaps only Notre Dame among all Catholic schools has a reputation comparable to the Ivy League schools. Other Catholic universities—such as Fordham, Georgetown, Boston College, St. Louis, Detroit—have distinguished scholars in residence and support first-rate academic departments and schools, but almost none possess the resources needed to support well-rounded, high-level university programs.

Catholics seem to have done rather well in medicine, perhaps because of the training opportunities open in church-connected hospitals. By contrast, though many Catholic universities maintain law schools of better-than-average reputation, Catholics generally have been in the minor leagues of the legal profession. The Catholic in the Wall Street law firm, for example, is a rare specimen. Indeed some of these influential firms customarily select only one man each from Fordham and St. John's, even though these large law schools are in New York and almost next door to Wall Street offices.[6]

For these reasons and because they are covertly discriminated against in many fields, Catholics are grossly underrepresented on college faculties. While practicing Roman Catholics numbered about 47.5 million in the United States in 1969 (or about 25 percent of the total population) they represent only 11.8 percent of all college and university faculties. Only in four fields do Catholics approximate their proportion of the total population. They represent 27.2 percent of all faculty in nursing, 24.7 percent in re-

[6] Erwin O. Smigel, *The Wall Street Lawyer,* Bloomington, Ind.: Indiana University Press, 1969.

SELECTED ATTRIBUTES
OF CATHOLIC ETHNIC GROUPS IN U.S.

	Irish	Germans	Italians	Poles	French
Have completed high school	77%	62%	51%	46%	42%
Hold prestige jobs	32	31	13	17	22
Earn over $14,000 a year	24	19	17	18	7
Belong to Democratic Party	70	65	67	77	70
Score high on general knowledge	18	9	7	3	5
Score high on open-mindedness	52	48	42	43	40
Consider themselves "very happy"	41	36	35	27	40
Score low on anomie	64	51	47	43	49
Score high on piety	32	31	13	30	22
Score high on religious extremism	19	20	24	34	28
Score high on racism	44	46	54	61	51
Score high on anti-Semitism	29	47	43	52	54
(Number of persons interviewed)	(328)	(361)	(370)	(184)	(177)

ligion, 19.7 percent in philosophy and 17.6 percent in languages. All these are marginal fields in contemporary scholarship. Catholic faculties are concentrated in Catholic institutions, and are present in little more than token numbers in other institutions.

While practicing Protestants represent about 33 percent of the total population, they were 45.3 percent of faculty. Jews, 3 percent of the population, were 6.7 percent of faculty. About a quarter of all faculty indicate they have no religion at all. Most of these were brought up as Protestants.

A 1963 survey of Catholic ethnic groups by the National Opinion Research Center (NORC) gives us the best information we have about these groups.[7] The survey shows that the Irish are better off than other Catholics in most ways. They are the most educated and prosperous, the most open-minded, informed, happy, pious and the least anomic, racist, anti-Semitic, or extremist group in religion. The French, a relatively small group, are in many respects the worst off as a group, with Italians and Poles vying for second place. According to this survey, Poles are more pious and more biased than Italians. Except for the Irish and Germans, much less than a third of each group hold prestige jobs. All groups are overwhelmingly committed to the Democratic Party.

Some of these characteristics are artifacts of tenure in the New World. The Irish, for example, have been around longest and so, quite naturally, have done better than others. When we compare only high-school graduates of third or later generations, we get a better picture of the relative success and satisfaction in each group. Even though the number of those interviewed is small, some interesting contrasts are suggested by the study.

[7] National Opinion Research Center, "Information about American Ethnic Groups," printed in *Why Can't They Be Like Us?*, Andrew M. Greeley, Institute of Human Relations Press, 1969.

SELECTED ATTRIBUTES OF CATHOLIC
ETHNIC GROUPS IN U.S.—HIGH-SCHOOL GRADUATES
OF THIRD OR LATER GENERATION ONLY

	Irish	Germans	Italians	Poles	French
Hold prestige jobs	31%	34%	12%	32%	21%
Work as professionals or managers	45	47	37	22	31
Earn over $14,000 a year	26	22	3	21	11
Belong to Democratic Party	67	61	51	62	76
Score high on general knowledge	26	17	20	11	9
Score high on open-mindedness	51	56	51	34	40
Consider themselves "very happy"	47	38	26	32	48
Score low on anomie	74	60	44	61	60
Score high on piety	32	32	10	20	39
Score high on religious extremism	14	15	20	31	26
Score high on racism	39	30	54	61	29
Score high on anti-Semitism	25	38	32	59	43
(Number of persons interviewed)	(131)	(102)	(29)	(24)	(31)

In this comparison, we find Germans leading the Irish by a nose in job status, but again the Irish are the most knowledgeable, the happiest, the least anomic and anti-Semitic. Poles, followed by Italians, are the most racist. Poles are also the most anti-Semitic and extremist in religion, even though relatively few score high on piety. Racist sentiment among Poles is concentrated in the mid-West, where many tend to live in large ethnic ghettos. In the East, Poles are no more racist than other Catholic groups.

Italians are of special interest. There are so many of them and (in this small survey sample at least) they have trailed far behind other Catholic groups in job success. Italians are much less likely than other high-school graduates, according to the NORC survey, to hold prestige jobs or earn more than $14,000 a year. They are the most anomic, the least pious, and the least likely to think they are very happy. Considering all this, they are relatively open-minded and unbiased.

Italians have not done well. Relatively few go to college or enter the executive class or prestige professions. No man with an Italian name has ever sat on the U.S. Supreme Court. Few have headed leading corporations or universities (Giannini of the Bank of America is one of the few). The only really prominent Italian name in American science has been Enrico Fermi, who emigrated here as an adult, having earned his degrees in Europe. In Congress, John Pastore is the only Italian who ever headed a leading committee. John Volpe, a member of President Nixon's cabinet, is only the second Italian to rise to that level. The most famous of all Italian political figures, Fiorello La Guardia, four times mayor of New York City, ironically was a Protestant and part Jewish by descent. On the whole, Italians seem to have done better on the West than East coast, perhaps because capital and opportunity were not so tightly controlled by WASPs on the frontier. Certainly there is no lack of talent, ability, brains, energy among Italians, as the substantial cultural and economic achievements of Italians in their homeland clearly demonstrate. Explanations for this relative failure in America may lie mainly in prejudice and institutions that have held them in place.

Another NORC survey found that among college graduates Jews and Irish Catholics have the most liberal racial attitudes (the Protestant Irish having among the *least* liberal). Among college graduates, Jews and blacks are the most sympathetic to student militants.

Jews are the most likely to belong to neighborhood organizations, and Poles the least. Of all ethnic groups studied, Italians are the most likely, by far, to live in the same neighborhood as their parents and family, and to visit them weekly. Of all ethnic groups, Jews are the most open-minded, the most liberal politically, socially the most active, and financially the most successful.

The attitudes of Jews toward Catholics, however, have not only failed to improve but have significantly deteriorated in the last thirteen years. At the same time, the attitudes of Catholics toward Jews became significantly better. Jews were more likely in 1965 than in 1952 to say that Catholics did not respect Jewish beliefs, that Catholics did not want to intermarry, that their clergy were not intelligent and did not promote understanding, that their magazines were not fair. In 1952 Jews had better attitudes toward Catholics than Catholics had toward them. By 1965 this was reversed. The biggest increase in anti-Catholic feeling was found among the younger, more religious, and college-educated Jews. Such changes of attitude may derive from the college boy's recent inclination to think of the ethnic working-class as honkies and pigs, as many black militants do. Anti-Catholicism, it is said, is the intellectual's anti-Semitism. Such studies seem to validate the claim.

WORDS WITH AN ETHNIC

Henry Lorenz, 53,[8] lives in Chicago, one of a family of 13. At 12 he dropped out of school. He has been a carpenter and is now a house painter.

"The big question in my mind is how long I'll be able to sit comfortably here—in this neighborhood. How long this is going to last. I have an instinctive fear. I don't know why, that it could end at any time. I feel very uncomfortable living in the big city. For some reason or other, I

[8] Studs Terkel, *Division Street: America*, New York: Pantheon, 1967, p. 151.

dread the thought that me and my family will find ourselves swimming in some kind of blood bath. There's not
a question in the world about it. Any thinking man or
woman will see this. If they don't, they're deaf, dumb, and
blind to the facts of life. In black-white relations, we
haven't got a solution and I don't see any solution in sight.

"My feeling about the Negro is this: I never try to think
of him in terms of is he equal to me or isn't he equal to
me. I don't know and he doesn't know. I admit to this:
I am a man and he is a man. I can't say to a Negro, 'You
are equal to me.' Some are, some aren't. The average Negro
is not. I am not saying he won't be and that he might not
surpass me one day. My father came here when he was
seven years old from Europe, couldn't read or write the
American—the English—language. He had no relatives
whatsoever, outside of one cousin who was just about in
the same boat he was. Yet he made his way. Scholastically,
he got nowhere. Insofar as making a lot of money, he didn't
get anywhere. But this is one of the lessons I've learned, it
is not so much what you make or how you make it as it is
what you do with it after you've made it. And here is where
the Negro is not very smart. Because the average Negro's
mind, when he gets a given amount of money—he could
forward his education with it—but the average Negro
thinks about how big a car he could buy, how many clothes
he could put on his back, and whether or not he could
afford a diamond or two.

"I fear the Negro today. By and large, the Negro represents violence. I don't think the issue involves civil rights
any more. It's gone beyond. Right now in the heart of the
average Negro is vengeance. You better believe it. They
intend to make me pay for what my great, great, great
ancestors did to them. I am completely innocent of this.
Even the so-called good Negroes. In their hearts they are
too timid in themselves to come forward, so we don't think

they feel this way. But you would be amazed, if we could open and bare their hearts, how many of them have this feeling for revenge in their hearts.

"We talk about this constantly on our block. In tones of how can we stop it? What can we do to stop it? But there is a feeling of defeatism in everything they say. You detect it. A feeling as if they have been sold out. They feel as though their government has sold them out.

"I tried to analyze this in my mind and I see the Negro is going to make great strides by virtue of the fact that he has the force, the militant force of the government behind him. This is the only reason he is going to make these strides. I am going to gain access to your home, but only because there is a man strong enough to break your door down behind me. You fear the man behind me. I haven't gained much in admittance, have I?

"Now it's an odd thing, the white people on every hand are screaming about what we owe the Negro, they're telling us the wrongs we have done, the wrongs we have committed against the Negro in the past, and they're doing everything in their power to alleviate this thing, to change it, to make it right. But each damned one of them, you better believe this, each one of them is wondering how much money have I got at my command? Where can I move if he moves next door to me? How far can I get?

"Depending on where they fit in the economy, where they fit distance-wise from the Negro, you can tell who is going to speak the loudest and the hardest for the Negro. The farther he is away from him and the more money he has, the more harder he will fight for him. But let the Negro breathe down his neck!

"I was raised in a Bohemian Catholic family. I remained a Catholic until I was about thirty. And then certain things became untenable. So I grew away from it. Maybe I'll be condemned to a certain kind of damnation, I don't know.

"Man is a creature of habit. He gets something, he grows to like it, he possesses it, he hates to give it up. Sometimes he'll defend a thing to the death rather than to give it up and it actually may not be worth anything. You've got to release some of the old ideas. If something's going to live, you've got to let something die, too. I mean, you can't have life without death.

"If Jesus returned to earth tomorrow and the average person were to see Him on the street, they would look at Him, point a finger and say, 'You lousy bum, why don't you go back to Old Town? Why don't you shave? Why don't you take a bath? Why don't you wash the garments you're wearing?' You better believe it. I think He'd be crucified, condemned as being some kind of crackpot. This I'm sure of."

14

The Irish

We choose to focus on the Irish for several reasons. One, they typify white, working-class middle America. Two, they are said to be the most likely ethnic group to slip out of the liberal alliance. Three, they are influential in our national life—in politics, unions, the Catholic Church. Four, they give us many clues about black-white relations—what they are and what they should be. Five, they illustrate some of the virtues and vices of ethnicity. Six, we know more about them than about other ethnic groups.

Kevin Phillips, a young Irish "brain truster" of Attorney General John Mitchell and Richard Nixon (both claiming to be part Irish), insists that the Irish are a significant part of the emerging Republican majority in the country, and will be increasingly so.

Among the ethnics, the Irish may be the first to slip into the arms of the WASP hegemony. Strange indeed, for it is these very Gaels whose loathing of the British and all that is WASP—based on genuine grievances—has driven them to almost permanent rebellion and centuries of guerrilla warfare in their own country, lasting to this very day. The Irish, along with the Jews, have been the most vocal spokesmen for the white minorities. While they retain this role and remain the most liberal of the Catholic minorities on many issues (as we have seen in the NORC study), there has been a conspicuous movement to the right from their ranks. They have not deserted liberalism, but they are moving away in more than a trickle and making fast friends of old foes.

As with other ethnics, a chief manifestation of Irish disaffection is backlash. They are "fed up with riots, drugs, and black demands for special privilege." It is paradoxical yet predictable that the Irish should be in conflict with blacks. According to what we might term the "proximity theory" of human responses, people tend to abuse those who are on the next rung down on the social ladder, those who nudge them most and are easiest to kick. Blacks are only a rung or so down from the Irish.

Except for skin color and the head start the Irish had in this country, the two groups are not dissimilar in history and culture. The basic experience they share is a long, bitter and recent history of colonial suppression and slavery. The masters were the same in both cases—the English upper classes. The Southern plantation and slave owners were, almost without exception, English aristocrats. The Irish had the same masters, an English upper class that occupied "John Bull's other island" for centuries.

For those who are not familiar with the sources of rebelliousness in the Irish character, William V. Shannon's
description of the hard years, continuing well into the
nineteenth century, is enlightening.

The Irish "toiled in squalor for English landlords and
merchants who possessed three-fourths of the land and
two-thirds of the trade. For three centuries, the Irish farmers had been sinking into the status of a landless peasantry.
They by now had no legal right or even fixed tenure to
the soil. They held their cottages and their pinched acre
or quarter-acre only if they paid annual rent to the land-
lord, often an absentee in London or Bath who never
showed his face in the neighborhood from one end of his
life to the other. To this economic subjugation, the English
added after 1691 the Draconian penalties of a new Penal
Code. Under these laws the Irish were beggars in their own
land, deprived of civil rights, mercilessly exploited, and
subject to hanging or deportation for trivial offenses." [1]

Under the penal code, the Irish language was forbidden,
and formal education became almost extinct. No Irish
Catholic could teach school, go to a university, work for
the government, or become a lawyer. No Catholic tradesman could have more than two apprentices. No Irish
Catholic could own a horse worth more than five guineas.

No Irish Catholic could vote, carry a gun, enter the
military, or serve on a jury. Priests were often arrested
and deported. Irish Catholics had to pay toward the support of the established Anglican Church. No Catholic
church could have a spire, and no Catholic could marry a
Protestant or buy land from one.

To retain any large piece of land, the Irish had to swear
allegiance to the Anglican Church. When a Catholic died,
his estate was divided among his sons, and thereby frag-

[1] William V. Shannon, *The American Irish,* New York: The Mac-
millan Co., 1966.

mented. If his eldest son became Protestant, the whole estate would go to him.

The code was applied for about 125 years, forming the character of the Irish into what it was when they came to the New World, and long after.

These brutal masters, of course, were the same Englishmen who ruled the American Colonies up to (and even after) the Revolution—the same people who imposed colonial rule on the people of India, Africa, Asia—and brutalized the agrarian and working classes of the British Isles. Some of their descendants still hold the bulk of American wealth and power.

Out of such histories of brutalization, the Irish and the blacks became subjected peoples. Like others in such a state, they didn't know whether to fight or be raped. Some fought. Some smiled, relaxed and tried to enjoy it. Many Irishmen and blacks shared the same dual impulses: hostility and acceptance, anger and good humor, bad temper and sweetness, earnest rebelliousness and the happy-go-lucky drunkenness, the desire to kill and the desire to please, hatred of the master and the need to woo him.

Many Irishmen became intractable rebels, passing their youth in borstals and jails. They filled the British prisons as the blacks fill ours. The Irish spawned terrorist groups (the Fenians in Ireland, the Molly Maguires in America) just as blacks recently have. On balance, the Irish zeal (in the old country at least) for guerrilla war, selective bombings, random acts of violence far exceeded (and still does) any comparable tendency among blacks. Like blacks, the Irish were great and willing street fighters, but they lacked the discipline (or the opportunities to develop discipline) needed to form effective military units. The Irish Republican Army was more formidable in legend than in fact, as the Panthers may prove to be.

The police who imposed the authority of the hated British on the Irish rebels were called "peelers." The Irish invested as much loathing and contempt in that word as blacks do in the word "pig."

The Irish sing proudly of their rebellions, as in this favorite tune about a hero of the Irish Republican Army, Paddy Mulligan, the man from Mullingar:

> The peelers chased him out to Connemara for beating up
>   the policeman O'Hara.
> And when he came to Ballymar, he stole the parson's car,
> and he sold it to the Bishop in the town of Castlebar.
>
> 700 peelers couldn't match him.
> The chief sent out the orders for to catch him.
> And when he came to Dublin town, he stole an armored car,
> and he gave it to the IRA brigade in Mullingar.
>
> Well, the peelers got their order to suppress the man at sight,
> so they sent for re-enforcements through the country left
>   and right.
> 3000 men surrounded him; they hunted near and far,
> but he was with the IRA in Johnson's motor car.
>
> They came with tanks and armored cars. They came with
>   all their might.
> Them peelers never counted on old Paddy's dynamite.
> On the 13th day of April when he blew down to July,
> the name of Paddy Mulligan is the pearl of Ireland's eye.

Many chose not to resist. They became Protestants, in this way winning favor with the English. Many became toadies, lackeys, sniveling servants. They were Uncle Toms before the word was invented—the "good" Irishman, the faithful servant, the loyal but lazy darkie, the lovable fellow who smiled, shuffled and said "yowser" a lot. What can you do with "the man" on your back?

Out of their servitude, the blacks and the Irish both became talkers, charmers, comics, minstrels, song-and-dance men. They talked easily and well because they were denied literacy and had no other way to communicate. They talked to charm each other and the master—lacking the power, wealth, or arms with which to establish more profitable relationships. They talked because they had no money for other entertainments and because, being often jobless, they had a lot of idle time for chatter.

The Irish talked, preached, orated, persuaded, amused, instructed. When they finally learned to write English, they turned to literature with a vengeance. Out came Shaw, O'Casey, Wilde, Burke, Yeats, Synge, Joyce, Behan and many writers in the States. (Their skill with language went back to days when Irish monasteries trained many of Europe's priests. In the ninth century, it is said, anyone who knew ancient Greek was either an Irishman or had learned Greek from an Irishman. The monasteries were closed by the English.)

Music and dance were extensions of the talk. Blacks and Irish *had* to sing and dance—to express themselves and to please "ole massa." These folk arts reached deep into the society, tapping the expressive resources of the lowliest toilers, yet speaking to people at all strata. The power of this folk music (reaching down into the guts, the soul of a people) and its impact on American arts, culture and youth can hardly be estimated. American country music has origins in Irish song, as jazz and blues have theirs in black music. The Beatles are Irish boys from Liverpool. Folk-rock has one foot in Harlem and the other in Dublin.

The Irish songs were sad and melancholy, like the black spirituals. They expressed underground sentiments, submerged or forbidden opinions, the common man's fears, longings, sorrows. The Irish love song and black spiritual often had double meanings. The Irish sang softly and patriotically of Ireland as the beautiful Kathleen Mavourneen, My Dark Rosaleen, etc., while blacks told stories of flights of freedom—"passing over into camp ground," "following the drinking gourd," etc. (Jamaicans sing of the "yellow bird, high on the banana tree"—the mulatto who is passing into white society.) The Irish songs were also, like black music, gay and spirited. The Irish jigged, tap-danced, soft-shoed, shuffled, and so did the blacks. Gene Kelly and Bill Robinson were the prototypes.

The Irish made jokes and fools of themselves, just as blacks did. The Irishman became the stereotyped "Pat and Mike" vaudeville comedian, scraps of which are still seen in Jackie Gleason. And the ordinary Irishman resented it as much as blacks do Amos 'n' Andy.

The English masters regarded the Irish as dirty, lazy, ignorant, superstitious, quarrelsome, uncultured. In a sense, they were right: to the extent that the Irish were enslaved and impoverished, they were indeed all these things. They were ignorant because the English closed their schools, forbade their language and excluded them from universities. They were superstitious because they were poor and ignorant—as blacks have been for the same reason. They were lazy because they had no work and no prospects. They were dirty, again, because they were poor and had few sanitary facilities. They were quarrelsome because they hated their condition and their oppressors. They have never regarded themselves, however, as uncultured and have always been as legitimately proud of their culture and history as blacks are of theirs.

The Irishman's sense of his culture and its violation are seen in this Irish-American song: ". . . The women in the upland digging praties speak a language that the strangers do not know. For the stranger came and tried to teach us their ways. They scorned us just for being what we are. But they might as well go chasing after moonbeams or light a penny candle from a star."

In both the Old and New Worlds, the Irish have known what the black man knows: the pain of being poor, being told by strangers to learn new, supposedly better ways, being treated as culturally inferior (if not innately stupid), and having to assimilate all the ugly (as well as the good) ways of industrial culture.

As for ambition, there was a rugged road ahead. If you have nothing to work for, what's the point of working at all? If the man is only going to keep you down, what's the sense in trying to get up? Take it easy, drown your sorrows, get a good luck charm. Many Irishmen became infatuated with booze, idleness and the pot of gold at the end of the rainbow. The Irish sing of Mrs. Durkin: "In the days that I was courtin' I never tried resortin', to the alehouse and the playhouse and the other house besides. I'm tired of all my pleasures, so now I'll take my leisure. Goodbye Mrs. Durkin, I'm sick and tired of workin'. The next time that you hear from me, I'll be diggin' lumps of gold. . . . No longer I'll dig praties. No longer I'll be poor."

2

When the Irish fled the pratie famine and came to the New World in the middle of the nineteenth century, they found lots of alehouses but few pots of gold. The Irish were, as a group, the dirtiest and toughest immigrants to disembark on American soil. Most Irish neighborhoods were sodden with saloons—surely as many drunks to the block as there are alcoholics and addicts in similar black ghettos today. Their neighborhoods in New York were so rough, bloody, dangerous that no one in his right mind, not even the police, ventured into them. The Irish became cops in New York, among other reasons, because only the Irish could enter neighborhoods like Five Points, Chelsea, Hell's Kitchen or Greenwich Village.

Many of these immigrants were called "pig-shit" Irish.

At the other extreme were the "lace-curtain" Irish who, like the "black bourgeoisie," adopted the manner and ambitions of the master. The ordinary Irishman, the average "decent man," who far exceeded in numbers the extremes at both ends, resented both the pig-shit and the lace-curtain types as disgraces to his race.

In the New World, the Irish were hated and feared—just as blacks have been. There were so many of them, they came all at once, they were so "dirty, lazy, hostile." More than that, they were "Papists," who would, if they could, put the Pope in the White House. Because they imported an alien religion, in this sense they were worse off than blacks, who at least practiced the master's religion.

Fear and hatred of the Irish produced the most "successful" racist party in American history—the Know-Nothing party. Before the Civil War, Protestant rioters invaded Catholic neighborhoods en masse, burned down Catholic churches, and savagely beat any Irishman they could lay hold of. The Know-Nothing party elected about seventy-five Congressmen in 1854–55, and carried most of New England, Maryland, Delaware and Kentucky. Its appeal was exclusively anti-Irish and anti-Catholic—as Wallace's appeal is largely anti-black. The Know-Nothings came out of an embittered Protestant "lower class," which, sensing the approach of a terrible civil war, wreaked its anger on a class even lower in the pecking order. Poverty and oppression do similar terrible things to all people.

History often repeats itself in this respect, each class turning on the one below it. The Irish draft riots during the Civil War were the worst in the history of any American city. The scapegoats in those riots were blacks, the only group worse off than the Irish. These draft disturbances were a classic illustration of the "proximity theory." Though the Irish grievance was with the class above them, they struck the class below. The upper-class, WASP North-

ern industrialists and abolitionists decided to make war—
and because the Irish lacked the three hundred dollars
needed to buy a son out of military service, they were
drafted to fight in numbers outrageously disproportionate
to their population.

When the draft riots broke out in New York City, the
Irish, who made up a third of the city's population,
looted, burned, killed for four solid days. During that time
they burned a Colored Orphan Asylum, hanged many
Negroes and beat up many more.

The Irish were pitted against blacks not only by industrialists who wanted war but by employers who wanted to
break strikes. In 1863, for example, blacks were used to
break a strike of Irish longshoremen, and frequently from
that date on were used everywhere to undercut the Irish
in the job market.

The Irish, plagued by bias, discrimination, and the
legendary signs NO IRISH NEED APPLY, thought they were
worse off than slaves. For this reason, they opposed the
abolitionist movement before the Civil War, and wanted
neither secession nor civil war. Still, swarms of Irish volun-
teered for the Union Army and served well the anti-slavery
cause, in numbers far exceeding their quota.

"The only difference between the Negro slave of the
South and the white wage slave of the North," said Con-
gressman Mike Walsh in the House of Representatives in
1854, "is that one has a master without asking for him and
the other has to beg for the privilege of becoming a slave
[getting a job] . . . The one is the slave of an individual,
the other is the slave of an inexorable class." He saw what
is obvious, except to the blacks and the Irish themselves:
that blacks and Irish were two peas in an Anglo-Saxon pod.

Most Irish are not strivers. Most value holiness, good
songs, good friends, more than material success, but they
cannot be happy to see others making it while they merely

hold on. Their thwarted affluence, the failure to find the crock of gold, along with their enforced servility, may account for some of their nascent conservatism.

As immigrants, the Irish had a marked advantage: they could speak the English language when they got off the boat. Their easy familiarity with the master's tongue gave them the prospect of rapid advance in the New World. They also came over here some half-century before many other big migrations. But despite these advantages, the Irish have not been able to compete successfully for the riches of the WASP, perhaps because they never really aspired very much to wealth.

The Irish have generally succeeded in fields where charm, talk, holiness and a tough hide are valued, but not in the Anglo's domain of wealth and economic power. The average Irishman is a true middle American—a low-ranking civil servant, a semiskilled factory worker, a salesman, a small merchant, a building tradesman, a dock worker.

Despite the many similarities in their backgrounds, Irish and blacks have collided—largely because they are in competition with each other and must share the same institutions, and because they are neighbors.

The Irishman is, typically, a Northern city dweller. As such, he collides with blacks everywhere—in his neighborhood, in the schools, on the job. The Irish seem less likely or able than other blue-collar groups to move to exclusive suburbs in order to avoid the collision. The Church and parochial schools have also held them, as well as Italians, physically in their old neighborhoods, as has their fondness for city life.

The Irish policeman has collided with the black youth; the Irish mother with the black mother on school busing. The two groups have confronted each other in the building trades and on all levels of the civil service. But, while they have been engaged in such conflict, their very proximity has brought many of them into close and agreeable contact.

3

Backlash, the proximity theory, the failure of the Irish to see what they have in common with blacks represent only one group of factors influencing the movement of many Irish to the right. Other factors are:

—The fact that Irish are no longer called "pig-shit"; some (like the Kennedys) have made it big, while others now own a little house they regard as their castle. Many have succeeded by learning to ape the master's values, covet his shoddy merchandise, serve him faithfully.

—The fact that many Irish boys have been drafted, and killed, in a war against communism.

—The fact that, out of a history of suppression, landlessness and foreign rule, many Irish tend to be rather pugnacious and patriotic.

—The fact that the Church and the Irish are so closely identified, and that exaggerated anticommunism exists in some quarters of the Church.

Irish thought is dominated by the Church, and vice versa. The Irish clergy, like their parishioners, at one time leaned heavily toward liberalism on many social issues, especially those not touching on marriage and the family. The so-called "American Schism" in the Church has to do with whether or not Rome would support non-Catholic trade unions and other social movements. Liberals like Cardinal Gibbons, Archbishop Ireland and Bishop Spaulding finally prevailed upon Rome to support American Catholic participation in the Knights of Labor during the late nineteenth century, and the Church in this country became Americanized and liberalized. The hierarchy in

New York, however, remained conservative—a tradition carried on by Cardinal Spellman in recent years. Since the advent of the Cold War, conservatism on the issue of relations with the communist world has become far more the general position of the American Irish Catholic clergy. Many churchmen feel that communism is the anti-Christ. This conviction probably has many sources: the suppression of churches in Russia and China, and the "atheistic" proclamations of these nations; defense of private wealth, of which the Church has a great deal; competition for the hearts, minds and souls of men. Such a conviction also comes out of plain hysteria and fear.

Radicalism, black and white, that leans toward Maoist, Castro or Soviet politics, sounds a shrill alarm to many clergymen and devout Irishmen. McCarthyism is simply dormant, not dead: any sudden swerving to those brands of radicalism could revive it—more demonic than ever. Already the combination of New Left and black militant politics has opened Joe McCarthy's grave a crack.

By contrast, the Church in Italy has somehow managed to live with the largest Communist party in the Western world, with few visible signs of anguish. The Irish, many of whom are ideological purists, have made fewer adjustments than Italians to the changing currents in world politics. When they get hold of a devil, they do not easily let go.

In some Latin American countries, the position of the Catholic Church with respect to the key issues of expropriation, land reform, nationalization and social welfare is almost identical to that of the communists.

Perhaps the greatest miracle the Church could perform for its members, the international community and middle America would be to modernize its position, in the Pope John style, reconciling its stance to the changing conditions and survival needs of the modern world.

In Ireland, ironically, the Irish tend toward statism in the conduct of domestic affairs. They have, recently at least, been rather quick to take public initiatives in solving social problems. Far more of the Irish economy is publicly owned or subsidized than that of the States, and apparently nobody thinks these public initiatives are communist, immoral or atheistic. Moreover, like most Catholic people, the Irish tend toward a communal view of life—a rather strong sense of mutual responsibility, community welfare, the brotherhood of man and the sharing of assets. On their own sod, they show almost no respect at all for the "capitalist way of life," either as an inspiration for individual conduct or as a means of organizing the economy.

At least on their own island, the Irish do not venerate rugged individualism, striving for riches, or industrialization. They seem to dislike industry, smoke, superhighways, big cars, big factories, plush hotels. They even have mixed feelings about tourism. They like homespun, handicrafts, a bit of green land, some fat sheep, small textile plants and a public house. Most do not care much for big money and big profits, and will not change their life to accommodate industrialization. As a result, the Irish Republic is officially listed by the U.N. as one of the "developing" nations of the world. The major "industrial" city of the Republic—Cork—is as charming and pastoral as the British industrial cities—Liverpool, Glasgow, Cardiff, Belfast —are ugly and oppressive. Paradoxically, all these British cities contain large Irish populations, impoverished migrants who are as unhappy there, and as belligerent about it, as they were on landing in New York. In all these places, however, they are learning to conform to the Anglo ideal, which is quite different from the one they cultivate on their native soil.

Another factor that has contributed to the Irish swing to the right is clannishness, a quality nourished by a history of oppression in their homeland, and passion for their incredibly beautiful island. The quality was born at home in the rebellion, but it has not withered in the New World. Many Irishmen are reflexive patriots: give them a song of battle to sing, a glass of ale to drink, a flag to wave, and they are fulfilling their ancestral heritage. This ready sense of patriotism often shifts to their new home country: Irish patriots become American patriots.

Still, the Irish in America today are not happy about the war or the draft. Both issues generate discontent. Gallup and Harris polls indicate that the Irish don't like the Vietnam war any more than anyone else does, though many are foggy about whether or not there is any justification for the war. One thing they are not foggy about is equality of sacrifice. The Irish are pre-eminently draftable, being—as a rule—literate, physically fit, and less likely than many other groups to go to college. They are not at all happy that the college boys, the sons of the affluent and rich, are exempt from service. And, with their sons being shot at by real enemies, they are not likely to be pleased by Panthers dressed in Castro-esque uniforms, or college rebels waving Vietcong flags.

4

Irish culture is strong. It is not easily bent or transformed, and it resists offending codes. It is distinguished by several qualities. Some of it springs from the Irishman's brand of Catholicism, with its rather extreme puritanism with regard to sex and the family. The Irishman does not entertain "indecent" thoughts about women or any unnatural or illegal sex objects. Probably there is less sexual deviation, pornography—but more frigidity and frustration—in Ireland than anywhere else in the world. Marriage and the family are so sacred and binding that, in Ireland, many men are afraid to partake of them at all. (On this score, the Irish, and the blacks—who are more relaxed and less puritanical in these matters—have something to teach each other.) The Catholic League of Decency, a powerful national organization, which flourished for some decades of this century, for the purpose of censoring books, films, etc., was an Irish creation. Though it is gone now, its spirit lives on. Many Irish are still deeply offended by immodesty, violation of marital vows, sexual perversions, pornography. Many are alarmed by radicalism that threatens the Church or by coercive regimes, as in the communist world, that resemble British colonialism.

To know the Irish is to know their experience, their strengths and weaknesses. The Irish have faults, many of them, but they also have real needs and grievances. Theirs is not a "pig culture."

In the Irish vernacular, the word "decent" sums up a code of personal morality and a style that is old-fashioned but not "pig shit." A "decent man" is a good and respected one. Modesty is his proper standard of behavior. He must dress modestly, treat women with respect and modesty, be humble before God. His language in front of women and children must be decent. Preferably, he should have modest ambitions. The revered heroes of the decent and modest man are the saints and scholars.

The life's reward of the good Irish mother is to have a son, preferably the most promising, enter the priesthood. In honor and prestige, the priest ranks above all those who tend the material and temporal world (doctor, lawyer, merchant, engineer). The honest craftsman (carpenter, plumber, pipe fitter) is also more honored than in most other cultures.

The Irishman's basic resistance to industrial culture has somewhat tempered the fierce competitiveness of American society. His leisurely style of life is needed more than ever in our uptight society, as are his good humor, decency, quick tongue and simplicity of style.

We may stretch ourselves, as we should, to understand the black man's culture so that we can appreciate him and work with him. We may support, as we should, black studies for students. Yet if we really seek a brotherhood among men, this understanding must be broadened. We must not, in our attempts to elevate one culture, turn away from another culture and disdain its values. If we examine the Irish perspective, we may see some justice in what they and other ethnic cultures say. A revival of ethnicity, and pride in ethnicity, can perhaps reduce the excessive standardization that is enveloping American mass culture.

Much more to the point, the Irish and blacks themselves, along with other ethnic outsiders, need to identify their common interests and common enemies and, with this knowledge, reconcile their crippling differences. The Irish Catholic, out of his own history, should be able to understand the fervor of the blacks. Out of his own experience, he should be able to join with blacks and others in advancing a common cause against the oppression of wealth.

15

Workers

The blue-collar working class is neglected, misunderstood and villified by stereotypes and false images. So much garbage is written about workers—when anything is written about them at all—that it is hard to know where to begin an honest portrait. As authors we were confronted with an absence of research from which to draw documentation. Therefore we can only write about workers out of our own firsthand experience with them, an experience which has spanned many years.

In some ways workers are like the classes above them, only less so—modified versions of their "superiors." In other respects, the working class has a distinguishable culture all its own. Though this culture has a central tendency, there is much deviation from it. The working class is far less homogeneous than the middle class, since fewer selective factors are operating. To rise into the middle class, aspirants must, almost by definition, conform to a rather limited set of norms, which *are* the middle-class life style. They must pass standardized tests. They must meet certain rigid qualifications. They gain admittance to this group early in life if they attend the right schools and use their education to find jobs acceptable to middle-class standards. Admittance later on is usually predicated on a business promotion to a position of relative economic or social prestige. The worker, on the other hand, is part of the working class by virtue of the simple fact that he works.

Considerable variation is found among workers, even in matters of style and dress. When employers try to impose uniform dress codes in shops, they are usually met with passionate resistance from workers. On the job, workers can shout, sing, argue loudly, curse and do almost anything as long as it doesn't slow production. There are no "office codes" of decorum, nor would workers permit their imposition. Such verbal license is also part of life off the job.

Many outlets for expression of rebellion are open. Language need not be pure, correct, clean. Long hair (e.g., the duck-tail) and exotic hair fashions (e.g., the mohawk, the pompadour) have always been common with working-class boys. Until the middle class adopted maxi-length hair styles, working-class boys typically wore their hair at a modified midi-length, and still do in the British working class. The "skin head" protest among English youth is a negligible phenomenon.

To those who find in others only the thrill of the chase, who see only money, power, status in the eyes of cocktail companions (contacts for moving-on-up), the working class offers little. Many young workers have real vitality and individuality, but if they stick to their jobs for long or fail to acquire a skill, their jobs may make them spiritless and uniform, like the parts stamped out on their presses. Even then, it is remarkable what a diversity of styles the working class can sustain.

Working-class culture is rarely polished, pleasing or sophisticated, but at its best it is honest and unpretentious. Because workers tend to be honest and blunt with themselves and others, as parents they usually avoid the charge of hypocrisy that is leveled against many middle-class parents by their rebel offspring. A worker is more likely to get angry with his kids, to tell it to them like it is, without resorting to manipulation and emotionally dishonest "child-rearing" concepts.

Early sex knowledge and experience (for boys) is also part of working-class culture, along with a frank and earthy acceptance of the animal nature of mankind. At the same time, strict prohibitions on the sexual conduct of women are common. Middle-class youth is at last breaking the sex barrier—looking at "art" films, writing four-letter words on campus walls. Working-class males have already been there, having arrived at a very early age.

Working-class youth are not as likely as middle-class youth to revolt against materialism, since their parents, while perhaps overly occupied, are not obsessed with material things or the accumulation of wealth. They are, moreover, still struggling to acquire basic necessities. Workers seek material possessions more for the sake of comfort and security than for status and power.

Though far from satisfied with their lot, workers are usually not so hungry or striving, so intent on getting ahead as classes above them. They want the good life, of course, but their concept of it is a house big enough for the family, the material conveniences, some money in the bank, an interesting job. For this very attribute, which is surely more a virtue than a vice, they are criticized by those writers who talk about "failure to postpone gratification" as a source of working-class failure in school and work.

The "upwardly mobile" behavior involved in pleasing (or brown-nosing) teachers, bosses, "superiors" is quite foreign to most workers, hence many of their problems in school, work, life. Yet in this way workers escape the fakery that can undermine self-respect and the sense of identity. Workers are less likely than the upwardly mobile to conceal their real feelings and thoughts in an effort to please or manipulate others for the sake of favors.

Similarly, workers are not likely to fake optimism and good cheer. They do not always smile, look at the bright side of things, expect the best. Yet they are generally cheerful rather than gloomy. They usually take life as it comes and do the best they can. Working-class youth—wanting less, expecting less, accepting more—can often tolerate more frustration and develop more staying power than middle-class youth.

Though we have spent a lifetime with workers we have never seen one slobber at the dinner table like Joe, in the film of the same name. What is different about their manner is that they rarely knock themselves out to please others in the more superficial ways—open doors for women, shake hands with everyone, introduce people, see that guests are served first.

Because life is harder for workers, with greater scarcity and more pushing and crowding, they tend to be rather distrustful of others. Some of the wariness is caused by insecurity and a sense of impotence, inability to control their

own destiny, reliance on others for decisions. At the same
time they often place their unshakable faith in a few
leaders.

Among the negative features of the worker's life is his
built-in remoteness from the outside world. He is almost
out of touch with the world for eight hours a day, or however long he works. He doesn't have a phone at his elbow,
as office workers do, nor even easy access to a phone. He
doesn't move around in the world as a salesman, professional, merchant, or executive does, but is usually shut up
in the plant during his working day, with no outside contacts at all. Nor do outsiders come to him, as they do to
retail clerks or restaurant workers. Often he doesn't even
travel or vacation but spends his leisure, instead, viewing
the world via TV. Inevitably such remoteness limits him
as a person.

What George Orwell said about the British working
class a few decades back still applies, with modification,
even to the American working class: "This business of
petty inconvenience and indignity, of being kept waiting
about, of having to do everything at other people's convenience is inherent in working class life. A thousand influences constantly press a working man down into a passive
role. A person of bourgeois origin goes through life with
some expectation of getting what he wants, within reasonable limits. Hence the fact that in times of stress 'educated'
people tend to come to the front; they are no more gifted
than the others and their 'education' is generally quite
useless in itself, but they are accustomed to a certain
amount of deference and consequently have the cheek
necessary to a commander."

The American worker is too often inclined, in absorbing the American way of life, to give up the old and simple
things for the new.

2

Like most Americans, he is a compulsive consumer in a mass market of food, furniture, clothes. The ethnicity of his home is often traded for a tasteless imitation of new styles. Old fashions and handcraftsmanship are abandoned for chrome, limed oak, fancy figurines, bad reproductions. The supermarkets and super shopping-centers, from which he buys his food, offer him an imposing array of products—most of them bland, hothouse, ersatz, tasteless. The shopping and buying themselves are presumably made palatable by the pursuing presence of canned, ersatz, twinkling music, the music of the super canned society.

Workers from rural backgrounds are close enough to the earth to remember what good home-grown food tastes like. Yet so utterly supermarket-oriented has the worker's shoping become, that the direct purchase of food from farmers is almost unknown. Hothouse tomatoes are bought during the tomato-growing season. So much is frozen or "processed." There is usually no fresh fish. No fresh corn; it's all shipped a week old. No tree-ripened fruit. The chickens are tasteless and juiceless. Then there is the delicious, and symbolic, apple—beauty on the outside and blandness inside. Nothing is homemade, irregular, unique. Some workers—those closest to the soil—show their distaste for the tasteless by turning back to old-fashioned country cooking—hominy grits, country ham; but most simply go along with the supermarket trend.

In the same way, much of what the worker consumes—the furnishings in his house, the television he watches—is not his choice or taste at all, but that of the mass media and mass producers. In the arts, however, the natural expression of workers often still comes through. A man can't produce his own TV shows, but he can strum his own guitar, dance and sing. None of these require capital or corporate power. The worker's tastes, creations, recreation, intelligence and culture are assaulted by those professionals in the mass media who impose their own style and taste on workers, and by those in the academy who cloister Art and Culture and admit only the elite to their inner sanctums.

Professional television people come with two approaches to their work, though the results are basically similar: there are the mass-market people, who erroneously think they will capture most buyers by repeating clichés about cowboys, secret agents, doctors, cops and robbers, the Jones family; and the "cultivated" people whose "educational" presentations often kill the viewer's desire to learn and feel. Neither understand their audience a bit. That they are a mile off target can be seen in the thunderous popularity of the televised football game, the one program that TV professionals have absolutely no control over. By comparison, the contrivances of television producers get meager ratings.

Among the other professionals who typically ignore or exclude workers from their consideration are those who preside over libraries, universities, projects for the "creative" use of leisure, parks and recreation, art institutes, performing arts centers, public theaters, museums. They are the chosen custodians of Culture. From their high perch they shine and polish their treasure and protect it against the invading hordes. They are brilliantly successful at keeping workers out.

The overwhelming bias of professionals is illustrated in the place given to courses for adults and workers by universities. It is practically no place at all—with almost no standing, status, or funds. Some philanthropic souls take an interest in laborers, but usually on their own terms.

They have all the questions and answers; the worker has no chance to come through.

All these artists, experts, professionals, teachers conspire against the working class, and workers pay them handsomely for it. The average worker gets so confused by such misappropriations of his taxes that he comes to doubt his own impulses and tastes. "I don't understand it," he says, and leaves it at that. If professionals bothered to expose their wares or talk to him man-to-man (listening as well as lecturing), some of them might be able to enrich the worker's life, as the worker has enriched theirs with his improvised arts.

Workers are not without expressive talent. Most American popular and improvised music originates in the working class. Jazz and rock come from black workers; country and folk from white workers. The grand-daddy of white rock, Elvis Presley, is the son of a truck driver. Johnny Cash is thoroughly working class, as are many Southern musicians. Some of the best folk music came out of the mines, from men like Merle Travis ("Sixteen Tons" and "Dark as a Dungeon").

Middle-class youth have taken over this music because it has more guts and feeling than the stylized music of the academy. The music that inspired Bob Dylan, for instance, was played by hill folk and Southern workers many decades before he picked it up from Woody Guthrie and others. Sinatra, who has no peer in American popular music, came straight out of the Jersey City Italian working class. In Britain working-class musicians abound. Among their most popular exports to the States are the Beatles, Joe Cocker, Tom Jones—all working-class in background and style.

Still, those who write or otherwise depict the doings of our society studiously ignore the lives and talents of workers. While the British give some dramatic recognition to the working class, as in the films *Saturday Night and Sun-*

day Morning, This Sporting Life, Loneliness of the Long Distance Runner, if we are to judge by American films and television, nobody works for a living except doctors, trial lawyers, sheriffs, spies, cowboys.

Occasionally a worker will appear in a film. *Woodstock,* for example, featured one worker going about his duties: a "sanitation man," cleaning out the portable johns. The man is interviewed as he sloshes the johns with his hose. His responses—which seemed unusually intelligible relative to other things said in the film—were *translated* for young middle-class viewers into English subtitles, to underscore the ridiculously alien quality of the man.

Then, at last, came Joe, a working-class "hero." Joe is presented to us in the film of the same name as a raw slice of working-class life. He is large, rather burly, Irish, probably in his early thirties but bald. He has a fat belly; he talks a lot and loudly, in a thick Bronx accent; he belches loudly when he eats; he gobbles his food and eats with his hands. When he learns that a nice middle-class man has killed a drug-peddling hippie, he becomes the killer's fan and companion. The odd part about this slice of life is that actor Peter Boyle, who plays the lead, makes Joe such an authentic and winning fellow, a man incapable of real cruelty, under all the belches and racism, that very little he does in the film seems possible, at least to people who know any Joes like him. The film's director took the traditional comic Irishman, the vaudeville buffoon of another era, and turned him into a killer. The trick fails and the viewer, seeing Joe with his guns, half expects him to go into a soft-shoe dance.

While the violent racism of some blacks is often understood and forgiven by many New Classmen, similar dispositions among white workers are deplored. Such blacks are tough and militant, while their white counterparts are authoritarian and repressive. The language of the ghetto

is imitated, while the language of white workers is regarded as simply ungrammatical.

Workers, we are told, love authority and hate change.
"The privileged," says Louis Harris, in an extravagant
display of objective pollstering, "have become the pro-
genitors of change, while the underprivileged whites have
become the steadfast defenders of the status quo."

He misunderstands. Workers simply oppose change that
always benefits others and hurts them. In this, they resemble many who serve on college faculties. That is, they
resist change that threatens them personally, and can afford to take grandstand postures on issues that do not.

According to a 1968–69 survey of 60,447 faculty members in higher education around the country, faculty sentiment runs strongly toward liberalism in politics and
toward conservatism on those academic issues that affect
their self-interest. (Of the respondents, we must note, 82
percent were male and 94.4 percent were white—reflecting
the fact that higher education is one of the sturdiest
bastions of white male privilege in the country.)

In general, the faculty members were very unsympathetic
to the methods and often even the goals of student pro-
testors. They tended to reject all criticism of higher education and proposals for its reformation. The American
professoriate, concludes the surveyor, "looks much more
liberal than the general population or than other professional groups on national and international considerations.
But when you shift to questions of campus demonstrations
or educational change, where they are directly involved,
you find a very marked shift in orientation. There is a
striking and clear shift toward a more conservative attitude where the faculty's immediate self-interest is involved." [1]

[1] *The Chronicle of Higher Education,* Carnegie Commission on
Higher Education, April 6, 1970.

The image of blue-collar workers as racist and conservative is a gross stereotype. The worker who thinks that dissenters should be shot or deprived of civil liberties exists, but he is not typical. The same variety of bigoted and reactionary responses is prevalent in other groups. The worker has been maligned, assaulted, ignored. Lacking the means to defend himself or his image, he turns to the Wallaces and the Agnews who make vituperative speeches in his behalf but clobber him economically. Aside from economic issues, perhaps nothing grieves the worker so much as the contempt universally displayed in our society for his culture. His anguish is intensified by the fact that he has no articulate defenders or champions.

16

Unions

With the exception of the schools, no American institution has come in for as much public criticism as unions. Schools have been on the front burner only in the last several years, while unions have been there since their inception. Almost every social lapse and irregularity of unions is featured in the press and, with some exceptions, the best-known union leaders are those who have been embroiled with the law. Much of the criticism is richly deserved.

Critics charge that unions are mostly wrong on Vietnam. The critics are right. The official policy of the national AFL-CIO is shaped by two men. One is George Meany, a

seventy-six-year-old Irish plumber from the Bronx, a
Catholic from the archdiocese of conservative Cardinal
Spellman. The other is Meany's foreign policy adviser Jay
Lovestone, once a communist leader and now a rabid anti-
communist, a sophisticated ideologue who provides the
polished rationale for these policies.

Even hawk Lyndon Johnson met with Soviet premier
Kosygin. Nixon went to Moscow and met with Khrushchev.
George Meany not only will not enter the Soviet sphere
but will not speak to anyone from that sphere who comes
here. Nor will he let the State Department allow "unionists" from that sector to enter the States. "Capitalists"
and representatives of virtually every American corporation move freely into and out of the Soviet countries, but,
to our knowledge, no craft union leader has ever made the
move.

But labor unions are not homogeneous. Many unions
are far over at the other end of the hawk-dove spectrum—
including the two largest unions, the Teamsters and the
UAW, which together represent more than 3.5 million
workers. Other unions also dissented from official AFL
support of the war, including the clothing workers, public
workers and meat cutters. In some cases the dissenters
joined in late, but the same can be said for many liberals
and leftists.

The war cannot be passed over lightly for it reflects our
national purpose, ideology and the interests of the mili-
tary-industrial complex. Important as it is, however, war
is not the only issue in the nation. It is not even the only
issue of concern to students and young people. Nor can it
be the only issue that concerns critics of labor, since most
of them were equally critical of labor before the Vietnam
war began.

Many unions and their leaders have been guilty of
thievery and the grossest undemocratic and antisocial acts.

The savage murders of Joseph Yablonski, his wife and daughter, appear to be connected to the courageous opposition he put up to the United Mine Workers' Union leadership. Some others have met a similar fate. More often, those who sought to change the union or question the practices of union officials have been beaten up (as recently happened in the National Maritime Union), barred from union ballots by specious and frivolous qualifications, or counted out by dishonest managers of union elections.

In some marginal industries of the big cities, the small "independent" unions are ruled by racketeers. Membership in these various unions may run into the tens of thousands. In most cases the victims are black and Latin workers who need the protection of unions perhaps more than anyone else. Aside from the Association of Catholic Trade Unionists, however, almost nobody has paid much attention to the scandalous operations of these "independent" unions.

Some union leaders are vain and impossibly arrogant. Some are "on the take," while others have been corrupted by the luxurious emoluments of their positions. Still others have been subtly corrupted by invitations to Presidential balls, and social acceptance by their "betters," who have admitted them to their fancy clubs, fed them at their posh restaurants, put their names up for public awards, and in other ways played on their vanity.

All of these things are well-known. Moreover, while it is possible to discuss the role of most institutions without personifying their villainies, the same doesn't hold for unions. Con Ed (polluter of our air) is not personified, nor is GM (maker of a car "unsafe at any speed"). These giant corporations have presidents, yet we never see their faces in the media. Discussions of unions, however, usually feature particular "villains"—Meany, Powers, Shanker, DeLury—whoever happens to be bothering people at the

time. They are highly visible "devils" while the corporation executive is nameless and faceless.

The truth about union leaders is that as a class, they
are rather quiet men who, away from their jobs, simply
fade into the general lower-middle-class landscape. Very
likely less than 5 percent of full-time union officials make
as much as $20,000 a year. Nor are huge incomes hidden
behind fat expense accounts. The highly publicized International Presidents and Secretary-Treasurers who receive
$50,000 a year are the rare specimens. There are not more
than twenty of them. Compared with leaders of other
large institutions, even these are not grossly overpaid. Our
most informed guess is that the average salary of full-time
union officials is probably around $15,000 a year.

Take an average American worker, imbue him with
some sense of class injustice, make him somewhat more
militant than average, bless him with the capacity to articulate his grievances and with some everyday political
skills, and you will have an approximation of the average
union leader.

Unions, of course, have little right to complain about
their treatment in the media. The public has a right to
expect higher standards of unionists. The union movement
has certain moral pretensions. Union leaders often purport
to speak for social justice and emancipation. Their sole
justification for being is their claim to be concerned about
human welfare. Given such pretensions, they cannot expect to be judged by the entrepeneur's standards, which
justify any antisocial act in the name of efficiency, productivity, higher profits.

Unions are like churches, as Walter Reuther used to
say. They must accept all comers as members, sinner and
saint alike, but they cannot afford to put the sinner in the
pulpit. Too many unionists are insensitive to this simple
truth.

The proverbial open mind, however, often snaps shut when unions are mentioned. On very few subjects is so much misinformation taken as fact, nor bias so readily considered objective judgment. Every dog—even if he is "old," "bureaucratic," "decadent," "undemocratic," "selfish," "corrupt," "counter-revolutionary," "communistic" —deserves his day in court.

The perspective of those who live in New York City may be subject to special distortion. New York is a center for light manufacturing. Construction, trucking, shipping, garment making, service trades—and white-collar jobs— are found in the city. It is *not* an industrial center. Hence, neither industrial workers nor industrial unions inhabit the city in significant numbers.

This is unfortunate. New York is the center of communications in our society. Radio and TV, book and magazine publishing, *The New York Times* and *The Wall Street Journal*, the foundations that support writers and researchers are all there. Not incidentally, it is the financial capital of the country and the headquarters of most major American corporations. But most New Yorkers may search in vain for industrial blue-collar workers or for contact with industrial unions. The closest many will come is the marginal Puerto Rican garment worker, the hardhats (whom few New Yorkers talk with anyhow), the cabbie, the cleaning woman, the waiter. None of these is an industrial worker.

London is so much saner and sweeter a city than New York because—among other reasons—the real working class is so liberally mixed in with the New Class and whitecollar residents of the city. Out of this mixture (and the far more intimate size of the country) come exchanges and awareness that lead to a meaningful political collaboration (albeit, a stormy one) between intellectuals and workers— and the creation of a Labor party which, for all its flaws, has dragged the Tories almost into our era and created, even out of scarcity and a loss of empire, a reasonably viable and happy society.

Not only New York but also Washington, D.C., center of political power, has a critical shortage of blue-collar workers and even industrial union headquarters. It is a city almost exclusively of public administrators, corporate lobbyists, white-collar workers, service workers and the poor. The view of unions from either center is skewed, yet it colors much of what is said and written about unions in the media.

2

Not all students are bomb-throwers. Not all blacks are enraged, and not all are passive. Not all Italians are gangsters, and not all are saints. Jews are neither all rich capitalists nor all poor communists (nor *poor* capitalists and *rich* communists). Nor are all Irish either pig-shit or lace-curtain. In the same way, unions are not a single entity. Not all unions are righteous, and not all are reactionary. They run the whole gamut. Within the worst and the best—including most craft unions—are good elements and bad ones, enlightened policies and indecent ones.

For example, most New Yorkers are keenly aware—as they should be—that the Sheet Metal Workers and other building trade unions in the city have bad racial policies. The problem is that these New Yorkers are not equally informed about other unions. Most New Yorkers seem unaware that many unions in the city, even some in the skilled trades, have exemplary racial policies. Large unions such as District 37 (State, County and Municipal Workers), Local 1199 (Drug and Hospital Employees) and District 65 (Distributive Workers) include in their ranks and leadership tens of thousands of unskilled blacks and Puerto Ricans who have fought their way to better social and economic status through their unions. Yet these groups are never taken as typical (and indeed they *aren't*), though the Sheet Metal Workers, which has excluded blacks for generations, *is* taken as typical (though in fact it *isn't*).

Harry Van Arsdale, hard-working leader of New York's electrical workers and Central Labor Council, typifies the city's union leaders as much as do the publicized hard-hat leaders. He has reached out to bring minorities into his union, and he did it before the issue had attracted much public attention. Through an active recruiting campaign he brought more blacks into local 3 of the IBEW than were in all other locals of that union combined. Moreover, he has sponsored large education programs for members, helped organize the unorganized, marched on picket lines for grape workers, and done other good works. Yet his "nonpartisan" policies lead him to oppose Lindsay and support Rockefeller, and his conservative style leads him to loathe hippies and student rebels. His politics and style are too conservative (from the authors' point of view), but that ought not to obscure his many solid virtues. In fact, he is far from the loathesome union bureaucrat of the popular caricature.

Unions are usually neither as good as District 37, nor as awful as the New York Sheet Metal Workers. Some have excluded blacks and other minorities, and some, like Cesar Chavez' United Farm Workers (AFL-CIO) have championed the excluded. The grape workers were nobly served by the young idealists who manned picket lines in good weather and bad, months on end. But they were also served by thousands of members from various unions who, responding to Chavez' call for aid, raised money for the strike, and walked picket lines in working-class towns around the country. According to Chavez, the union's major sources of financial aid were the AFL–CIO and the UAW. Without them the union might have been starved into submission.

Similarly, the struggles of black hospital workers and sanitation men in Charlotte, Memphis, Atlanta, Jackson, have been led by AFL-CIO unions and supported financially by the national AFL and the UAW.

The conventional, and erroneous, wisdom about unions has deepened the schism between black and white workers and kept blacks from making progress through the labor movement.

Young blacks who turn away from unions might ask themselves: How can the *majority* of blacks (who in overwhelming numbers are workers) achieve any real status in the society *soon,* other than through unions? Isn't it obvious that efforts to promote "black enterprise," even if successful beyond Roy Innis' fondest dream, cannot affect more than a handful of black people? Blacks should, of course, control institutions and enterprises in their own communities, but even if they win such control, the effects on most ghetto residents will be minimal.

Though their representation is inadequate, blacks have won more influence in unions than in any other social institution. A study of black powerlessness, conducted for the Urban League in Chicago and Cook County, Illinois, found that unions had a larger percentage (13 percent) of black "policy makers" than any other private institution.[1]

In welfare and religious organizations, whose constituents were often largely black, 8 percent of policy-making posts were held by blacks. The universities (including Chicago, a citadel of radical academic opinion) had a

[1] Harold M. Baron, with Harriet Stulman, Richard Rothstein and Rennard Davis, "Black Powerlessness in Chicago," *Trans-action,* November 1968.

negligible 1 percent representation. Most of the universities had few black students, faculty, or administrators. The University of Illinois had one black policy maker. Roosevelt University was the sole institution that had a number of blacks at the top. Only *five* out of 380 policy-making posts in these universities were held by blacks.

In all of Cook County only 11 percent of all policy makers hold either political or union office. Yet *almost half* of all the Negro policy makers were found in these fields.

In three-fourths of the former CIO local unions, blacks were represented in leadership. In two-fifths of the former AFL locals, *no* blacks were represented, *but one-third had leaderships that were 15 percent or more black.* Even the AFL, in this study, looks better than Chicago's universities, churches, welfare and other organizations. Some of these institutions are learning that they can't cop out by claiming there aren't enough "qualified black applicants"—any more than the Sheet Metal Workers' Union can.

In the UAW, Negro membership may reach 400,000. About 25 percent of workers in auto's Big Three are black. About eighty blacks serve as full-time international representatives of the UAW. Perhaps only the NAACP and the Urban League employ a larger block of black policy makers. Two of the twenty-two members of the UAW's International Executive Board are black, as are the directors of some of the union's national departments.

Even in the carpenters' union, among the most exclusionist, black membership is about 2 percent of the total— higher than black proportions in most Northern college faculties. Craft unions are generally more integrated than the staff of *The New York Times Magazine,* in whose pages unions (all unions, not just some) were described as the "principal barriers" to black advancement—and certainly more integrated than the faculty of Princeton University, where the black author who made this charge has a temporary and token position.

More blacks belong to unions than to any other non-religious organization.[2] Black membership of the UAW and Teamsters (the Alliance for Labor Action) is perhaps 750,000, and as many as 2.5 million blacks are members of AFL-CIO unions.

Industrial unions are very likely the most racially integrated organizations in the country—not necessarily out of inherent virtue, but because the CIO saw from the start that it had to include black workers if it was to organize along industrial rather than craft lines. Though still far from equality, unionized blacks enjoy most of the advantages won by white members.

In the years of the official war against poverty, union victories at hospitals and in other service trades probably had as much economic impact on the ghetto as all OEO programs combined. In the South, blacks have begun to see in unions a promise of real social and political advance. Public employees have waged historic strikes in Memphis, Charlotte, Atlanta. Martin Luther King went to his death in one of these struggles, and Ralph Abernathy to jail in another.

[2] According to Bureau of Labor statistics, almost half the members of the 550,000-member Laborers' Union and of the 50,000-member Longshoremen's Union are black. In all, forty-five AFL-CIO unions have black membership that is relatively higher than the proportion of blacks to whites in the total population (about 11 percent). A number of large unions have more than 20 percent black membership. These include: State, County and Municipal Workers (400,000 total members), Meatcutters-Packinghouse (488,000), Letter Carriers (168,000), Postal Clerks (139,000), International Ladies Garment Workers (440,000), Building Service (398,000), Laundry Workers (25,000), the American Federation of Teachers (205,000), and possibly United Steelworkers (about 1.1 million).

Blacks in the ranks of the work force are increasing rapidly—from 520,000 to 752,576 black "craftsmen" between 1965 and 1969, and from 1.6 million to 2.1 million black operatives in the same period.

Social as well as economic benefits flow from black participation in unions. The union activist learns how to organize and work with other people; he learns how to get things moving and get things done. He learns how to settle his grievances—with his fellow workers and with his employers. A union is, by its nature, an orderly and organized alternative to individual frustration and violence.

Most significantly, in the *integrated* union especially, the activist learns the politics of coalition. This is part of the art of negotiation, but more basic. If a candidate wants to win an election, he must advocate a program with broad enough appeal to win him a majority of votes. A white racist in a largely black local can't win, nor can a black racist in a white local. Even if his local has only a minority of whites, a black candidate may lose an election if he turns that minority against him.

Finally, the integrated alliances formed among unionists seem far more an agreement among equals than are the working arrangements between blacks and middle-class counterparts or student militants—where a certain condescension and mutual contempt are often present. Certainly it is a far healthier relationship than that between residents and outsiders in the ghetto. White and black workers are much alike. They tend to be tough and pragmatic. They are far less snobbish in personal relations, social life and aspirations than middle-class people. Their relations are more natural because, for whatever reasons, the white worker seldom carries around the white man's burden of racial guilt. He does not work with blacks because he is "sorry for them."

3

Casual and ad hoc protest organizations of blacks, students, the poor or women have not yielded the results hoped for. Very little has happened, as far as the reordering of our society goes—not to mention the revolutionizing of it.

Though civil-rights and black-power groups have left their mark, the groups themselves are ephemeral. Student groups are even more transitory, perhaps because the students themselves are highly "perishable": they grow older, they graduate or lose interest. So they disappear—and their organizations along with them. These groups do not have a chance to become "bureaucratic"; they simply vanish.

The labor union's permanence gives it stability and at least the possibility af greater democratic control. To contend with corporate power, workers can hardly organize as casually as students can. They must have an experienced, full-time staff, offices, headquarters, a body of procedures, a dues structure—an organization that is tough, tried and durable.

The union's procedure and permanence give it the order and regularity usually needed in a democratic organization. By contrast, in an ad hoc group, minorities and elites can easily control or disrupt meetings. Anyone can vote and speak. An outsider (from administration or management, for instance) can enter a meeting, pack it with friends and relatives (who are also outsiders) and take over the meeting and the vote. Meetings can break up in chaos if each person is allowed to do his own thing, delaying and disrupting. Or, the chairman, unrestrained by procedural rules, can himself control and manipulate a meeting. Without a membership roster or procedural rules on elections, a single person or a small elite can easily elect or appoint itself to office.

The ad hoc group, of course, has certain useful functions. It can sometimes move quickly to needed action; it can sometimes discuss and clarify more easily than groups bound by procedures. It can also become a lynch mob, or one that is unable to control minority fanaticism.

Permanence and procedures do *not* automatically ensure democracy and majority rule, far from it. They can cripple democracy and deal harshly with minorities. But *without* them, over any period of time, democracy is subverted. Or if it can survive, it is usually only in small groups, where sentiments are shared anyhow. Let's face it, orderly procedures are "bureaucracy." But bureaucracies can be very good or very bad. The intent is to make them as responsive as possible both to the majority and to the minority. Unions cannot operate like floating crap games; they must have permanence and procedures: they *must* be bureaucratic.

In the Marxian schema, only organized workers can make basic changes in the economic structure of the society. Whether the Marxian view is accepted as true or not, the worker and his union do have certain advantages over other groups. The labor union is an economic organization, and contends with the major economic institutions of the society.

Because of their economic leverage, unions have considerable social power, and the potential for even more. They can shut down plants, stop production and profits. They can bring our economic life almost to a standstill by closing the postal service, the transportation system and other arteries of commerce.

Unions have power also because their jurisdiction is so vast. Since most of us work for wages or salaries, most of us are prospects for unionization. By contrast, the jurisdiction of groups organized by college students and blacks is far more limited. Unions are, by far, the biggest organizations in the country committed to social and economic change. They can reduce the powerlessness of workers, black and white. They can bring authority under control, and open avenues to social change. They can enable people in the lowliest jobs—garbage workers, for instance—to force the powerful to consult with them and negotiate the terms of their labor.

Well-organized unions are *inherently* powerful; that power is accessible to those workers who lead or influence these unions. Aside from the controls they have over wages, hours and working conditions, unions can lay hands on strategic levers of social change. They often influence and sometimes control their members' investments in pension and insurance funds. Some of the nation's largest housing developments have been built with such funds, as well as hospitals, clinics, resorts and other community facilities. (Under black influence, the constructive investment of these funds could enrich life in more than one corner of the ghetto.)

Unions collect and spend significant sums in political campaigns. They issue publications to their members. For eight hours each day they have access to millions of workers on the job. They can influence legislators. They spend money for salaries, office rent, supplies and services. They provide legal counsel for the victimized. They can buy time on radio and TV. In meetings, negotiations, strikes, conventions, they offer opportunity for the development of leadership skills.

4

One popular cliché says that unionism and blue-collar jobs are withering away. Actually, the 26.5 million employed blue-collar workers at the end of 1968 exceeded by 2.3 million the number employed in 1960.

The number of union members, while down somewhat from 1955 as a percent of the work force, has risen in absolute numbers to a record of about 20 million. More important for the future, the fastest growing unions (Federal Workers; Teachers; State, County and Municipal; Teamsters) are organizing in the services that are most rapidly expanding. When unions organize the South, as they will one day, they will tap another fast-growing work force. Unions and workers are obviously relevant, growing not withering, and so it will remain for many decades.

Not only do unions flourish in the blue-collar field (despite automation and technological change), they are making inroads into expanding white-collar, technical and professional fields. During the three years ending in 1969, unions added 3 million members, mainly from the white-collar work force. Union members are now 30 percent of the total nonagricultural work force; they are still only about 11 percent of white-collar workers.

Geography (more specifically, *the South*) is a large barrier to unionization. As the South rises and its cities grow and industrialize, workers are turning to unions. Employer resistance is strong, however, and often savage, as in the days of the sit-downs, some forty years ago. All but seven of the states with the lowest proportion of union membership are in the South and Southwest.[3] Some Southern cities are ripe for organization. The Southern Christian

[3] UNION MEMBERS AS PERCENT OF NONAGRICULTURAL EMPLOYMENT, 1966.

Most unionized states:				*Least* unionized states:			
W. Va.	44%	Mo.	36%	S. Car.	7%	N. Mex.	16%
Mich.	41	Ohio	36	N. Car.	7	Utah	17
Wash.	40	Mont.	34	S. Dak.	10	Ark.	17
Pa.	38	Minn.	33	Miss.	12	Vt.	17
N.Y.	37	Ore.	33	Fla.	14	Kan.	17
Ind.	37	Calif.	32	Texas	14	Ariz.	18
Ill.	36	Alaska	30	N. Dak.	14	La.	18
				Ga.	14	Ida.	18
				Okla.	15	Neb.	19
				Va.	16	Tenn.	19

Leadership Council, with its national headquarters in Atlanta, follows Martin Luther King in its zeal to unionize black workers. Success there may spread to other industrial centers of the South.

Union power is far more decentralized than critics assume. Only three unions have more than one million members. The largest, the Teamsters, has only 9 percent of all union members. The five largest have 30 percent of membership. (By contrast, in Germany, the five largest have 60 percent.)

Most unions are baronies rather than kingdoms. That is to say, much local autonomy exists. The local, district, or regional union usually has more power, funds and function than the national union. Industrial unions tend to be more centralized than craft unions—simply enough because they deal with bigger and more centralized employers. The craft union is also less homogeneous in its character than the industrial union. It is misleading to talk about *any* craft union as though it had a single quality or character that applied equally to all locals or districts. Local autonomy makes the craft union wildly heterogeneous in character. While George Meany is thought to be *the* spokesman for a united labor movement, in fact, his power is quite limited, as is the funding of the national AFL-CIO. Mainly the power is in the separate national unions and their locals.

Most collective bargaining is carried out at local and regional levels, as are most strikes. *About half of all strikes involve fewer than a hundred workers.* Such decentralization of structure and bargaining suggests that unions may be closer to members and their sentiments than is usually assumed.

For the most part, says the chief economist for the Bureau of Labor Statistics, union constitutions and union operations recognize majority rule, rights of minorities, and safeguards to fair elections.[4] Union officials are regularly voted out of office, not only at the local level but increasingly at the national level. Incumbent presidents who were defeated in recent years include those of Steel; the IUE (Electrical Workers); State County and Municipal; and the Insurance Workers. Moreover, union presidents fought hard for reelection in Textile, the Mine Workers, District 50 and Government Workers—and strong opposition kept incumbent presidents from running in the Chemical Workers and the Federation of Teachers.

Of 186 national unions, 22 percent changed presidents during the two years ending in 1967. At lower leadership levels, the turnover is even greater. At these rates, union bureaucracies cannot be totally encrusted.

Members can affect and change their unions in other ways. Most importantly, they can reject agreements negotiated by top leadership. In 1967 alone, over a thousand agreements were rejected by the membership—or more than 14 percent of the cases in which the Federal Mediation Service was involved. Members may also vote to decertify their bargaining representative. Still, only about 5 percent of all representation cases coming to the National Labor Relations Board involve decertification petitions. That *most* union elections are honest and democratic may be underscored *by the fact that less than 150 election complaints are filed each year under Landrum-Griffin, out of about 18,000 elections for union officers held annually.* Dishonesty and fraud occur in some union elections, but they are exceptional.

Some critics of unions claim that labor and management are so close that the strike is becoming obsolete. Yet strike losses during 1967 were the highest since 1959 (still less than 3 percent of total work time). About a third of

[4] Peter Henle, "Some Reflections on Organized Labor and the New Militants," *Monthly Labor Review,* July 1969.

these strikes came during the life of the bargaining contract. Most involved a small number of employees and were
of short duration. Many were "wildcats," in violation of
contract. The persistence and growth of strikes certainly
suggests that individual members are not without means
of protesting their collective grievances.

Other critics of unions (often the same ones, in fact) insist that there are *too many* strikes and too much time and
production lost in them. Everything is relative. While 22.9
million man days of work were lost in strikes during 1964,
for example, *forty times* that number of work days were
lost in unemployment. And about *twice* as many man days
were lost from work injuries as from strikes. If "lost time"
were included from injuries occurring in past years but
continuing into 1964, the loss would be about *eight times*
as great for injuries as for strikes.

5

The mythology that obscures the features of
working-class life derives partially from the "success story"
of unions and what observers have made of that story.
Unions have made real gains. But they started from very
far back, and they still are far from the millenium. Since
our society has been late and miserly with social insurance, unions have had to push hard in collective bargaining for benefits that don't show up in pay checks.
Their focus on such goals has some negative side effects.
Fringe benefits mean more to older than to younger workers—and it is the young who are drawn to men like George
Wallace.

But unions have an obligation to the aging, as much as
to the young. Pensions had to be fought for and won. Pensions cost money, and these costs were subtracted from the

wage package won at the bargaining table. Also, older
workers need more hospitalization and medical insurance.
These too came out of the total package, leaving less for
wages. It was humane to help the older worker, and it
enabled him to retire with dignity and make way for
younger workers. But it was costly. In the UAW alone,
more than 200,000 members have retired and received
pension benefits of over $1.5 billion. Unions have some-
times overresponded to the older worker, as in seniority
and vacation benefits, but one can hardly look at the life
of the aging worker and say he has too much.

Unions need to pay more attention to the needs of the
young. An aging and sometimes feeble union leadership
needs to refresh itself with new leadership recruited from
younger workers. Unless the young become partners in the
union movement, they may end up wrecking it. The
dramatic rise in the rate of rank-and-file rejection of union
contract settlements is a clear signal of workers' disapproval
of the top union leaders who negotiate these contracts.
Usually, veteran unionists report the increased rejections
result from organized opposition among young workers.

Unions are, however, limited in what they can do for
members. First, they are limited by the willingness of their
members to go into battle, to strike. Then they are limited
by the public's willingness to accept strikes. The middle-
class liberal, for example, is often offended and sometimes
outraged by strikers. He may say, "They're only out for
themselves." When the desperately poor hospital workers
strike, he will say, "Pity the poor patient." But he will
offer no clues as to how else the hospital worker can get
some measure of justice. When subway and sanitation
workers strike for a modest $3.50 or so an hour (to per-
form some of the most disagreeable jobs known to man),
many middle-class liberals still complain.

Above all, unions are limited by the overwhelmingly

superior economic and political power of the corporations and other employers with whom they deal. That a union can go into the ring at all with a corporation like GM or GE, for example, is remarkable enough; that they can stay in and land some punches is nearly miraculous.

Unions depend for their power on the morale and solidarity of their members, and on their desire to fight and work for what they seek. As far as financial power goes, unions aren't in the big leagues. The total net assets of all unions are somewhat over $2 billion. General Motors alone, with *one* year's income (let alone assets), could buy up all the assets of all the unions in the country and still have left, after taxes, almost half a billion dollars. To speak, as some do, of "big unions" and "big corporations," as though they had joint title to the assets of the nation, is misleading. Unions have their holdings almost exclusively in the consent and initiative of their members.

It is said that unions are only interested in higher wages and production, regardless of the public interest. Unions are indeed interested in higher wages and better working conditions. Given the depressed living and working conditions of their members, they should be. They are also interested in what they produce, but there's not much they can do about it. Such are the facts of alienation among workers, the separation from responsibility for the product of their labor. Neither workers nor unions have *any* control over *any* production decisions. None of the key production decisions made by management—such as those concerning the kind, quality or quantity of goods produced—are under union control. They are all prerogatives jealously guarded by management. Unions can raise some of these issues in negotiations, as auto workers have raised the auto pollution issue, but such demands have almost always given way to management resistance and the more pressing and immediate needs of workers.

Production issues are a matter for general social policy and require *legislative* action. Here the record of unions is better. They are, indeed, the only major organized power bloc in the country that consistently and actively supports legislation to protect the interests of consumers and regulate management production decisions.

This balance of power brings us to a riddle. Unions strike because they have to—because pay checks fall behind inflation, because the condition of the working class *is* as impoverished as we describe it. For all this, the union worker is demonstrably better off (financially and otherwise) than comparable workers who are *un*organized.

But corporations can set prices at whatever level the market will bear. Thus price rises finally erode wage increases. Clearly, other instruments are needed to buttress the strike and the wage hike. The economic competition of publicly sponsored enterprises with private producers, through pace-setting companies is, in some countries (Sweden, for example), one way of reducing profits and prices somewhat. Such pace-setters, financed either with public or cooperative money, could be developed here also, to compete with private industry in monopolistic fields and to generate the price competition that many large industries now lack. Competition from *publicly* financed pace-setting industries would, as in Sweden, raise quality and hold prices down.

What members and their unions engage in is not "class struggle" in any classic sense. Their conscious antagonists are the employer and the conservative legislator, not the "capitalist system." Yet their efforts have sweetened that system considerably. Unionists have tasted enough of victory to know that this is not the "final conflict" for which the "prisoners of starvation" must arise. Unionists will not be found mounting the barricades. They have learned hard lessons after almost a century of fierce bloodletting on the picket line. Probably they have been too moderate in this respect, for open conflict is one good way to rally people and get what you want. But they have learned many other good ways to get on with it. Unlike some militants, they will not be found burning down their neighborhoods to prove a point, or otherwise sacrificing their own ranks in unproductive or self-defeating conflict. Industrial unions, of course, and unions of the poor and black tend to be far more "class conscious" and to have a longer tradition of militant class conflict than the older and more conservative craft unions, some of which never even carry on strikes.

American unions are not "revolutionary" organizations. If we mean by revolution what the Jacobins in France and the Bolsheviks in Russia meant by it—killing the king, seizing power and property by armed force, carrying on civil war with political adversaries—then American unionists are truly *counter*revolutionary. Only a handful of workers and unionists would want to march on Washington or Wall Street, bayonets drawn, and try to seize power.

If by revolution we mean something much less "glorious" than a Molotov cocktail in the police washroom or the flaming rhetoric of unconditional surrender—if we mean by revolution "profound change in the social system," then most unionists would go along, but more in fact than in principle. The advocate of "profound change" must be *very specific* about what he wants and how he's going to get it before unionists will give him a sympathetic ear. They will not take a pig in the poke or exchange poor conditions for intolerable ones. Great variation will be found in opinions about the kind, the speed, and the strategies of change, but the average union activist will favor change in most social institutions.

If unionists want change, why don't we get more of it? Partly because some unions are not militant enough about it, and partly because they don't know what to do or how to do it, but mainly because they don't have the power to shake things up.

Interested outsiders can help with all these things. The career of Ralph Nader has shown clearly enough what can be done. His vitality, integrity, dedication have probably stimulated more unionists than the collective work of all writers and scholars around the country.

Joe Rauh, another Washington lawyer, is a second case in point. Rauh has taken the initiative in a sweeping variety of issues that interest many unionists. He played a leading role in seating the Mississippi Freedom Party at the Democratic convention. He has been directly and centrally involved in the plight of miners and the Yablonski elections. He had a critical part in the defeat of Carswell and Haynsworth for the Supreme Court.[5] All are tangible and constructive acts performed by an outsider in collaboration with unionists.

Like Nader, outsiders can help unionists to understand the principle of planned obsolescence as it operates in the economy. They can help them see how shabby, dangerous, undisposable, overpriced and unnecessary is so much of the junk turned off our assembly lines. Workers also *consume* and they are no happier about what they buy and what they pay than anyone else.

Unions have been anything but sensitive to their common interests with the intellectual community. Out of fear of "long hairs," union leaders have failed to oppose— sometimes even joined—campaigns of intellectual repression. They have not seen that when a society closes down on the nonconforming social critic, it will surely follow by

[5] In the Carswell and Haynsworth cases, Rauh worked with the labor movement (including George Meany), which was, by common acknowledgment, most responsible for these significant and unprecedented Presidential defeats.

throwing the union agitator in jail. They need only to look to the South for evidence of that, or to Joe McCarthy and Barry Goldwater, stalwart enemies of unions and "long hairs" alike—or to George Wallace, who combines slick anti-unionism with hatred of intellectuals.

On their side, intellectuals might be expected to see that a nation where workers are atomized and powerless, as they are without strong unions, is unlikely to provide a congenial setting for the serious social critic.

As students and others see the true fascist elements revealing themselves in our society (as early civil-rights workers saw them in the South; and as they were seen in Memphis, Kent State, Chicago, Dallas), they may see *some* unions in a different light. Against that background some unionists may even seem progressive.

The old radical movements once trained union leaders. Even today a large number, especially in the industrial unions, are out of that movement. Unions still need to be refreshed from time to time with intellectuals, ideologues, social critics—the Jesuits of the union movement—but ones who will offer tangible programs, not pie in the sky.

We believe it will be difficult to build a sane and equitable society, or establish the coalitions we have referred to, unless many people in the society, on both the right and left, give some concentrated attention to unions—and unless unions, for their part, dramatize themselves and their causes enough so that people can see them for what they are.

17

Alliances and Policies

In a sense, all people, from menials to million-aires, share some interests in common—but some share more than others. In the past, the people at the bottom—the poor, ethnic minorities, blacks, youth, workers—have shared many interests and, together with enlightened members of the middle class, they have formed political alliances to advance those interests. In general they have shared a desire to acquire some of the power held by the very wealthy. They have also advocated programs of full employment, a high and equitable living standard, and adequate health, education and welfare.

The political alliances of these groups have been stormy

and volatile, as may be seen in the relative disorder of
Democratic party conventions as contrasted with Republican ones. Recently, these erstwhile allies have behaved
more like enemies. Many workers scorn the poor, blacks,
welfare recipients, youth and other political allies. Many
blacks charge that all whites are enemies, and many former
middle-class allies see workers and unions as reactionary
and racist.

The schism between workers and middle-class progressives has been deepening for several decades. They were
closest during the New Deal, brought together by objective
conditions—Depression, war, and the charismatic personality of Franklin Roosevelt, aristocrat, Harvard man,
WASP, and hero of the workingman. Since then, relations
have been rather disjointed. Aristocrat Adlai Stevenson
spoke more to the New Class, and aristocrat John Kennedy
more to the working class. Eugene McCarthy, a college
professor, elected to the Senate with trade-union support,
turned to the New Class in the 1968 campaign. Humphrey
lacked appeal to either group, in the end.

Eugene McCarthy told a university audience during the
Oregon primary that Robert Kennedy was running best,
"among the less intelligent and less educated people in
America. And I don't mean to fault them for voting for
him, but I think that you ought to bear that in mind as
you go to the polls." McCarthy, Arthur Schlesinger comments, was attempting something novel in progressive politics—" a revolution *against* the proletariat."

Many issues need clarifying if we are to reunite old allies
and reconstruct our society along democratic-humanist
lines. We believe that middle-class opinion makers need to
awaken to some realities of American life. Many of them
live at rarefied levels where almost everyone's income is at
least $15,000 a year. *Less than 10 percent of the nation's
families earn that much.*

Opinion makers, most of whom are in that 10 percent,

think of themselves as open-minded and sensitive, and sometimes they are, but too often their politics are intro- spective—concentrated only on issues that touch them, plus a now-fashionable interest in the poor and blacks.

Their politics are sometimes expressed in the kind of vinegary liberalism that led Senator McCarthy, in his en- dorsement of Humphrey, to plead for the rights of honest draft dissenters but to say nothing about the draft's dis- crimination against blacks, the poor, the working class— and make no significant comments about other social and economic issues. The Senator's failure to ignite fires out- side the middle class can easily be understood in the light of that arid statement.

The chemistry of the Kennedys has been different. The contrast was highlighted in Senator Edward Kennedy's appeal to supporters of his two slain brothers to reject the "dark" and "extremist" movement of George Wallace. "Most of these people," Kennedy said of Wallace support- ers, "are not motivated by racial hostility or prejudice. They feel that their needs and their problems have been passed over by the tide of recent events. They bear the burden of the unfair system of Selective Service. They lose out because higher education costs so much. They are the ones who feel most threatened at the security of their jobs, the safety of their families, the value of their property and the burden of their taxes. They feel the established system has not been sympathetic to them in their problems of everyday life and in a large measure they are right." If a meaningful new politics is to work in this country it must be based on the kind of empathy expressed in those words.

A turning point in the Presidential campaign may have come when Humphrey began to see something Wallace had always understood: that while many "experts" said the "old issues" were dead, millions of American workers angrily disagreed and wanted a better life.

Wallace's bigotry finally did him in among many Northern workers. Industrial workers generally have closer relations with blacks than any other class, and the big factories in steel, auto, rubber, glass, etc., are probably the most integrated work places in the society. Most workers who were drawn to Wallace because he spoke their economic language must have fallen away from his camp as his campaign became more violent in tone.

When opinion makers bothered to talk with workers they found to their surprise that not all were racists. After talking with Wallace supporters in Flint, Michigan (said to be a hotbed of Wallace sentiment), Mike Hubbard, a student editor of the University of Michigan *Daily,* wrote: "Certainly these Americans do not identify with red necked racism . . . No one ever taught them Negro History, but they grew up with blacks . . . They don't dislike blacks, they just feel black men shouldn't be given a bigger break than anyone else. The white UAW members as a whole do not believe Wallace is a racist. All they know is what he told them, and he never said he hated blacks. Even the most militant Negro workers I talked to didn't feel there was large scale prejudice in the Union. They dislike Wallace, but not the men who are voting for him."

An effective coalition must consider the special interests of each participant. Radical blacks, for example, have been lukewarm in support of groups whose overriding concern has been war and peace, to the neglect of other issues. Antipollution activists, similarly, have been denounced by black activists for distracting people from "the real issues." None of these groups can win the needed support until they *join* issues.

In politics, we all seek satisfaction of our own needs. When we insist that there is only *one* really important issue (or even two or three), we are demanding that others accept our priorities. We can make some friends that way, but we can make a lot more enemies, especially when our terms are non-negotiable or when we make no effort to persuade others who have pressing claims of their own. Isolation, frustration and political extinction are inevitable for those who refuse to accept the realities of coalition politics.

Progressive coalitions are heavily handicapped. They are up against the traditional conservatism of great wealth and concentrated power which, with relatively minor exceptions, supports the Republican party. To hedge their bets, some of the wealthy also contribute to liberal candidates, but such support is comparatively negligible. Since *everyone* in the nation, from the wealthy to the small-town voter, suffers from recessions brought on by Republicans, the steadfast support of conservative economics by these groups defies reason and self-interest.

Progressive candidates cannot compete in a market where elections increasingly are bought and sold. In the 1968 Presidential election, for example, Republicans spent about three times as much as Democrats. While elections were once won by door-to-door and personal contact, now candidates are more likely to enter homes on expensive television time.

In a democratic society all electoral politics must be based on coalitions. Both the Democratic and Republican parties are coalitions, as are all other mass parties in the democratic world. A third or fourth party in the United States might include forces not now adequately represented in either of the major parties, but even these would necessarily represent coalitions if they wished to rally mass support or even sustain themselves. The Labor party in Britain and the New Democratic party in Canada are also coalitions of groups that are only somewhat less disparate than those in the Democratic party.

It is a false dream that a party wedded to a finely detailed ideology can win power in the foreseeable future, though it could play an effective educational role, and might achieve power in a period of deep crisis. Or, as has happened in some European countries, it might win a kind of tenuous power after decades of persistent mass education and organization.

The American political temperament may not be suited to such patient political commitment. Radical groupings come and go. Most cannot persist in the face of frustration and rejection. When they last, they are usually held together by small bands of true believers. Such groups are often unwilling to settle for the long haul and the gradual accretion of numbers and influence that are necessary to build a new electoral force that might give voice to the aspirations of the American left.

Dissident political groups that turn to independent electoral activity usually spin their wheels in fruitless campaigns. They are left exhausted, frustrated or angry, and cut off from the people to whom they should be speaking. Such campaigns often leave scars that are beyond healing. In their weakened condition, radical groups almost never make it back into the mainstream before the time comes to set the whole process in motion again and run another campaign.

Perhaps changes in the electoral system could make it easier to form new parties. Proportional representation, for example, could make it easier for minority parties to elect candidates. In this way disaffected minorities could forge a clearer political identity, as they do in many European countries, and experience more success within the electoral system.

Electoral politics, however, is not the only vehicle for political participation. Many dissenters apparently can't think of political activity in nonelectoral terms, though history is replete with examples of movements that have shaped political events, though their leaders did not contend for public office.

Martin Luther King can hardly be written off as a political nonentity, though he was always reluctant to endorse candidates and his organization was nonpartisan. The prolonged struggle of the NAACP for civil rights was in most respects successful, though nonelectrical. Cesar Chavez has been much more than a union leader. He has drawn more sustained attention to the plight of the migrant workers, especially Chicanos, than anyone before him. The boycott of grapes by the Farm Workers Union was a political education campaign, one that profoundly affected the way young people and others view society. Thousands of rather conservative and unconcerned young people participated on the side of the dispossessed in that campaign and came to identify with their cause.

Ralph Nader has perhaps moved as many people to important social activity as did the campaign for Eugene McCarthy. The various antiwar movements that sprang from original beginnings in SANE have affected the nation's political climate and forced public officials to deal with peace demands. In Britain, the tiny Fabian Society put its stamp on nearly a century of British public policy.

When public opinion changes, so do laws, public officials, political parties. Fifteen years ago, some Republicans were calling for the return of TVA to private hands; twenty-five years ago, for the abolition of Social Security and unemployment compensation. These demands were abandoned because they meant political suicide. As Vice-President, Richard Nixon was the most warlike of hawks, calling for an invasion of Indo-China when we had no commitment there. His proposal was scornfully rejected by President Eisenhower. Nixon as President, however, has given grudging ground to pervasive antiwar sentiment.

It is said that nothing can stop an idea whose time has come. An idea's time arrives when the way has been prepared for it. The time has come for all kinds of ideas about how to deal with the problems of our time. The *will* to deal with issues imaginatively is needed, as well as the energy to organize for public education and action around proposed solutions.

Even without effective national leadership, for example, local citizens have slowed down and often stopped the urban renewal and expressway bulldozers in many cities. What is lacking is a set of ideas that might make up into a national program, one that could give people in affected communities some hope that they can defend their loved enclaves without accepting the blight that still remains where the bulldozer stops.

2

We offer here not a statement of policy for a political party but a series of suggestions around which a program might be created that would appeal to the largest mass of Americans—the poor, minorities, blue- and white-collar workers, students, war protesters and enlightened members of the middle class. Such a program cannot be based on introspection or concern only for one's own family and friends. Our society is being torn apart because, while serving almost no one well, it fails utterly to deal with the problems of the overwhelming majority. Large numbers of middle Americans will continue to resent the poor, the black, the Mexican Americans, the Puerto Ricans, as long as they fear for their own security and feel that others are getting unjust shares of the rewards. Political programs that ignore this fact will further divide progressive sentiment in the country.

As a society grows more complex, clearly it becomes more difficult to administer rationally from a centralized point.

The effort to impose upon local programs rigid federal guidelines leads to frustration and ultimately to disaster. On the other hand, many programs must be national if they are to be effective. Control over pollution of the air and water, for example, can be managed only by a federal agency which can dictate standards for rivers and lakes that run through or border on communities in many states. The air over New York City is polluted by cars in Manhattan, but also by the oil refineries and factories in the New Jersey meadows—and Chicago's air is fouled by the outpouring of refineries and steel mills in nearby Indiana.

Traffic and transportation in many big cities is an interstate problem affecting not only the central city but the suburbs that are often located, not only outside the city, but outside the state.

Also, problems such as education (which can probably be effectively administered only at the local level) cannot be funded except through the federal government's power to tax real wealth, which is national in character, and so situated that it cannot be taxed by local groups.

So, while the problem of local control is real, and movement in that direction must be made if democratic forms are to survive, the movement must be a partnership between local communities and the federal government. In most cases the money must come from Washington, with control over funds being given to local groups and authorities whenever possible.

All programs depend on local initiatives and organization to define needs, agitate for change, engage in direct action where needed. Direct action by citizens can prevent, and often has, the imposition on communities of undesired state and federal programs—as in highway construction and urban renewal. The problem with cities, however (perhaps aside from New York), is not that too much is imposed from outside but that the cities are starved for funds and are grossly neglected by the federal government, which *has* access to money.

Ideas have been advanced for raising private capital locally, for local programs and to support the diversification of local industries. Jane Jacobs argues that the growth and health of cities depends on diversification but that capital is often unavailable, or deliberately withheld, from new types of industries in localities that are dominated by a few giants.

To be relevant, a political program must start with a declaration to end the war in Vietnam as quickly as American armies can get out. An end to the war will make it possible to begin the work of internal social reconstruction. After the war, the pendulum will probably swing against the military. Before the momentum slackens, a campaign for reduction of the more insane items in the Defense budget should be mounted on a continuing basis. Weakening of the military in this way would have the effect of undermining the most powerful reactionary force in the society.

The basis for creating a powerful coalition against military spending already exists in the Members of Congress for Peace Through Law, which has a combined membership of Representatives and Senators totaling about a hundred. This committee predicts that its proposed cuts in the military budget would result ultimately in savings of $95 to $100 billion.

We have accepted for so long the Defense establishment's every demand that we no longer comprehend its staggering dimensions, nor the floodgate of possibilities that would open to us if the military's power could be curbed. Some of the proposals made hereafter may appear grandiose, but all could be underwritten for at least a few years if the ABM were abandoned and plans for aircraft carriers and new tanks scrapped.

Programs of physical reconstruction, especially in the cities, can give millions of embittered people some hope for the future, unite deprived whites and blacks, and reduce the anger that drives many to the arms of demagogues.

The following proposals are not at all comprehensive, nor do they cover even all the issues raised in this book. They are merely suggestive of the kind of program that might appeal to and rally a majority of decent and progressive voters.

—Underwrite the development of attractive prefabricated housing by industry, preferably by consortia of companies now in the war business. This would ease the transition for both workers and business from war to peace.

—Provide mortgage subsidies to housing cooperatives to underwrite large-scale housing and redevelopment at interest rates between 3 and 4 percent to members. Such a measure would give cooperatives a market advantage over the wildcat real-estate developers who create suburban blight across the country. Since such mortgages would be federal, they would be available only to groups that are integrated, thus providing powerful incentives to break segregated housing patterns.

The combination of prefabrication with cheap mortgage money could make excellent housing available at not much more than $100 a month. Through such cooperatives, even welfare families could become home owners and the blight of race- and class-segregated housing reduced.

A clue to the kind of housing that might be produced is found in the trailers that have pre-empted a large part of the single-dwelling-unit market. Sleazy as many are, and often produced by underfinanced fly-by-night operators, they still offer housing that can't be matched in conventional markets for less than twice the $5,000 to $15,000 they cost.

If General Motors can build and market a large Chevrolet, equipped with power brakes, power steering, air conditioning, automatic transmission, radio, deluxe trim at $3,500 to $4,000, it could build precast and prefabricated modular housing components in high-grade two- and three-bedroom units for not more than three or four times that amount.

Even if building tradesmen were paid $8 to $10 an hour to erect such units, the on-site labor cost in modular buildings would probably not be much more than $500. With an interest subsidy of 4 to 5 percent, the unit could be sold without down payment at from $100 to $125 per month, depending on location and taxes. Steady and plentiful jobs could be made available for union construction workers in the process.

—Provide federal subsidies to regional authorities to develop high-speed mass transit. Money could be made available on a matching basis. Areas unwilling to cooperate through regional authorities simply would not receive money.

In this way a giant step could be taken around the now-archaic local government structures that impede regional development. Sometimes as many as a hundred governmental units operate in a single county. Regional governments are needed to tie these fragments together and cope with metropolitan problems. Such federally subsidized authorities would help prevent the starvation of central cities. They could also, through federal authority, require black representation on regional boards.

—Provide subsidies for the development of experimental high-speed electrical and steam-powered minibuses for use in central cities, for air-cushioned vehicles to be used in interurban transit; and similar technological experimentation that might replace cars with mass-transit facilities.

—Give grants to regional authorities to promote clean air and clean water programs on a regional basis. Such money (supplemented by local funds at the rate of one dollar for every five of federal funds) could build the most modern sewage treatment plants, clean up rivers and lakes, detoxify the smoke output of public buildings, beautify unsightly dumps.

—Make federal investments to reorganize the nation's job and career training facilities, with special emphasis on the expansion and enrichment of community college programs to train people for work in new careers—in medicine and other fields of developing shortages. No program of national health care can provide decent care with the present impoverished level of medical manpower. New occupations, beginning with the doctor's assistant and going down the scale—jobs at which people can learn while they earn—need to be developed across the country.

Thousands of women now working as registered or graduate nurses could be upgraded to aid doctors and serve as the equivalent of the old-fashioned family doctor. Similarly, nurses' aides could be upgraded to replace the registered nurses who move up. Young men with field experience as medics in Vietnam and other war zones could be trained for similar occupations and quickly put on jobs where they could earn and learn at local hospitals and community colleges. They could be paid from manpower training funds as much as $3,000 a year, to be supplemented by similar amounts at the local level. Their tuition could also be paid for out of public subsidies.

In the field of mental health, people who wish to work part-time could be trained as companions for older people, many of whom could be kept out of public institutions if regular visits (three or four times a week) were made by trained people who could help with simple tasks and re-

duce the isolation of the aged ill. Thousands of paraprofessionals could be trained to work at home with people
who have been released from mental hospitals, but who
may still need guidance and assistance.

In the new field of pollution control, manual workers
could be quickly upgraded to jobs as water inspectors,
clean air inspectors, water technicians, landscapers, etc.

Generous expansion of community colleges could de-
mocratize the class structure by providing more accessible
opportunities for the poor and the working class—and by
postponing for two years the class segregation that now
takes place at the time of high-school graduation.

Universities and colleges could give up the job of educating freshmen and sophomores and deal only with those
who, being somewhat more mature, may be better able to
use what the university has to offer. By postponing the
decision two years, the late starters would be better able
to qualify for the university, and the student body in
higher education might thereby be democratized.

Also, the depersonalization many students complain
about could be minimized by reducing university size, and
requiring students to take their first two years at a community college. If they could qualify for a career after two
years, many young people might decide to go to work for a
few years before entering the university. Thus the community college program, adequately financed, could have
an altogether beneficial effect on American education.

At all levels, there should be subsidized experimentation to give students experience with the real world—in
and out of schools—and develop in them the ability to
cope with reality.

As it is, the schools cloister youth much too long, keeping them from productive endeavors and from the exciting
and tough world of real life. The schools are often far more

confining than liberating. They often dampen rather than excite curiosity. Surely we can do better . . . and if we don't we may have a full-blown student mutiny on our hands, reaching down to the lower levels of public schools. Very likely, were education to be made more a part of the real world, the poor and the average American would be far less disadvantaged in the new setting than they are now. They have a stronger thirst for practical knowledge and a greater aptitude for it than the more "academic" minds that are cultivated in affluent society.

—Offer grants to state universities to establish educational and noncommercial TV stations, based on the population of the different states. Every state could be guaranteed at least one outlet, and states such as New York, California, Illinois, Texas might get as many as five each.

The university would operate the stations with the guidance of advisory committees, appointed by the Governors and representing all elements of the population. After the initial grants, stations would receive subsidies on a per capita basis. A national production center and news-gathering agency could be set up by university consortia.

Such a network could provide an antidote to commercial TV and a yardstick for measuring news presentation. It could offer the best teachers in various credit and non-credit courses, for use by high schools, community colleges, adult education programs, etc.

—Establish a civilian conservation corps to provide education and training at the community college level and to perform useful work in the national forests, hospitals, schools and on pollution projects. Such a nonmilitary educational program would pay participants not less than $2,000 a year, plus room and board. Participants would be able to earn community college associate degrees in from three to four years while working and learning in the program. The corps would assist regional authorities with the development of mass transit plans, local park systems, regional health programs, etc.

Through real tax reform, the federal government can take steps to redress the income inequality from which lower- and middle-income groups suffer. Such a reform program should, among other things, give *earned* income credit to wage and salary workers, of from 5 to 10 percent of income (up to a reasonable salary ceiling). Income from work is the only kind of income that never, except at the top executive level, gets special treatment under our tax codes. Such a tax credit to a working family head who earns $8,500 a year would result in tax savings of $5 to $15 a week.

The average man can keep his head over the poverty line only if he has a job and works full time. Central to his concern about economic issues, therefore, is the basic question of full employment. Joblessness is still the mainspring of poverty, racial discrimination, job insecurity, low wages, inadequate income, inability to buy schooling, health care, goods, etc.

Yet jobs are often unrewarding, monotonous and fatiguing. Historically, however, to the extent that we have improved the conditions of labor, we have done so through bargaining in the job market. When labor is in short supply—as it is when employment rates are high—the worker can reject unpleasant jobs and force employers to make work more attractive. He may not be able in this way to make his labors positively gratifying, but he can make them more tolerable.

Central to the problem of underemployment is the fact that our economic capacity is grossly underutilized. The problem has been particularly acute under Republican administrations.[1] Needed, according to Leon Keyserling, is a growth rate averaging 6 percent and, after reasonably full use of our resources has been restored, an annual growth rate *in the production of useful goods* of 5 percent.

Between 1953 and 1968, failure to use our full economic capacity cost us $917.8 billion dollars in GNP, he estimates —money that could have bought decent housing for everyone. The true unemployment rate (including concealed and part-time unemployment) was 5.6 percent in 1968 and rose even higher in 1969. In those years about 10 percent of our productive capacity was not used. Put to good use, this capacity could have made up many of the deficits suffered in middle America and financed many of the public service programs we need.

When we do not make use of full capacity, millions are jobless and the whole society pays. Only one percentage point of economic growth amounts to about $10 billion in production each year—the value of about 500,000 dwelling units. If our rate of growth falls to zero, as it may, we will lose about $40 billion in production—enough to bail middle America and the poor out of most of the problems we have discussed.

An enlightened government would begin by providing jobs for all able-bodied citizens through "government as the employer of last resort" programs, in which workers would earn enough to maintain their families at levels in keeping with the Department of Labor "adequate" family budgets. Such programs could be organized with federal grants to regional authorities that would plan for area reconstruction and reclamation. In rural communities the work might include cleaning up waterways, creating roadside stop-off places, reclaiming mined-out farm and timber

[1] From 1953 to 1960, our average annual growth in GNP was only 2.4 percent. In the Kennedy-Johnson years it averaged 4.7 percent. In 1969, it dropped back to 2.4 percent.

land, replanting the land left barren by mineral exploitation. The jobs might keep thousands in the rural areas,
where many no doubt would prefer to live if they were
not forced to move to the city in search of jobs.

In urban centers the programs could cut in whenever
local unemployment reached some specified level—say 3
percent, and could provide for amenities such as parks,
tree planting on streets and boulevards, new beaches, cultural and recreational centers, preservation and refurbish-
ing of historic buildings and sites.

Such programs could grant federal corporation tax reductions to industries that create new employment opportunities in Appalachia, the Mississippi Delta, and other
areas where the displaced are concentrated. In return for
the subsidies, the employer would be required to maintain
wages and working conditions comparable to those prevail-
ing in national markets—as employers have been required
to when bidding for some defense contracts. In areas of great
need, new industries might be forgiven the full federal tax
bill for as much as five years, with taxes being imposed
on a gradually increasing scale each year thereafter, until
the maximum was reached. The loss to the federal treasury
would be somewhat compensated for by placing on the tax
rolls workers who now earn little or nothing, and must
turn to the public for tax-supported welfare.

For those who are unable to work—the mothers of young
children, the sick, the handicapped, the aged—income
would be guaranteed in a more humane national system
to replace the welfare system that in many states keeps
families teetering almost at the edge of starvation. Again,
such a system could slow down the flight from rural to
urban areas, by providing as much, or nearly as much,
support for a family in Mississippi as is now provided in
Chicago, Detroit, New York.

For the special, though not exclusive, use of now-unemployed mothers, there could be established a network of day-care systems that would free them for training and for work outside the home. To some extent such a system could feed upon itself through the involvement of welfare mothers as paraprofessionals in training to staff the day-care centers. Obviously such a program would have great appeal also to working-class and middle-class women who are now kept out of the labor market because of their inability to arrange for the care of their children. It would do much to liberate women generally, and would greatly enrich the country by enabling women who are now economically unproductive to contribute their skill, learning, productive capacities.

Incredibly enough, a real beginning could be made in the implementation of all the foregoing, and more, simply with the money that would be saved by abandoning plans for the already obsolete B1 bomber, on which a $20 billion price tag has been placed by the Members of Congress for Peace Through Law.

According to Republican adviser Kevin Phillips, a rather stable majority of about 57 percent Republican voters will emerge when and if Wallace succumbs to Republican challengers. This majority will be white and it will be made up of the rapidly expanding Sun-Belt South and Southwest, the backlash urban vote, the Heartland vote (Midwest, mountain and Appalachia border states), and the remains of the Republican establishment.

According to this strategy, Republicans can win and hold power without making any concessions to liberalism. They can, therefore, forget the Negro vote, the Northeast, the liberal urban vote, and a few states like Michigan and Minnesota. The Northeast and the cities are in decline anyhow, in this view, and besides, the liberal votes contained therein are not needed to put together a solid conservative majority.

The strategy counts on a major and permanent erosion of the Catholic vote, which has already begun, it is claimed, in the rightward swing of Irish Catholics in New York. It predicts that the race issue will have the same impact on voters as the Civil War, making a lasting impression on their voting habits, and it postulates that the principle force breaking up the Democratic party is the black socio-economic revolution.

We hope that this strategy is mistaken. The Republican victory in 1968 was hardly auspicious. Democrats won both houses of Congress. Nixon won only 43 percent of the popular vote, and if Robert Kennedy had lived, he would probably have gone to the White House. Still, a conservative victory based on the racial polarization of voters is ominous.

Much depends on what happens to the white vote in the South and to the Catholic vote in the cities. In many ways the South is becoming more like the rest of the country. Liberalism is growing there, along with reaction. Visible progress *has* been made in civil rights. The South *is* industrializing, and will in time generate the same urban and working-class vote that has supported progressive programs.

Among Catholics in the North, progressive traditions are still strong, and these traditions, if racial tempers can be cooled, will not easily turn to conservatism.

Even in late 1968, only about a third of voters identified politically with the Republican party.[2] Such was their identity, not their voting behavior. What happens in the future will depend on how successfully we can cool conflict among progressives. It will also depend, among other things, on

[2] Survey Research Center, University of Michigan.

how effectively unions can organize, especially in the
South, and how well they can mobilize an integrated and
progressive urban vote.

        Can Humpty Dumpty—or, a left-liberal alliance
—be put back together again? Not instantly and miracu-
ously, certainly, but perhaps with new insights and much
effort. The New Deal coalition grew informally, in response to FDR's leadership on a wide range of social issues.
Roosevelt came to symbolize the desire of a majority to end
laissez-faire economics and enact significant social legislation.

Some were no doubt attracted by FDR's rhetoric and
promise to "drive the money changers from the temple."
Most responded to specific acts—the forty-hour work week
and federal minimum wage law, the Social Security act,
bank deposit insurance, legal guarantee of the right to
unionize, the creation of TVA and the promise (unful-
filled) that other public power authorities would follow,
the CCC and WPA and PWA, the unemployment insurance system, the first housing programs for the poor,
schemes for distributing land to poor farmers, efforts to
save the family farm. There was something for everyone,
including the remarkable WPA theater and music projects,
the employment of artists to create murals on public buildings, and of writers to prepare the famed WPA regional
and state guidebooks.

The New Deal rallied a majority. No one had to explain
to the poor, the blacks, the workers. They saw with their
own eyes what was happening, experienced it, and got their
hands on some money for the first time in many grim years.

There were no special calls to the intellectuals, but the
appointment of Tugwell, Cohen, Frankfurter, Wallace and

hundreds of other brain trusters to key posts gave intellectuals reason to identify with the Administration.

Political candidates must be more than one-issue men. Coalitions are composed of people who, while disagreeing on many issues, agree to work together for those issues they regard as basic or timely. Too often, middle-class activists seek association only with their own kind—the ideologically and stylistically pure. Their standards of behavior are rigorous but often more applicable to candidates for an exclusive sect or club than to those mortal men who seek public office. Many value the WASP and the Ivy style even more than political performance. They will easily forgo the second, on many occasions, when only the first is offered by a candidate. Adlai Stevenson was a case in point. He offered measured prose, good manners, gentle wit, genuine modesty. But he was, and did not pretend otherwise, an almost classic conservative in politics. Few liberals saw beyond the style and into the political man. By contrast, the right is seldom fooled by a pretty manner. Right-wing Republicans would not buy performances by Ronald Reagan and Spiro Agnew if these two all-American boys were not at the same time reactionary all the way, like themselves. They are no doubt pleased to have two such "glamour boys" speaking their lines—but only as an added attraction, not as the main event.

Political movements whose leaders conform to a single style give the impression of being monolithic and exclusive, however loudly they proclaim a devotion to democracy and populism. Groups such as the New Democratic Coalition, Americans for Democratic Action, Reform Democrats of New York, Independent Voters of Illinois, California Democratic Clubs have been notably unsuccessful in attracting blacks, Latins, workers, the poor. Even a man with the name Duffy (Joseph), ADA leader, turned out to be that rare bird, an Irish Protestant and a minister at that. In his campaign for the Senate in Connecticut, however, the Reverend Duffy stepped out of the mold and campaigned vigorously among workers, blacks, ethnic minorities.

On the other side, Nelson Rockefeller, the ultimate patrician, drew support from New York's hard-hats not because he promised to keep blacks out of their hair, but because, through his vast State building programs, he offered guarantees of continuing employment in their trades. Given the condition of New York's housing, hospitals, schools and public institutions generally, the left could have outbid him on this score, but apparently nobody was really interested.

Political support is won by persuading people that their self-interest is at stake and that they should act to defend it. For one reason or another, some individuals define self-interest more broadly than others, but finally all political decisions are made in consideration of one's personal welfare. To win support, political appeals must be made in those terms.

The difference between the political left and right is that the left claims to be acting for all the people, or at any rate in the interest of large majorities—and its appeals must justify that claim. Coalitions embracing majorities will come into being only when left-leaning activists can look beyond style and purity to discover issues that move majorities—silent or vocal.

Putting Humpty together will certainly require a new perspective on our relations with the communist and Third worlds. While previous wars have solidified and nationalized our people, Vietnam has fragmented them. Another such "counterinsurrection" will crack the social bond beyond repair.

The left-liberal alliance and our very lives depend on

making better sense of our relations with the communist world, and with the world of impoverished people who as yet have no political identity.

A re-alliance will require an examination of stereotypes and false images. Not all young people, or even many, take hard drugs or blow up ROTC buildings. The Weathermen are few in number, not typical of young radicals. Large numbers of young pople are eager, healthy, idealistic.

The middle class embraces individuals who promote their own selfish interests, impose their style and culture, and strive to exclude others from institutions they control. But this class also supplies much of the leadership, expertise, openness and financing that a left alliance needs.

Similarly, the violent blacks are relatively few compared to the overwhelming majority who will no longer submit, but who earn their own way and consistently support populist programs.

Many police are brutal but many are not; they are just ordinary men trying to make a living.

And some, or even many, workers and unions are conservative or racist—yet a great many, most, in fact, are decent, populist in natural sentiment, eager to make better sense of their lives.

Two maladies especially—violence and hard drugs— sustain the cleavages and stereotypes. The mending of alliances and images will not be possible until these diminish.

A suitable climate for a populist society will depend on a thorough reformation (revolution, if you prefer the term) in the schools—and a switch from didactic and regimented teaching to learning that is real, problem-solving, and cooperative rather than competitive. Such education would integrate rather than segregate youth, bringing them into real roles in the real world.

The kind of learning that is valued by the middle class— the kind offered in the "better" suburban public schools, the big-city private schools, the Ivy League universities and colleges—cultivates respect for "individual excellence" and predisposes students to the acceptance of elitist values. People so trained can rarely believe that the ordinary man —the "mediocrity"—has a place in political life.

The first thing they question about a candidate is his education. They are really asking: Does he hold a degree? Is it an advanced degree? Was it awarded by a reputable university? Or, lacking the degree, does his language conform to accepted standards?

Though some of the worst "bandits" and foulest reactionaries in our history won degrees at fancy Eastern universities, many middle-class activists cling to the belief that only such schooling qualifies people for political leadership.

Public affairs must be open to more than those with money, style, youth and education. Movements that, in spoken and written word, appeal to "the people" but choose their spokesmen only from the New Class can't have wide appeal. Foot soldiers in the army cannot pick their officers. But in civilian life, the infantryman does have a choice, and he is unlikely to elect leaders only from the officer class. Middle-class activists have begun to see the need to include blacks and other minorities in leadership, but they still draw the line at ethnics, plebeian Catholics, workers. The foot soldiers will not serve in movements that exclude them and their peers from places of leadership.

Probably the economic bungling of conservatives, the end of the Vietnam war, and the common interests of these natural allies will be enough to put the alliance back together. Still, it will take a lot of doing.

Young people, because they have so much vitality and leisure and so much to gain by change, must be important catalysts in the shaping of alliances. They will need, however, to work with others who share their interests. The young can help change the nature of the educational institutions that house them. In the work force, they can help change the nature of work. They can, above all, influence the participatory institutions to which they have access—especially unions and political parties. The millions of young people who belong to unions, by organizing in a self-conscious way and working *with* experienced unionists, can profoundly change those institutions. In a similar way they can help change the political system by organizing themselves for participation. The middle-range young person will be most useful in accomplishing this work since the fanatic tends to divide rather than pull people together.

Can it work? Who knows? We think it can. Such a coalition has worked in the past, with more or less success, beginning with the New Deal. It was turned around by the death of Roosevelt in office (and the succession of Truman), by the popularity of war hero Eisenhower, by the assassination of John Kennedy in office (and the succession of Johnson), and by the assassination of Robert Kennedy. It has been turned around by the black revolt and mass migrations into 'the cities, by the ideological conflict between capitalism and communism (neither of which, in power, offers much to working people and average citizens). It has been turned around by the sudden affluence of the New Class and their neglect of have-nots and working people.

Many critics on the left think our society too corrupt and decadent to be saved. We don't. But we do think the alternative to reformation is violent revolution. We repudiate this alternative, but we know that something like violent revolution may occur in this country under cataclysmic conditions—depression and war. Under such circumstances, a revolution of the right is far more likely than a revolution of the left.

The only alternative to that bleak and bloody prospect, we believe, is the reconstruction of a left-leaning coalition that can move the nation forward somewhat, stave off Armageddon long enough to permit development of programs that may help the American people make sense of their lives, and begin to create the measure of peace and tranquillity that is indispensable to national survival.

INDEX

A